Adventures in the
Wine Trade

Published 2023 by Académie du Vin Library Ltd
academieduvinlibrary.com
Founders: Steven Spurrier and Simon McMurtrie

Publisher: Hermione Ireland
Editorial Director: Susan Keevil
Designer: Martin Preston
Art Director: Tim Foster
Index: Hilary Bird

ISBN: 978-1-913141-45-5
Printed and bound in the EU

Adventures in the
Wine Trade
DIARY OF A VINTNERS SCHOLAR

BEN HOWKINS

Foreword by Hugh Johnson

ACADEMIE DU VIN LIBRARY

Contents

Foreword

Ben entered my life when I had the bright but crazy idea of kick-starting the moribund reputation of Tokay – once the world's most expensive wine. The communists had trashed the treasures of Eastern Europe, its finest wine among them. No one doubted the former greatness of this ultimate sweet white wine. Other wines claim to be 'the wine of kings.' Tokay really was, and of emperors and tsars; no one else could get hold of it.

Dreamer and optimist that I am, I reasoned that if it had once been so great, it could be again. The same vines still grew in the same ground. The same climate ripened them on the same hills above the same rivers that provided autumn mists. Sauternes has similar conditions. Everyone knows Château d'Yquem. But Tokay got there first, and still, in my opinion, has the edge in sweetness made sublime by complexities of flavour and invigorating acidity. I had tasted Tokay from the 18th century still almost alarming in its energy. Opulence and energy: a world-beating formula.

All of which brings me, and in 1993 brought me, to Ben.

My co-dreamer in trying to revive Tokay was Peter Vinding-Diers, the Danish winemaking genius who had already started a revolution (and a new university department) in Bordeaux by his understanding of yeasts. Peter had seen the opportunities created when Communism collapsed. Peter also knew Ben and his reputation as a super-salesman of, at this juncture, the finest port.

I needn't recount here how we struggled, with zero resources, through the mess left by the communists, both physically (the vineyards were almost unworkable) and morally (no one trusted anyone: Hungary was in deep trouble). We needed a candid native with local knowledge. Istvan Szepsy, of the family that originated Tokay, agreed to advise us. And we needed someone with huge knowledge and experience of how fine wines are marketed, distributed and sold worldwide. Enter Ben.

We have been friends now for 30 years – indeed, we were at school together, though we didn't know it. If London is recognized as the worldwide centre of the trade in fine wines (and it is), Ben embodies the tradition and the skills, the know-how (and, it must be said, the unshowy charm) that put it there.

So Ben's book is a journey through the complex and highly enviable life of a top-seed wine merchant of the old school, where relationships are paramount. Port and Sherry (he has written books on both) played a great part in his life before he entered the realm of the Rothschilds. Where next? China, of course. The world's top wines are wanted wherever culture meets privilege, and indeed power. Famous (and occasionally frightening) names crop up all the time. Bagging something exclusive, indeed creating it, making it desirable and finding the right customer is an art Ben seems to have mastered, and if it takes him all over the world (or at least the luxury world) you certainly won't hear him complain.

Hugh Johnson, London 2023

Introduction

Defining moments in our careers, indeed our lives, may be simple or complex; they may happen by chance, at a meeting, or at a dinner party. Mine was an interview, in 1963, with a highly decorated soldier in the Court Room of Vintners' Hall in the City of London. I was being proposed for the annual Vintners' Scholarship.

The Wine Trade in the 1960s was very traditional, very niche and largely family-led. Fine wine was enjoyed courtesy of the wine lists at the Savoy or Mirabelle, or plucked from the damp cellars of grand country houses that held a seemingly inexhaustible supply of dubious Nuits-St-Georges. At the other end of the scale, us chaps would clumsily court young ladies with endless bottles of Mateus Rosé, Blue Nun or Bull's Blood in dimly lit, Gingham-table-clothed bistros, where candles flickering from straw-covered Chianti flasks lent a suitably romantic touch to the proceedings.

This is a story that connects that amateur and delightfully innocent yester-world of wine with the highly professional and global business of today – one that sits at the very heart of our Western lifestyle, and which continues to open doors that other businesses do not. It is also about the characters who presided over that transformation – people who, for the most part, enjoyed their craft and whose chief aim was to put a smile on our faces.

I was fortunate to have a ringside seat as many of these changes unfolded – as communications with overseas suppliers switched from telegrams to telexes, thence to faxes and to the internet; as 'wines by the glass' became common-place in pubs and restaurants; as people with far more talent than I set about creating wine and spirit brands that consumers could follow and trust.

Just as the UK gradually became a wine-drinking nation, so, too, did the United States. Contrary to popular opinion, it was the noteworthy Bordeaux 1970 vintage that first caught the attention of American retailers, a decade before journalists got behind the excellent 1982 vintage. Consuming wine was considered more classy than drinking spirits, and TV shows switched their characters' preferences accordingly. Dry martinis at the bar gave way to sommeliers' suggestions at the dining table. Formal wine education became big business.

And then came China, where a whole new generation of wealthy individuals emerged in what seemed like a blink of the eye, intent on learning what made Western culture tick. Among the luxury items firmly in their sights was fine wine, and like a generation of Americans before them they started at the top – in China's case, with Château Lafite Rothschild. Again, I was fortunate enough to have close links with the Rothschild family, and also to be involved with two other luxury brands, Royal Tokaji wine and Last Drop whisky, that were perfectly positioned to capitalize on this burgeoning and highly profitable segment.

Three quite different markets. Three wonderfully welcoming places to visit. If there is an 'Englishman, Irishman, Scotsman' story here, it might go like this:

Before he opened his bottle of fine wine, the beaming American collector would extol the virtues of the scores and ratings that this particular vintage had received; expectations would run high, perhaps too high, but all would be analyzed and all would be well.

The Chinese host would boast of the provenance of his fine wine and also the price that he had paid for it. As he and his friends raised their glasses to their lips, all would exchange inscrutable smiles while perhaps not understanding exactly what they were drinking.

Meanwhile, the English wine merchant, after taking his first sip of a similarly fine wine, would turn to his fellow imbiber and murmur with a twinkle in his eye: 'Not too shabby, eh ?'

Fortunately, there is room in this world for all of us and it has been my privilege to be a part of it.

Ben Howkins, London 2023

CHAPTER ONE

Lost in France

'Monsieur le President des Etats Unis est mort' – or it could have been *'Monsieur... le President des Etats Unis est mort!'*. Either way, it was not what I was expecting to hear when I stopped to fill up with petrol one cold, dark November morning just south of Calais. But the sleepy Frenchman who was kindly filling up my tank kept repeating it as though in a trance. It was, of course, the morning after November 22rd 1963, just moments since that awful tragedy in Dallas, Texas. That is where I was on that fateful day, in a petrol station in France.

I limped back to England with the devastating news echoing in my ears. It brought me back to earth in more ways than one. My diary records that the day before I had enjoyed 'my last lunch in France with François and Robert Hine and four bottles of wine plus cognac'. Between three of us. It is fair to say that I do not remember exactly what I did after lunch. Hopefully, a little nap?

What I do remember – sort of – is that I drove the eight hours plus from Cognac to Calais through the night to catch the morning ferry homewards, having spent five and a half months, spread over France, Spain and Portugal, of unadulterated fun interspersed with some serious learning. Or maybe it was the other way around.

It had all started on June 10th of that year when I caught the 4.30 after-noon ferry from Dover to Calais in my red Mini-Minor 306 COX. Armed with top-level letters of introduction to the most important wine producers in Europe and to the controlling bodies of each region, I was officially representing the Vintners' Company.

To say that I was proud would be an understatement; to say that I was nervous would be nearer the truth. In those days the Vintners' Company was the very embodiment of the wine trade; it was the wine trade.

For over 600 years, the City of London-based Livery Company[1] had, *de facto*, been at the centre of England's, and therefore the world's, wine trading activities. Each year, as part of its remit to further knowledge among the UK wine trade, the Company grants a scholarship, in those days worth £300, to allow the fortunate recipient to study in Europe's leading vineyards. I had chosen to focus on Champagne, Burgundy, Bordeaux, Oporto and Jerez – then the main quality wine regions in Europe, and by extension the world. My wine trade employer at the time was Phipps Northampton Brewery Co Ltd – hardly known for the quality of its wine portfolio. It owned a retail wine shop called Lankester & Wells and my business card, specially produced for this venture, described me as 'Representative of Lankester & Wells, Northampton, Wines & Spirits Trading Organization (Midlands)'. Brown & Pank was their wholesale division – hardly in the same league as Berry Bros & Rudd or Harvey's of Bristol. In truth, the closest I had been to a vineyard, apart from a mini-trip to Louis Guntrum in Nierstein, Germany, was to handle bundles of wine labels with evocative names such as Gevrey-Chambertin, Nuits-St-Georges and Pommard. This was in the brewery's wine bottling hall by the River Nene in Northampton. The bottlers had nicknames for such foreign-sounding names, so these three became respectively 'Geoffrey', 'Nutty' and 'Pommie'. Bottling in the UK was common practice at the time and it must be said that sometimes, just occasionally, if there was a shortage of, say, 'Nutty' labels, then 'Geoffrey' was called upon to finish off the cask.

---

[1] Having received its charter of incorporation from King Henry VI in 1437, the Vintners' Company's position as 11th of the 12 great Livery Companies was decided in 1516. Had the date been fixed earlier, when the Company was at its zenith, it would have been ranked third or fourth in this ancient hierarchy.

But Vintners' Scholar I was, and on June 11th 1963, at the age of 20, I arrived in Reims to be welcomed by François Lanson as the house guest of Lanson champagne. As a retailer with wholesale ambitions, my company had links with several of the great champagne houses. So it was that my first visit to a wine producer was to Irroy, owned by Tattinger, where I was lunched with Irroy 1959 and afterwards enjoyed the 1955 with the *chef des vignes*. Later that day, back at Lanson, I was offered Lanson 1955 at teatime and dined with the 1959. Not bad for a first day's study, I thought: I think I can manage this.

A week in Reims was followed by a week in Epernay. Lunches at Le Cheval Blanc and La Chaumière loomed large, and delights such as escargots, lobster and strawberries made an astounding change from my usual fare of roast and two veg. Francois Lanson showed me my first vineyards; M Chapman from Heidsieck introduced me to *marc de champagne*, a taste from which I have never recovered, and Henri Krug kindly explained over a glass of Krug 1959, that Krug, the champagne king, did not in fact own any vineyards.

My diary then records that I took off to Paris for the weekend with a sleepy hitchhiker (who he?). We spent most of the evening in Les Halles with a former OAS officer who had just returned from Algeria[2], only to then be joined by a drunken deserter from the same regiment who kept repeating '*Je ne regrette pas à tuer; mais je regrette à tuer pour rien*'. We assured him that the Algerian War was now over, but feelings in France were still running high.

For the first, but certainly not the last, time on this venture it seems I was unable to find a hotel, so at 4.00 am, I snatched a couple of hours sleep in the car by the Jardins de Luxembourg.

My week in Epernay began with a welcome by Patrick Forbes of Moët & Chandon, who then took me to their luxurious Château de Saran. If my

---

[2] The Algerian War (1954-62) was an extended and often bloody conflict involving the Algerian nationalist FLN, the French government, and the right-wing paramilitary OAS (*Organisation armée secrète*) who resisted de-colonization. It was resolved in March 1962, when Algeria finally achieved independence from France.

previous week in Reims had set my sights high, being installed at Saran was stratospheric. Moët, then as now, was the leading champagne brand. It had the name. Other houses were, and are, smaller with prestigious reputations, but Moët led the way to the consumer. The key was its unrivalled expertise in public relations. It did not advertize. It welcomed its target market to its house in Epernay and to its home at Saran.

It soon became very clear that in order to work for Moët, you needed a title. Patrick was the next best thing –an elegant Old Etonian. The wonderful Hon Myra Campbell greeted us at Saran, assisted by la Comtesse de Maigret. In turn, Elizabeth Whigham, who I shyly blushed at whenever she did the flower arranging, was the niece of the Duchess of Argyll. Joining us for lunch on that first day were the Comte and Comtesse Chandon-Moët. Public relations at its zenith. Hospitality and friendship at its best. We seemed to exist on the 1955 vintage. It is fair to say that at one point I had a modest *crise de foie*. Of course, it must have been the food – and it certainly didn't stop me from enjoying a J&B whisky nightcap most evenings, or rather early mornings.

All our lunches and dinners were sublime. One day I ventured into the kitchens to chat to the chef and to Louis, the butler. At most dinners we had been enjoying Champagne's own red wine – from Bouzy, mainly the 1959. On the chef's table I spied a 1929. 'When are we going to enjoy that?' I enquired. 'Monsieur, it is too good for the drinking; it is for the sauce.' Such an exquisite put-down.

Saran became a wonderfully select meeting place for us young'uns – the starting point for many of the friendships that I would forge along the vinous way. I remember having an animated conversation one evening with Anthony Hanson, who went on to become a Master of Wine (MW), co-founded the respected Haynes, Hanson and Clark wine merchants, and wrote the seminal book on Burgundy entitled simply *Burgundy*. Anthony's background was his family's brewery, but wine was very much his first love.

It was almost obligatory to spend some time in the vineyards and the cellars if you wanted to get on in the wine trade. Getting to know your supplier better was a much-repeated mantra. The original purpose of the coveted Master of Wine examination was to enable leading UK wine buyers to get fully up to speed with essential vinous knowledge, all the better to negotiate with, or combat, their suppliers. The suppliers were mainly French wine producers, who in turn were always keen to sell their annual produce to the world's number one export market, Great Britain. Vintages varied a great deal more then than they do now in these days of modern technology. It was imperative that the English consumer be protected from the wiles of the French.

In fact, it was at Saran that I decided not to become a Master of Wine. How precocious was that? One evening before dinner I was chatting to two senior members of the UK wine trade, one of whom had been chairman of the Wines & Spirit Association in 1952, and one, or perhaps both, were in the original intake of MWs. While they extolled the virtues of becoming a Master of Wine and insisted that this should be my goal, I remember feeling that the exams were not commercial enough. How on earth did I know that? I decided that I would not benefit from taking the MW exams and I never did.

During that week, I also visited Pol Roger, where family member Christian de Billy kindly invited me back to lunch with his family; and Bollinger, where, in the absence of Madame Bollinger, who was in Copenhagen, her charming nephew Christian Bizot kindly showed me some pre-phylloxera vines. It was not the best timing: his wife was expecting a baby that day.

This visit also represented my first essay at making contacts – or networking, as it is now more generally known. Patrick Forbes, before he became MD of Moët London, was busy writing his splendid opus *Champagne* but had found it impossible to connect with Madame Bollinger. He asked me if I could smooth the way when I met Christian Bizot and I did. I still have a postcard from Patrick thanking me for my 'diplomacy'.

My father had always wanted me to join the Foreign Office, but I was now too deeply into wine.

En route to Burgundy I stopped for a couple of nights in Alsace – that most picturesque of wine regions, which has hardly changed in hundreds of years. There, the same families – Hugel, Dopff, Beyer *et al* – rule as they have done for generations, producing classic wines that at the time were the 'go to' style for English wine merchants. René Dopff of Dopff & Irion showed me their cellars, which date back to 1549, before lunching me with Clos des Murailles 1961. All wine producers are gourmets and none more so than in Alsace. We feasted on eel, truffles, lobster, quail and strawberries during my short stay.

On the recommendation of my Honorary Colonel in the Northampton-shire Yeomanry, Colonel Nigel Stopford Sackville, grandfather of the dynamic Tom Sackville of Goedhuis Wine Merchants, I tracked down Leon Beyer of the eponymous producer and we drank each other's health with a sumptuous 1961 Riesling.

It is a truism in the wine trade that once you have been made welcome by a producer, scanned the *terroir* and tasted the fruits thereof, you will remain for-ever loyal to that brand. It certainly works for me. Today, Leon Beyer's Alsace wines still appear on the wine list at Brooks's, my London club, although they are now furnished by his delightful son, Marc – one of the world's true gour-mets.

From Alsace it was on to Beaune – inevitably after a good lunch and another tasting. I decided to stop for the night in Dole, which turned out to be a magnet for motorbike 'ton-up' boys. Since no hotel was available for less than FF25, my limit, I drove three kilometres to a disused aerodrome and bedded down in the car amid continuous rain.

Paul Bouchard, of Bouchard Aîné, was to be my host during my three-week sojourn. Forewarned that Paul, Downside-educated and fluent in Eng-lish, had a good sense of humour, I felt the trip boded well.

On my first day at Bouchard Aîné, June 28th, I was offered a VBC – a *vin blanc cassis* – by Paul's father, Georges, before lunch *en famille* at the office. This novel concoction of white wine from the roughish Aligoté grape mixed with a dash of cassis, or blackcurrant, liqueur is mind-blowing both in its deliciousness and its simplicity. It would go on to become universally known as 'Kir' after the colourful Felix Kir, first Mayor, then Canon, of Dijon, who was a great advocate of this very moreish drink. Felix also happened to be a good drinking friend of Georges Bouchard, though I imagine 'Kir' was shorter and easier to pronounce.

Beaune in those days was a small walled city with a happy atmosphere. Deux Chevaux Citroëns puttered about, but most of the offices and wine cellars were within walking distance of each other and there was an abundance of handy shops, cafés and restaurants. The city was also a melting pot of young *stagiaires* – English (mainly) youngsters embarking on a vinous version of the Grand Tour. It was where I met many of the friends who are still friends today, such as David Butler Adams – the immaculately dressed scion of the old-established Adams wine merchants, who I first encountered in the company of two other Englishmen at Louis Latour. I noted in my diary that all three were 'generally and perpetually in wine'. I think it was a compliment.

It is one of the more pleasing aspects of society that people who are destined to like one another gravitate towards each other – sometimes because of nationality, sometimes through mutual interests and sometimes by pure happenstance. Those abroad from similar backgrounds naturally tend to form cliques and we were no different. We were young, and we were very fortunate. We may occasionally have welcomed the odd Dane or American into our circle, but, essentially, we were Brits abroad.

We soon discovered that Place Carnot, in the city centre, was indeed the centre of life in Beaune. It was but a short walk from where we were all housed, it hosted our favourite meeting place, Bar Concorde, and it was no more than a step away from our favourite nightclub, L'Aiglan, which was run by a very decorative 19-year-old Tahitian who had married at 15.

Most of us had driven out to France and at one point I noticed that we had six Minis between us. Often after dinner we would foregather to race around Place Carnot. One such evening, the square resembled the scene in *The Pink*

Panther (ironically released the same year) in which a bunch of would-be jewel thieves dressed as gorillas roar past a bemused trattoria owner, yelling at the top of their voices before all crashing into each other. Thankfully we managed to avoid the crash bit, though we did spend many hours in our respective garages getting this or that mended.

But back to the day job...

The majority of Burgundy wine houses are based in Beaune, with only a few in Nuits-St-Georges, so day trips were very much the order of the day. Each house took great trouble in passing me on from one to the other, so little time was wasted. At the start of my visit, I managed to fit in a quick trip to Bichot, where Benine Bichot proudly, if hurriedly, showed me his new caves. I also called on Pierre Ponnelle, where Louis Ponnelle, his sister and I enjoyed a quick beer. These two were the only visits without tastings.

Blind tastings were everything. That is what we did: taste, spit, taste, spit, taste, spit, and taste again... learn, learn, learn... concentrate... focus... learn... compare and contrast... go back and taste again. Note the colours and aromas... balance is always key (but balance between what?). Tannin, acidity, fruit. Short finish, long finish. Old vines, new vines. South-, west-, east-, north-facing slopes... Which appellation, which slope, which vineyard?

So it went on, albeit under kind and patient tutelage, purely for the benefit of our greater understanding. Or perhaps so that we would appreciate paying higher prices for the end result?

Interestingly, grape varieties were seldom, if ever, mentioned. It was taken as read that champagne was a blend of Chardonnay, Pinot Noir and Pinot Meunier, all of which were made into white wines, and that in Burgundy Pinot Noir was made into reds and Chardonnay into whites. Alsace had Riesling. Beaujolais had Gamay. Bordeaux had Cabernet Sauvignon, Cabernet Franc and Merlot. That was about it.

Trade visitors were always welcome in Burgundy, but very few of the wine houses had tourist facilities. Patriarche, with its new tourist centre, was the notable exception – but would the idea take off?

This was, of course, the time when wine supertankers were occasionally summoned northwards from Algeria to 'help out' with grapes that had failed to ripen in the Burgundian sun, leaving the wines with a low sugar content. Such was the case with the rain-afflicted 1963 harvest, when rich, red wines from the sunny south were warmly welcomed to add body to the local produce. I remember being awakened in the early hours by just such a convoy of clunking lorries. I turned over and let them do their job. Some 10 years later, however, the EEC put paid to all that, and Geoffrey, Nutty and Pommie were officially restored to their pristine purity.

Back at Bouchard Aîné, I encountered a splendid *stagiaire*, William Knight, who had been sent out to Beaune to learn the ropes by his English company. While William toiled away in the caves, I was lording it in the tasting room. After hours, though, we soon became firm friends and enjoyed many a jape together.

At Bouchard Père, Claude Bouchard, possibly the senior of the (by now) two quite separate halves of the same family, kindly took me through a solo tasting of no fewer than 27 red and white wines. In Burgundy it was the custom to taste red before white.

At Chanson, Philippe Marion conducted a fascinating tasting at which a fellow student, from California, described the Chambolle-Musigny 1962 as having 'its fruit grown inside'. We all agreed that this hit the nail on the head without actually having a clue what he meant. We then inspected flooded vines in Morey-St-Denis before hot-footing it to Clos Vougeot. Louis Latour of the eponymous company took us to Aloxe-Corton for another fascinating tasting. I was chuffed to identify, blind, the 'Geoffrey' Chambertin Premier Cru. At Faiveley, Guy Faiveley took us to Nuits-St-Georges for a most interesting tasting in the cellars – this time quite literally blind. Unfortunately, the electricity cut out at noon, leaving us trapped there. Undaunted, I found a candle and we happily carried on tasting '61s and '62s from cask. One day at lunch at Bouchard Aîné we met their broker in Beaujolais, M Chagny, who was dismayed that one of his daughters had just become a nun and one of his sons a monk. To cheer him up, Paul Bouchard uncorked a delicious Meursault 1955.

By this time, I had become aware that every single Brit I have mentioned thus far was an Old Etonian. I could give my views on the subject, but that is how it was. Among them was Jeremy Burroughes, a stalwart fellow who always chose his words with care. We were to share many excursions together in my red Mini.

Georges Bouchard kindly took me to Chablis for the day, where I enjoyed a Petit Chablis 1959 and noted that Chablis is 'not so pale as one thinks'. A chance visit to Reine Pédauque explained why I had received no introduction to this house. 'A *dégustation* of the most r*v*lt*ng wines that I have ever tasted' was the verdict recorded in my diary.

At Calvet, Messieurs Roche and Prieur were most generous with their time, giving me an in-depth tasting of their 1959 reds. I plumped for a superb Vosne-Romanée. Later, on my way to meet Paul Bouchard, I bumped by chance into Nick Clarke, who had been awarded a Vintner's Bursary. Nick, cheerful as ever, congratulated me on my scholarship and we wished each other bon voyage on our respective travels.

On my last day in Beaune, we surged south to Mercurey to visit Antonin Rodet. It was the usual formula – caves, vineyards, tasting… All in a day's work, but my goodness, what enjoyable work. Then it was north to the Côte de Nuits, where I began by measuring out the length of the Romanée-Conti vineyard – just 58 metres by my reckoning. In those days it was better known for its diminutive size than for its land value.

After a final *au revoir* to all the lovely girls (Miss Redpants, Miss Sandwich, Miss Patriarche etc) at Bar Concorde, Jeremy Burroughes and I hit the road south on July 19th.

For the next 10 days, we oscillated around the Beaujolais villages of Fleurie, Julienas and Brouilly, visited the melancholy Monsieur Chagny at the Château de Chatelard, and were given a superb engraving of Château de Saint-Léger by Claude Pasquier Devignes. I also met Charles Piat, the golf-loving wine titan of Mâcon, whose wines were to play an important part in my life a few years later when I became brand manager for Piat at International Distillers & Vintners.

In addition, we found time to swim in the Saône and crash the odd car. Once, while engaged in the former, we spotted a rather good restaurant on the opposite bank and proceeded to lunch there, only to discover when the bill came that we'd left our wallets on the other side of the river. A quick swim back and all was fine. Afterwards, while admiring a magnificent gladioli garden, we were hailed by the owner – an unsung hero of the 1914–18 war who insisted on showing us his remarkable stamp collection.

Further south, we marvelled at the ancient Roman amphitheatre in Orange, where preparations were under way for an upcoming *son et lumière* performance; we also visited the co-operatives of Rasteau-Sainte Cécile, where we were impressed by a *cuvé* holding 2,000 litres. We were thrilled to visit Châteauneuf-du-Pape itself, and in Avignon we were given an intriguing tasting by Monsieur Bellicard. What we were not so good at was finding hotel rooms. By my calculation, by the end of July, I had twice bedded down on floors, twice among the vines, and once apiece under the stars, in a barn, amid rocks, in a garage, by the side of a mountain and on a deflated lilo.

After such hard work, I felt it was time to take two weeks holiday. It was, after all, the end of July trailing into August and I was not expected in Jerez until August 13th. Naturally, I headed for Cannes. I made a token stop at Villeneuve Loubet, producer of Pradel Rosé, moved on to Marseilles, and thence to Perpignan and over the Pyrenees.

As it turned out, by the purest good fortune, my sainted mother and cherished brother John had taken a gîte near the delightful Spanish fishing village of Cadaqués, once the home of Salvador Dali. Could I take a look at it, I was asked, to make sure that all was in order ahead of their visit. Since I had no other plans, I was delighted to oblige.

Lost in Cadaqués, I found myself knocking on a door of an English family who rather fortunately knew the owners of the gîte, a Captain and Mrs Roche. They surveyed the village square through a telescope, ascertained that the Roches were not in their usual café, and instead directed me to their house.

The door was cheerfully opened by Captain Roche, a retired BOAC pilot, and he and his delightful wife Karen made me most welcome. My intention had been to spend no more than a couple of hours in Cadaqués; I ended up staying for eight days, free, gratis and for nothing while my mother and brother had to pay for the privilege of spending a week in their garden. The guilt rests with me still.

The Roches kindly fed me in exchange for bottles of burgundy that I had collected along the way, and for the next four days I met and mingled with the best of them. The icing on the cake was when Captain Roche (did I ever know his Christian name I wonder?) asked me if I would mind helping him bring his five-and-a-half-metre sailing boat, *Nilo*, back up the coast from Barcelona. Yet another coincidence: the dinghy in which my mother sailed at a reservoir back in Northamptonshire was called *Nil*.

Captain Roche and I drove south to Arentz, outside Barcelona, where I left my Mini at the local railway station so that I could collect it when I returned by train after our voyage. To sail along this beautiful coast, weighing anchor every night in shimmering, brightly lit harbours, then going ashore to dine or buy provisions before returning to the gentle rocking of *Nilo*, was heaven. Yes, it rained, we got soaked, the engine cut out, thunderstorms raged and we found ourselves becalmed for six hours before the northeasterly *transmontana* finally blew us home on the jib alone – but what an adventure.

My *ad-hoc* holiday, though, was over and it was time to start work again – this time in Jerez, over 1,400 kilometres away in the south of Spain. I duly headed west to Zaragoza along the bumpiest road I had ever encountered, then south to majestic Madrid, on to Córdoba and Seville, thence to Jerez de la Frontera – my home for the next four and a half weeks.

CHAPTER TWO

Jerez, Oporto and Bordeaux 1963

What is odd from today's perspective is why I chose, or was advised, to spend four and a half weeks in Jerez, as opposed to a mere four weeks in Bordeaux and three in Burgundy. The latter were, and probably still are, the two greatest wine regions in the world, but the fact is that in the 1960s, sherry accounted for a huge proportion of wine we drank in Britain every year. Bordeaux and burgundy were niche; Sherry was universal. I suppose, too, that spending August in Andalusia in southern Spain could not be considered too much of a hardship.

The first book on wine that I bought was Tommy Layton's *Winecraft*, published in 1959. In the appendices, he lists vintages from 1876 to 1958 for seven European wine regions, Sherry included. This might seem surprising today, but in 1963 Sherry was regarded as up there with the best, with vintages every bit as important as those of champagne. The difference was that in Champagne, which was light on sunshine, they needed to blend their vintages and add sugar (*dosage*) to achieve consistency, while in Jerez, which had a surfeit, they needed to blend vintages and fortify the fully fermented wine to achieve the same effect. Here were two great wines, the world's finest aperitifs, that were made in quite different ways to compensate for their climatic deficiencies.

My hosts in Jerez were to be Rafael and Miguel Valdespino. On arriving at their offices on August 14th, I was handed 27 letters from family and friends –

my only communications link with the outside world. We chatted briefly about motorcycling, Miguel's passion, before going on a tour of Valdespino's two splendid bodegas, and within minutes I was offered my first glass of sherry in Jerez. It was Inocente Fino, still my yardstick for *finos* today and with the same outstanding label. Many years later, by which time I was working at International Distillers & Vintners, I asked a colleague why he thought the Gordon's Gin brand, not the export label, was so successful. He replied thoughtfully that its italic font, so often used in formal invitations, implied a form of welcome leading to enjoyment. The same could be said of Inocente and its sibling, Tío Diego Amontillado.

Jerez de la Frontera, to give the city its full title, was a hub of bustling, sun-drenched activity, interspersed with bouts of (essential) shady siestas. Tapas bars, beaches and bullfights, fiestas and flamenco set the pace. By contrast, the sherry producers' bodegas, where thousands of butts slumbered peacefully in the semi-darkness, were vast, cathedral-like edifices with open windows to let in the cool ocean breezes. An ever-present sight were *los mutilados* – poor souls, still in their Civil War uniforms, who by definition had lost an arm or a leg in that terrible conflict, and who now patrolled the streets finding parking spaces or hovering around bars, their hands outstretched for a peseta or two. It was accepted… an everyday sight. In those days, like everyone else, we called them cripples without ever pausing to consider what personal tragedy lay behind their present plight.

The previous year's Vintners Scholar, Michael Maguire, worked for Harvey's of Bristol, purveyors of the famous Bristol Cream. A great *bon viveur*, Michael had been sent to Jerez to keep an eye on things at Harvey's secret HQ, since the company did not possess a bodega of its own at the time. Taking Spanish time to heart, Michael duly arrived in his black Alfa Romeo Giulia to begin the day's work at 2.00pm. While we were waiting, a new Harvey's recruit, Robin Byers, greeted me and we agreed to meet up later at Los Cisnes – a splendid hotel, owned by the Valdespino family, that was the acknowledged hub of all social activity in Jerez. One thing led to another. We met up with Pepe Soto, who had an amazing collection of sherry books… we tasted a 100-year-old Madre de Dios at Pemartin... we met Beluca Pina-Sánchez, who invited us to her brother's wedding the following day involving an 8.00pm 'lunch' at Los Cisnes... I also found myself in receipt of a parking fine.

Somewhere along the line, I agreed to take the irrepressible Robin to Gibraltar, the nearest airport, to fly back to England. I took sanctuary in the bar while Robin bid a somewhat extended farewell to his then girlfriend before wandering back to my hotel, the Toc H. All fine, all dandy, I thought, and an interesting way to spend my 21st birthday – knocking back Spanish brandy in an airport bar.

Years later I got my own back, quite unintentionally of course, when I drove my 1928 4½ Litre Bentley to Paris and back to take part in the annual Beaujolais Nouveau run in early November. It was very cold. My wife (of whom more later) and I were nicely warmed in the front by the Bentley's stonking engine while Robin and his wife, Lavinia, gently froze in the back. I passed Robin a brandy flask that I kept in the glove compartment. His hands were too cold to grasp it...

The days and weeks passed quickly, as I visited many bodegas and was royally entertained. I learned something new in them all. Such names as Pemartin, de la Riva, Mackenzie, Misa, Manuel Fernandez and Garvey have sadly gone, lost in the ZRM/Rumasa juggernaut[1], while others – Domecq, González Byass, Harvey's, Williams & Humbert, Sandeman and of course, Valdespino – remain at the top of their game.

These were the days when Jerez's three different types of soil – the most desirable being the sublimely chalky *albariza* – really mattered and vineyards, or *pagos*, blessed with the best, such as Macharnudo and Balbaina, were highly

---

[1] In the early 1970s, the old Jerez order was turned upside down by a local businessman, José Maria Ruiz-Mateos, who began buying up both bodegas and *pagos* under the auspices of Rumasa – a 'pyramid' of dubious companies. The entire house of cards came tumbling down 10 years later, when Ruiz-Mateos was sent to prison, along with his sons. By that time, though, the sherry industry had been dealt a near-fatal blow, from which it took generations to recover.

sought-after. Back then, treading the grapes to kick-start fermentation during harvest time was still very much in vogue.

What has remained constant, and virtually unchanged to this day, is sherry's vinification process – the great *solera* system, nowadays called 'fractional blending' – that for centuries has produced the distinct styles of fresh *finos*, nutty *amontillados*, elusive-tasting *Palo Cortados* and robust *olorosos*. To the latter, add raisiny *PX* or the lighter Moscatel to create cream sherry.

Vintage, or *anada*, sherries are still largely unknown outside Jerez. Williams & Humbert, unique among the bodegas, I believe, have kept back a butt or two of each vintage since 1920 – originally to celebrate a birth in the family. Left to themselves, the 1934 had become an old *fino* while the 1936 had evolved into an *oloroso* – proof, if it were ever needed, that blending was the only way to maintain continuity.

Entertainment took many different forms. A cockfight was probably the least satisfactory. A bullfight was the highlight, especially during harvest time, when Jerez lived life in the fast lane. I had saved up just enough pesetas to afford a ticket in the *sol*; the price of a shady *sombre* ticket being beyond me. I mentioned this one day when in conversation with Maravilla Domecq. 'Don't be so silly, don't sit in the sun', she said, or words to that effect. 'Come and join me in the Domecq box.' I glanced at my *sol* ticket. 'Oh, don't worry about that,' she said: 'I will give it to our gardener'. Give it to the gardener indeed… my precious ticket.

The Domecq and González families were, and still are, Jerez royalty. Together with our front row, sombre seats there was a steady flow of half bottles of *fino* for the duration of the contest. I noticed that the Domecqs happily quaffed their rival's Tío Pepe, while the González family thoroughly enjoyed Domecq's La Ina. This was indeed party time, although bullfights were also the only events in Andalusia that ever started on time – 6.00 pm precisely, just as lunch ended. In due course I witnessed the legendary bullfighter, El Cordobes, being awarded one ear. Talk about the roar of the greasepaint and the smell of the crowds… this was the stuff of Roman amphitheatres.

In the meantime we had met up with Sam Sandbach, who appeared one day on his scooter, doing the rounds in his characteristically carefree way. There were always dramas with that scooter: sometimes Sam fell off, sometimes his luggage was stolen. In fact, our various Minis and other assorted vehicles were forever breaking down, suffering flat batteries or radiator leaks, or being crashed. Much of our time, it seems, was spent in garages, but so vivid are my other memories that I have almost no recollection of this aspect of our daily lives.

Harvest, or *vendimia*, time is celebrated by a week-long fair or *fiesta*, which in this particular year ran from September 6th to the 10th. My diary says: 'Nothing is best reported here,' and nothing was. Suffice to say that Jerez on those days was full of characters – Juan Pedro Simon, Paco de la Riva, Jimmy Fraser Luckie, Pepe Domecq (Prince Phillip's nephew) and the unforgettably named Wee Wee Diez.

The time had come to move on, hard as it was to leave such a friendly and hospitable place. While there, I had witnessed the first grapes being harvested in the Macharnudo vineyard with Miguel Valdespino… at San Patricio, I had marvelled at the three scales of *fino*, *amontillado* and *oloroso* specially drawn for me… at González Byass, I had had a somewhat animated discussion with an American importer about whether *fino* would or could ever replace the dry Martini as the aperitif of choice in the States… and I had revelled in being allowed into the various *sacristias* of each bodega, where the oldest and rarest sherries are kept.

Equally, I had also enjoyed introducing Jerezano society to the Twist, as well as witnessing their own incredible Flamenco dancing. But 'hasta la vista' it was, and William Knight and I bade farewell to all on September 18th.

* *

After two days on the road, thankfully in hotels this time, we arrived in Oporto as night was falling and navigated our way to the British Club, where we dined and played billiards. The following morning, we feasted again on a full English breakfast, or '*eggs y bacy*' as the Club's long-serving Rosa called it – the full extent of her English after 30 years.

The next evening, I dined with two great extrovert storytellers, Robin Reid and George Robertson, and George played the guitar until 3.00am. Robin ran Croft in Oporto, while George was his chairman in London. Irony indeed that seven years later I would become a director of Croft in London, though Robin did offer me a job during this visit.

Oporto is Portugal's business city. It is another bustling, noisy place, full of trams, cars and old buildings adorned with picturesque blue and white *azulejos* tiles. Across the River Douro to the south, the twin city of Vila Nova de Gaia is, by law, home to the port lodges – splendidly long, single-storey whitewashed buildings topped by red tiled roofs. Inside the lodges are thousand upon thousand of port barrels or *pipas*, each silently maturing for our collective benefit.

I quickly understood why all the port names that one instantly recognizes – Croft's, Taylor's, Graham's, Warre's, Dow's and so on – are either English or Scottish. These were the surnames, often of younger sons, who set sail to Oporto in the 17th and 18th centuries to trade wool for wine. In due course they founded their own port companies and their, or their partners', descendants are still here, many generations later.

They were the titans who carved vineyards out of the hillsides in the distant Douro Valley and invented one of life's greatest wines, vintage port. They were responsible for the outstanding vintages of 1912, 1927, 1945 and 1963. They also built two classic English edifices in Oporto – the British Club and the Factory House.

The British Club, sadly long since pulled down, was designed to make expats feel at home. Similar in many ways to the London clubs of St James's and Pall Mall, the food there was ordinary, the wines exceptional. We played billiards and snooker, enjoyed our glasses of port and read *The Times*. On one occasion, the snooker balls seemed to fly effortlessly about the room, breaking a window or two in the process. The next day the police arrived, but not before Silva, that most loyal of club stewards, had encouraged us all to leave in advance of their visit. We did, and nothing further was said.

The Factory House, so called because it is where, since 1814, wine merchants or *factors* have met to conduct their business under the auspices of the British Association, is an industry legend. It offers the epitome of fine dining, with two identical dining rooms – one for the food and wine, the other for port and cigars. Every Wednesday, since time immemorial, it has been the custom for the British port partners, social friends perhaps but also commercial rivals, to lunch together with their trade guests.

Back then, after lunch, the vintage port had to be tasted blind, to guess the vintage. Various cat and mouse conversations ensued, inevitably accompanied by a certain amount of banter:
‘Was this yours, Dick?’
‘Would this be John’s last vintage, hopefully…?’
‘Was this when you blended in from Quinta X?’
Never the surnames of Taylor, Dow or Warre; always the Christian names of the individuals who actually made the stuff. It was a fascinating exercise in openness amid such a closed community.

During my four weeks in Oporto I was fortunate to meet Dick Yeatman – a direct descendant of the Yeatman partner in Taylor Fladgate & Yeatman, after which the stunning Yeatman Hotel is named. I also met Reg Cobb, a scion of the Cockburn family, who greeted me off the train outside Quinta de Tua with the unexpected words: ‘Hello, I was at school with your father.’ I met Fernando Guedes, the genius behind Mateus Rosé, and lunched with Tim Sandeman and Colin Graham. I met Fernando van Zeller of Noval and the odd man out – Manuel Silva Reis, the leading mass producer of port. Under the guise of visiting the vineyards, or *quintas*, of the Douro Valley, I shot partridges with twins Ron and John Symington, whose sons and grandsons now own the company that includes Cockburn’s and Graham’s, among others. The *quintas* had to be visited regularly to check that each farmer’s vats or *tonels* were well looked-after and cleaned thoroughly before each new vintage. On one such visit to an outlying *quinta* with Robin Reid, we opened the little hatch at the bottom of the vat, only to have several chickens cluck their way past us. They had been happily nesting there all year. Croft did not buy from that farmer again.

At another *quinta,* I was fortunate to taste a deliciously dry tawny 1870 port straight from the wood. Such wine is known as a *colheita* port, denoting that it is from a particular harvest – in this case 1870. *Colheita* port is left in the barrel for many years, and sometimes for generations, unlike regular vintage port, which is bottled after two years. Many *colheita* ports are never bottled, but instead are drawn from the barrel when the family concerned wants to celebrate. They are, in effect, akin to family silver. Baked in the intense summer heat, *sans* air conditioning, they acquire a magnificent tawny hue that resembles the colour of a Portuguese sunset.

All the port shippers encouraged me to taste and taste because that was their job. I returned the compliment by listening and listening, since all their conversations at some stage led to port. In a way it was strange that these English names were a byword for excellence in port in much the same way as the vineyards of Burgundy or the châteaux of Bordeaux were for fine wine. Portuguese vineyard and village names were notable by their absence.

The number of visiting Brits swelled and swelled: chemists from London, buyers from the breweries and even more old Etonians. David Butler Adams and his friend Sam Sandbach were already here and at Cockburn's I met up with David Orr, who had not only been to Cambridge, but had what we considered to be a proper job. A delightful personality, David added a certain intellectual weight to our burgeoning group of friends.

I was placed under the wing of the charming Alfredo and Jean Hoelzer, as my company in Northampton imported their family's Calem port. Alfredo was really more interested in cars, as he owned the Volvo and Vauxhall dealerships for northern Portugal. His delight in showing me the new Vauxhall Viva was matched only by the boundlessness of the hospitality at his mother's Douro estate, Quinta de Val Figuera. At the end of the vintage, the tradition there was for all the workers to weave their way in a lively procession up to the various *quintas* to celebrate with the respective owners. On this occasion, however, Alfredo was still in his bath and had to be roused in the nick of time. The Hoelzers had a charming daughter, Julia, who I once took for a walk among the vines. This was much to the amusement of Jean, although Alfredo let it be known in his lovely, bumbling way that he did not approve. Tragically, Julia later lost her life, along with 130 others, in the Funchal, Madeira, air disaster of 1977.

A much-coveted invitation was dinner at Claire Bergqvist's Quinta de la Rosa – a delightful *quinta* perched high above the River Douro, just west of Pinhão. Claire's parties were famous for their hospitality, not least the 'unusual' food and 'different' drinks. In my diary I recorded that the borscht soup was so disgusting that we threw it out of the window. The drink selection was similarly 'exotic', consisting of gin, brandy, ginger ale and tomato juice – and that was it. Nevertheless, this was the last day of the famous 1963 vintage: flowers were presented to the hostess, we danced in the stone *lagars* full of fermenting grape juice and I somehow managed to break a loo seat. The following day, I happened to drive past the scene of the crime with Gwyn Jennings, who ran Sandeman in Oporto. 'Good God,' exclaimed Gwyn, gazing at the pink-stained landscape: 'What on earth is that mess? Looks like bloodshed.' Marginally embarrassed, I mumbled something about soup…

This dinner has since gone down in Bergqvist family history and recently, I was able to give Claire's delightful granddaughter Sophia, the present owner of Quinta de la Rosa, the exact date – October 12th 1963. I might add that these days, both the food and the wines at la Rosa are exquisite!

Guests at other dinners included Lord Newell, Mr and Mrs Baring Gould (who were great friends of the Duke and Duchess of Windsor) and Sir Dennis Whitley, the former Governor of Borneo. Such gatherings left a deep impression on this particular 21-year-old, who was beginning to realize that 'fine wines' in their broadest sense inspired awe among such establishment figures, commanded respect for those who 'knew about wine' and, above all, stimulated fascinating conversations about almost everything.

On October 18th I bade an emotional farewell to Alfredo and Jean, thanking them for their wondrous hospitality. My faithful Mini and I then wended our way across northern Portugal towards the Spanish frontier. Often the roads were little more than dust tracks hewn out from the wild and mountainous scenery.

On to Valladolid, north of Madrid, and thence to the Pyrenees. The normally indispensable *Michelin Guide* yielded few clues as to restaurants or hotels, and first Bayonne then Biarritz, passed before I arrived in Bordeaux at noon – two days, 654 miles and 76 litres of petrol later, at an average speed of 38.5 miles per hour. There I found myself billeted *chez* Madame Gré at 17 Rue Emile Zola, along with a Dutchman, a German, a Swiss and an old Harrovian. Jeremy Burroughes and William Knight were already there. Against the chilliest of backdrops, the party was about to begin.

It so happened that the winter of 1963 was the coldest in Europe since 1947. The vintage in the Douro Valley may have been excellent, but few good wines were produced in France that year, and certainly not in Bordeaux.

This was also the year in which Kim Philby defected to Russia, President de Gaulle vetoed Britain's entry into the Common Market, and the Profumo Affair, involving Stephen Ward, Christine Keeler and Mandy Rice-Davies, was in full swing. We were touched by the latter even in Bordeaux, since Stephen Ward's nephew, Jonathan Ward, a rather jolly chap as I recall, had recently opened a bar on the Quai de Chartrons. I encountered Jonathan in a fairground bumper car on my very first night. My own non-involvement in the scandal was that John Profumo, who at the time was Minister for War and who had served in the Northamptonshire Yeomanry alongside my father, had been due to visit our annual TA camp in May, shortly before I left England. Alas, this was not to be.

Such were the circumstances surrounding our study of Bordeaux, the most important wine region in the world. Certainly, there were visits to the various châteaux, but the main focus of our efforts was the region's all-important négociants. Georges Lung, grandson of Louis Eschenauer, was arguably the most knowledgeable, and was kind and generous in his attitude towards us young Brits. Samples were obtained from the leading châteaux before being tasted, compared and judged in Eschenauer's Bordeaux offices. Those selected were then bought from the château to be sold around the world, mainly to the UK.

Georges Lung held regular weekly blind tastings for all the *stagiaires* in town – always in the morning when the palate was at its most receptive. We were all unstintingly competitive as to how many Bordeaux regions, or even châteaux, we could identify. Could this have been because the 'winner', who made the most correct identifications, would receive an outstanding bottle of wine, such as Château Angelus 1955.

There were also times when Georges kindly invited to me join him for a trade lunch. On one such occasion, our guests were three visitors from the Finnish Wine Monopoly. Georges duly spoiled us with a Château Olivier 1959, a Haut-Brion 1953 and a Smith Haut-Lafitte 1920, although the Finns, keen imbibers that they were, drained their glasses in double-quick time without pausing to comment on such beauties. After they had left, Georges beckoned to me to stay. Head in hands, he lamented the fact that such important customers clearly had so little respect for such works of vinous art – that they cared so little for quality and thirsted only for quantity. I think this was the first time I had seen a wine producer's passion so candidly expressed.

It was at the first of Georges' tastings that I met the ebullient Rodney Briant Evans – another character with a proper job, this time at Sichel. So far as I know he was the only one of us who kept a photograph of his girlfriend by his bed. I was most impressed.

Although I had arrived at the tail-end of the much-lamented 1963 harvest, on my second day a group of us were taken to see the last of the *pourriture noble* grapes being pressed at Château d'Yquem. It was an extraordinary sight, not least because the pungent, raisiny aromas of the grapes attracted swarms of fruit flies, no doubt delirious at being presented with such a feast.

We thought nothing of criss-crossing from sub-region to sub-region in a single day, often in the company of enthusiastic négociants whose job it was to visit the various châteaux and collect samples of must (newly pressed wine) to be tasted back at their respective laboratories. Eschenauer, Bichot, Ed Kressman, Cruse, Delors, Calvet, Dourthe Frères, Sichel, de Luse and Schröder & Schÿler were among the foremost names, and during my stay I also met some of their major customers, such as Harvey Prince of Lebegue and John Grant.

One such journey was made in my Mini, along with Jeremy Burroughes and Jonathan Ward, to visit no less than six châteaux – Ausone, Nenin, Cheval Blanc, Canon, Figeac and Conseillante – before lunch in St-Emilion. Another time we hit the Médoc: Châteaux Beychevelle, Latour and Mouton Rothschild before lunch, Cos d'Estournel afterwards. One visit will always stick in my mind – to Château Loudenne, near Lesparre-Médoc, which was owned by the Gilbey family. This wondrous pink edifice was to feature in my life for many years, but my first visit was with Peter Dauthieu, whose father had just created the Peter Dominic[2] chain of retail shops in the south of England. Another former pupil of Downside, Peter was delightfully cosmopolitan. Annoyingly, he was also a better taster than I was and scooped more prizes. David Orr was also at Loudenne. Little did he know then that he would end his career in wine as the president of Château Latour.

We seldom lunched at the châteaux, and I am still unsure if this is because we were 'trade' or because no one actually lived in these incredible houses. We did, however, frequently sample the great 1961 vintage, that of Château Palmer being especially notable. (No, sadly I did not buy any 1961s.) We also regularly drank the 1953s and 1955s. The oldest vintage I sampled was Château Smith Haut-Lafitte 1892, which, as I noted in my diary, 'stood up remarkably well, refusing to wane'.

In those days Great Britain was by far Bordeaux's most important market; the States merely dabbled and China was far into in the future. At the time, the Bordelais were changing from shipping their claret in barrels to London

---

[2] Dominic was Peter's middle name, which his father quite rightly thought would be easier to pronounce than 'Dauthieu'.

or Bristol for bottling to bottling their wines at source – '*Mise en bouteille au Château*'. Bottling lines, though, were still rare in Bordeaux and the economies of scale worked against rigorous quality control, so it was far from plain sailing. In between all this hard work, we somehow managed to catch the releases *Dr No*, the first James Bond film, and Billy Wilder's *Some Like it Hot*. We also played soccer on the quai, rugger in the country, and enjoyed many bouts of *petit foos*[3] in various bars.

The first of two outstanding excursions was to Andorra, with William Knight, when my carburettor froze at 2,400 metres – the height of the (then) highest radio station in the world. On the way back, we chased a Renault 4 down a succession of Pyrenean hairpins; in between, we had lunch in Spain and I bought some very large silk scarves duty-free – for whom, I wonder? The other memorable outing was to the fabled Grotto of Lascaux with Jeremy Burroughes and Rodney Briant Evans – not just because of the fascinating cave paintings themselves, but because we were among the very last visitors to be allowed to see these astonishing works of Paleolithic art, which date back to 15,000 BC. Discovered only in 1940, the caves were closed to the public shortly after our visit due to a green mould that had appeared on the walls – probably due to the onlookers' gasps of astonishment. The Lady Fortune had indeed smiled on us.

For some reason, my daily travelogue comes to an abrupt stop on November 15th, although I did not leave Bordeaux until the 19th. Did I go AWOL? My final stop was in Cognac, where I spent four happy days visiting the region's four leading producers. First up was Rémy Martin, where the owner, a Monsieur Renard, kindly gave me a miniature of Louis XIII cognac, along with the advice that I must keep it for my wedding night. Almost exactly to the day, 13 years later, and much to the surprise of my new wife, I did precisely that. I still treasure that most elegant of bottles, which now sits sadly empty in my cellar.

Martell was next, followed by Hennessy, where I sampled some splendid

---

[3] Pron. 'petty fusse'; the popular French name at the time for table football.

old blends from the barrel. My last stop was to Hine, where the aforementioned François and Robert Hine so kindly gave me lunch. They also presented me with a bottle to take home, for which I still have the official customs document. It is stamped seize heures (4.00pm) on November 22nd – exactly 2½ hours before President Kennedy was fatally shot.

CHAPTER THREE

On the Road

Today it is fully accepted that everyone should be given the opportunity of a university education. In the 1960s, few of my contemporaries went to university. Those who did went to Oxford or Cambridge, or to Trinity College Dublin – Cirencester Agricultural College being the other choice. Gap years had not yet been invented. My route into higher education was somewhat different, in that when I left school in 1960, I was enrolled at Amherst College in Massachusetts for one year only. Nobody in England had heard of this liberal arts college, despite the fact that it was, and still is, one of the most difficult American colleges for prospective students to gain admission to. By a strange twist of fate, Amherst was also where President Kennedy made his last major speech, less than a month before that fateful day in Dallas. How I got there is a story in itself.

During the war, my father had been drafted into Churchill's War Cabinet and despatched to Washington DC to serve with the joint chiefs of staff. After the war, he chose to stay in the USA and settled in New York. My parents were amicably divorced and later my father married Elizabeth Penrose, who went on to become the first ever female news editor of *The New York Times*. My stepmother was evidently used to getting her own way. Despite the fact that I had never met her (nor indeed properly met my father), she suggested to him that I should attend an American university. I duly applied – without much enthusiasm, it must be said – to Princeton, Harvard, Yale and a handful of other American colleges, only to be turned down flat. Undaunted, my stepmother sent me an application form for Amherst. They turned me down, too. At this point my exasperated stepmother called the president of Amherst, the charming Calvin Plimpton, and informed him that since I had been to the best school in England[1] (a moot point, but who was I to argue?), it was the very least his college could do to accommodate me for a year on-campus. Three weeks later I received a letter from the equally charming dean of admissions welcoming me to Amherst[2] that September.

I enjoyed my year at Amherst, where my fellow students included the engaging Peter J Rubinstein, a future New York Senior Rabbi, and the brilliant economist, Joe Stiglitz, who became a double winner of the Nobel Peace Prize. I also have vivid memories of motoring down to New York City from my father's home in Connecticut in his 1952 Bentley Continental and of racing his 1928 Bentley 4½ Litre at Sebring in Florida, where he was the track marshall. At the end of my stint in America I ambitiously attempted to hitch-hike to California, only to end up in New Orleans. Then, all too soon, it was time to return to the UK, and to 18 months in the somewhat less-exotic surroundings of Phipp's Brewery, Northampton, where a job on the shop floor had been secured for me by a family friend. Fortunately, my brush with higher education was not yet over. Through my Vintners Scholarship, I not only learned the rudiments of the trade that would serve me wonderfully well for the next 60-odd years but made the sort of life-long friendships that others make at

---

[1] That school was Rugby, where Ben's father had gone before him and where his brother John would follow. Rugby was also the *alma mater* of Steven Spurrier and Hugh Johnson.

[2] It was at the Amherst 30th class reunion in 1994 that the author held the first ever tasting on American soil of Royal Tokaji (of which more in Chapter 10). The venue was the former Post-Attack Command and Control System Facility, situated a few miles from Amherst under Bare Mountain. This once top-secret 40,000 sq ft underground complex had played a pivotal role during the Cuban Missile Crisis of 1962. It was later repurposed as a library storage facility for Amherst and four other colleges.

university. It might not have been the most conventional start in life, but I have never regretted it for a single moment.

* *

Upon my return from the Continent at the end of 1963, my halcyon days as a student in the university of life behind me, it was decreed that I would become a salesman. My wares consisted of a motley assortment of wines. My terroir was the North Midlands – more specifically, Lincolnshire, Nottinghamshire, Derbyshire and Leicestershire. After six months spent hob-nobbing with the great and the good among the finest vineyards in Europe, it was a little like being posted to Siberia. I jest, of course, but like all good jokes this one contained more than a grain of truth.

The early 1960s was a time when wine was rarely served in pubs, when decent restaurants were few and far between, and when the denizens of working men's clubs knew nought but beer. It was about as far a cry from the sundrenched slopes of Andalusia as one could imagine, and it certainly wasn't what I was expecting – but still, there I was, chucked in at the deep end with only my company car, a Ford Anglia (much prized in those days) for company.

To learn the selling ropes, I was enrolled in an internal two-and-a-half week Watney Mann Dale Carnegie sales training course. My chief takeaway was that, in real terms, a salesman probably had only one hour per day to actually sell to his customers, the other 23 hours being taken up with sleep (8½), eating (4), travelling (3), waiting around (1), tea (1), relaxing (4) and desk work (1½). It was an appropriately sobering thought.

My office was in the newly constructed Glaisdale Industrial Estate in Nottingham. On my first day there, I faced a dilemma. A wine trade friend was giving a party in London that night: should I go or should I decline? Of course, I went. The M1 only stretched as far as Leicester in those days, but I hot-footed it to London regardless, enjoyed the party, then drove back to Nottingham in the small hours. The following morning my boss, the gallant Freddie Fewkes, offered to drive me around to some key accounts. Needless to say, I spent most of the day quietly dozing in the passenger seat, largely oblivious to the cultural desert in which I found myself.

Those accounts included working men's and miners' clubs, night clubs and the odd restaurant. My best seller was Justina, a Portuguese table wine that bravely held its own in an era of Mateus Rosé, Hirondelle and Black Tower. I soon discovered that coal miners liked beer – and that wine, in so much as it was for anyone, was for girls. The miners' clubs were renowned for their committee meetings, when it was expected that the visiting 'rep' would buy round after round of pints. After that, the committee might – or might not – place an order for your wine.

One such club was at the Pinxton Colliery in Derbyshire. 'Would I like to go down a coal mine?' I was asked. I would have been sissy in the extreme to refuse, so I duly joined a dozen or so miners in a cage lift and found myself bumpily descending the 200 feet or so into the bowels of the earth. There, lit by hanging lamps, were the glistening seams of coal that had first been mined in 1800 BC. We ventured along the various passages, half-bent in the semi darkness and feeling our way by touching the sides, when I was seized by a sudden urge to go to the loo. There was no loo of course: you just went where you were. And that's exactly what I did.

Back above ground, I asked one of the more rotund miners how many pints of beer he enjoyed each day – it was, after all, a hot, sweaty business down the mine. 'About 30,' came the reply, 'though on a good day, I can do 40,' No room for Justina here, I thought.

Stuart was the owner of Nottingham's premier night club, the Hippo. He bought plenty of spirits from me, mainly Gordons gin and Haig whisky, since vodka was virtually unknown at the time. Stuart had married a local stripper and lived in a spacious apartment overlooking the River Trent. He sometimes asked me to Sunday lunch, when he would cook a wonderful roast while I chatted to his delightful (and this time fully dressed) wife. On one occasion, we were interrupted by gunfire at the window. Jumping up from the table, dodging the bullets, we peeped gingerly outside only to see two or three men shooting at us. Apparently, they were a rival gang who had taken against my host. I made my excuses, as they say, and left.

Independent club owners never liked to pay their bills – and when they did, it was often preceded by a challenge. One club, on Ilkley Moor of Baht'at fame, boasted a ghost that was said to appear at midnight on certain dates of the year. If you waited long enough, you might see it; otherwise, you didn't get paid. Another club urged the unfortunate rep to stretch out his arms and place empty bottles as far away from his feet as he could. Place them the requisite distance and you were paid; fail, and you had to wait another week.

Sharing my office, as well as my sense of humour, was one Jeremy Fraser. Jeremy was much more successful selling beer than I was at selling wine, but to relieve the monotony of driving so many miles on one's own, making 10 or more calls per day, often on fruitless accounts, we would arrange to meet up at the same account to have lunch. The choice was limited to say the least, but our favourite watering hole was the welcoming Manor Hotel, at Long Bennington in Lincolnshire. On their list were some of our own wines. Where better to spend the balance of our respective expense accounts? Lunches at the Manor lasted well into the afternoons.

During this time, which was often punctuated with spare moments, an entrepreneurial friend, George Campbell Johnston, and I started a travel company, called Campbell-Johnston and Howkins. We focused mainly on selling chalet and hotel holidays in the Alps. Erna Low, Inghams and Murison Small were already in the market. David Lewthwaite asked our advice and then started Supertravel.

We found ourselves in the pioneering vanguard of what for many is now regarded as *de rigueur* so far as winter sports holidays are concerned. Until the early 1960s, families had tended to make their own bookings direct with hotels. We thought that taking a chalet for eight friends or block-booking part of a hotel would be much more fun.

During the treacherous (or glorious, depending on your view) winter of 1963, I remember that a two-week stay for 12 of us at the Grand Hotel Vereina in Klosters cost the princely sum £49 10s per person, including flights and full board (which in turn included a packed lunch). Ski boots were worn for the après ski tea dances but ties were mandatory for our four-course dinners with wine. Even hitting the nightclubs hard, it was difficult to spend over £100 per person. The deal was for the organizer to get a free holiday so long as he or she filled the chalet or part of the hotel – revolutionary then; commonplace now. Quite apart from that, the business presented numerous opportunities to chat up girls and sell wine – usually Justina – to everyone. What did Derbyshire miners and London debutantes have in common? Justina. Not an especially well thought-out brand positioning, but it worked for me.

Sadly, my four-year 'University of Life' education, interspersed with a moveable gap year, was about to end. In early 1966 I was summoned to London – to be exact, the headquarters of Brown & Pank in Stockwell. London was undoubtedly where I wanted to be; it was just a pity that the working environment was so sterile. It is fair to say that those offices on Stockwell Green were the yardstick by which I have judged offices ever since; it was the only place I have ever worked that caused my spirits to sink a degree or two the moment I entered. Whatever spring I may have had in my step as I crossed the threshold, I felt noticeably less positive. I don't really know why, given that all the offices I have entered since have given me a feeling of positive expectation.

That said, as London's fine wine salesman for Brown & Pank (the company name was often modified by a single consonant, which served to make it more memorable), I found myself out and about most days. This time my accounts were West End clubs rather than miners' clubs, while South Kensington restaurants took the place of rural eateries.

One of the latter was Land's, a splendid family-run restaurant in Walton Street with the telephone number KNI 7585. It was owned by the delightful Mrs Land, a Danish woman whose husband ran Carlsberg – or it could have been Tuborg. The manager was the brother-in-law of ex-King Farouk of

Egypt, a most friendly fellow, while the washer-upper was John Fairfax – the first person in recorded history to cross the Atlantic alone by rowing boat.

The owner and the manager often invited me to eat with them, the deal being that I brought wine samples while they fed me, and I sometimes used to wander into the kitchen to help John with the washing up. John was quiet but determined. One day he confided in me that he would soon be leaving the restaurant to row the Atlantic. The fact that he had no rowing experience was neither here nor there: he had lost his parents in a yachting accident in the West Indies and seemed to value life lightly.

William Knight and I came across him one day practicing on the Serpentine in Hyde Park. We chatted a while, then off he was again. Later, he practiced in the Thames Estuary.

John eventually made his trip across the Atlantic in the summer of 1969, braving sharks, storms and exhaustion during the six-month, 5,000-mile journey from the Canary Islands to Florida. In typical John fashion, he never once blew his own trumpet about this extraordinary achievement. I had offered to sponsor him with a few bottles, but he declined on the grounds that there was no room for them in his boat.

Other restaurants that bought wine from me included the Chanterelle in Old Brompton Street, telephone number KEN 0292, and L'Escargot in Soho, which was famously bought by Nick Lander, the future husband of Jancis Robinson MW. One order there was for a case of Château La Fleur Pétrus 1958. That was more like it.

Once, on a visit to a newly established wine merchants, Murray & Banbury at 227 Brompton Road, I was greeted by one Steven Spurrier. We had been at Rugby together and Steven was now their wine buyer. Ever on the look-out for the best and most interesting wines at the right price, I noted that Steven bought two cases of Château Pape Clément 1955 from me in November 1967.

John Davy, the enterprising free vintner at the Boot and Flogger, ordered

Volnay 1962. Nick's Diner and 19 Mossop Street, the Grenadier and the Chelsea Potter, all needed to be visited as often as possible – sometimes during the day, more likely in the evenings accompanied by girlfriends. This was, after all the Swinging Sixties and we thought it perfectly normal.

Meanwhile, I had moved flats from Manson Place off Queensgate to the centre of the universe – Cadogan Gardens SW3, opposite Peter Jones. Just before I moved, I had become involved in what one newspaper picturesquely described as 'Film Set Raid Story of Chelsea Plot', which I only mention since it threatened to blow my career in the wine trade career somewhat off-course. The headline was slightly inaccurate, in that Manson Place is in South Kensington, not Chelsea, but the facts were basically correct. A few friends –William Knight, Jeremy Fraser, Ran Fiennes and I – felt that a great injustice was being done in Britain's prettiest village, Castle Combe in Wiltshire, where 20th Century Fox were filming *Dr Doolittle*. To our minds it was a question of 'mass entertainment riding roughshod over the feelings of individuals'. We planned a night protest with the odd thunder-flash or two.

Fortunately, or unfortunately, there was a tip-off to the police that effectively put paid to our protest. Knight and Fiennes were taken into custody overnight, Fraser and I drove home. The main problem was that one of us was a baronet, which made it a top news story. My mother heard about it on the BBC one o'clock news while she was doing the ironing.

We were all subsequently fined for 'conspiring to create a public nuisance', which might have placed a serious question mark over our respective careers had not the judge remarked that we 'each had the invaluable asset of an excellent character.' Castle Combe was very much a *cause célèbre* at the time. We were fortunate that it just preceded the start of the Troubles in Northern Ireland, otherwise our little prank might well have had more serious consequences.

Ran was represented by Sir Peter Rawlinson QC no less, who had served as Solicitor General in Harold Macmillan's government. The elegant Giles Best QC represented me. By chance, he and I met up at the bar on a train to

Sussex a few years later where we drank each other's health. It was a fitting end to such an episode.

For the record, William Knight left the wine trade to enjoy a successful international banking career, Jeremy Fraser went on to become a successful and innovative artist, and Ran Fiennes – or to give him his full title, Sir Ranulph Twistleton-Wykeham-Fiennes Bt – left the Army to become 'the world's greatest living explorer' while I continued my vinous romp. Over 50 years later, we all remain great friends. In the meantime, the next instalment of my career was about to begin.

CHAPTER FOUR

Towards Enlightenment[1]

'Fun' is not necessarily the best adjective to describe one's chosen career. It smacks of insincerity, of lack of ambition and even disrespect. Yet in the wine trade of old, fun played an important part in all our lives, whether as colleagues or competitors. Maybe the wine helped? Most of us were just out of school (usually) or university (unusually) – fresh-faced, new to London and eager to play in what in those days was effectively the old boy network known as the 'wine trade'. At the same time, at least some of us realized that there was much to learn about wine, and we were more than happy to do so, as it was fun.

I have a letter in front of me from John Mahony, Secretary of the Wine and Spirit Association (WSA) of Great Britain, inviting me to attend a 'series of lectures on Wine and Spirits at the College for the Distributive Trades, 107 Charing Cross Road, London WC2 (opposite the Phoenix Theatre and next door to the Tatler Cinema).' It was written in December 1961 – that is, long before the days of WSET, the industry-leading Wine and Spirits Education Trust. The entire course cost one guinea. The subjects were Burgundy, Bordeaux, Sparkling wines, Rhine and Moselle, Sherry, Commonwealth wines, Italian wines, and Port and Rum. Wine, in those days, basically came from Europe.

---

[1] Parts of this chapter were first published in The Wine and Spirits Education Trust's 50th Anniversary book Best in Class, May 2015.

Interestingly, there was no mention of 'education' – that came later. One feature of these pre-WSET courses is that we were always asked to bring two glasses. That somehow implied a party, though we kept this until afterwards. The lecturers varied in their attempts to enthral us, but I think we all felt somehow bound to this rather fun world of wine.

Looking at my handwritten notes for the first time in almost 50 years, I am struck by two things: how much knowledge was actually imparted; and how, in spite of such worthy lectures, I still found time within them to write a naïvely steamy novel. I think the latter is best forgotten.

There was a happy sense of amateurishness on both sides. We students much enjoyed each other's company – an embryonic sense of culture and togetherness that appeared to have been a hallmark of the English wine trade since time immemorial. For me, it all started at 107 Charing Cross Road. We were 'in it together', we marvelled at the more engaging speakers, and we all felt a teeny bit privileged. We also enjoyed sharing a drink together afterwards – 'socializing' in today's parlance – before trailing home with our two glasses.

Ever since, I have been asked how or why I became involved in this world of wine. We did not drink wine at home, and during the previous year I had studied at a college where alcohol was forbidden until you were 21. Not for me the casual swigging of claret and port at Oxbridge. I left home when I was 18, so I made do with milk at meals and beer in the fraternity house – hardly an auspicious start. I joined my local brewery in Northampton because the directors were close family friends, and the shop floor was hardly a hotbed of vinous education. I remember on my first day, while I was being shown round, we passed a small room that my guide deftly stepped past, putting his finger to his lips. 'Shush… that is the where the computer is.'

It was under the wondrous tutelage of Don Lovell MW, with the encouragement of Bob Helliwell, that I started my education in wine. My records show that my first visit to a wine region was in September 1961. Where? To Germany of course – to Guntrum and Kupferberg. I cannot stress enough how important German wine was to the UK trade in those days. Another leaflet I have in front of me is entitled 'How to give a wine and cheese party' – a prototype, I suppose, for '*Abigail's Party.*' There was no formal training as such, but there was plenty of tasting. I can't quite remember what drove me on the most – the fascination of the different aromas and tastes or the fact that I could take home endless sample bottles.

It was in June 1962, following a pass in the aforementioned Examination in Wines and Spirits, that I was encouraged to apply for the Vintners' Scholarship. This was really quite grown-up. I duly presented myself at Vintners' Hall in the City of London to be greeted by a succession of besuited figures from similarly bespoke companies – Harveys, Hedges and Butler and the like. I all but froze: I was the outsider from Brown & Pank in the Midlands, for goodness sake. We took it in turns to be 'interviewed' – no mere exam, this. The Master, Brigadier Lorne Campbell VC, was fascinated by my American college experiences but eventually another Court member got round to asking me about wine: 'Tell me,' he said. 'Do you know how the *solera* system works in Jerez?' My hands gripped the arms of my seat. To explain this complicated procedure would take ages and left frightening margins for error. I decided to wing it. 'Yes', I replied as confidently as I could muster. Somewhat taken aback, my questioner leaned back with a slightly miffed – or was it relieved? –'Ah, good.' And that was that. It could be said that I won this coveted prize with just a single word.

This wholly unexpected experience was to change my life. Aged 20, I was to meet the owners of, and visit, the greatest vineyards in Europe some five years before I took the WSA Senior Certificate Parts 1 and 2, which was only a few months before WSET itself was incorporated. It also taught me a valuable lesson when interviewing: never ask a candidate a question to which the answer could be a simple 'yes' or 'no'. I was nevertheless eternally grateful that I had been asked just such a question.

First enlightenment: let's bring back interviewing as a means to an end. I believe the interview is genuinely underrated in our current age of exams and all-consuming grades. Yes, interviews take time, but today the Vintners' Scholarship is automatically conferred on the top student rather than given out as a prestigious and highly personal award. Let personality and character count for something, as well as the ability to pass exams; the yearly ambassador for the Vintners' Company should be interviewed, not automated.

I note in a further letter from the WSA in November 1967 that the organization now had an education officer, A G Bone, who I remember as a smiling, balding, busy and helpful character. A year later, an Education Department was established at 3 Lovat Lane in EC3. The director of education there was David Burroughs – professional, moustachioed and more than a little austere. Re-reading his letter concerning Senior (Parts 1 and 2) Wine and Spirit Course, it must have been him who initiated what I still regard to be an essential part of anyone's wine education – namely, management, even if at the time this was confined to subjects such as 'the Nature of Management' and 'Office Organization and Method'. In those days, schools and universities did little to prepare their students for office work: rather like marriage, it just happened; you got on with it.

For Part 1, during February and March 1968, the morning subjects were Bordeaux, Hock and Moselle (whatever happened to them?), Port, Loire and Italy. The afternoon subjects were Legal Matters, Customs and Importation, Marketing and Salesmanship, Scotch whisky (the token UK spirit?) and Spanish and Portuguese wines. For Part 2, during February and March 1969, the morning subjects were Burgundy, Champagne, Sherry, Alsace and Rhône. The afternoon subjects were Office Administration, Cellar Management, History of Trade & Current Affairs, Cognac (nice alternative?) and Other European Wines (to be covered in two hours).

Most of the lecturers managed to keep our attention throughout. Among them, John Salvi, Peter Hallgarten, Patrick Forbes, Guy Gordon Clark and John Clevely stood out; they were talented, knowledgeable and always enthusiastic. There were exceptions, though, including one fabled gentleman who insisted on solemnly reciting the 12 pages of notes that we already had in front of us. Yet overall, we began to gain a feeling of professionalism, coupled with a real sense of achievement. And again, the lectures became a meeting place – a melting pot for those of us coming to the giddy realization that by knowing more about wine, we might be more successful in the trade, whether buying, marketing or selling.

I think that the willingness of its senior members to give up their time (in those early days without payment) so that newcomers can learn has always been an underlying hallmark of the wine trade. It is a generous trade – one that engages in serious business while still finding time to enjoy the banter between colleagues and rivals alike. Much of this culture is due to open-heartedness of those early educational pioneers.

The 'Modern Cellar Management' paper naturally devoted much time and space to bottling. Punts were getting lighter, cans (whatever happened to them?) were being considered for red wines, a shortage of good quality corks was already being noted, and the pros and cons of SO_2 were much discussed. Wine labels still largely referred to their contents rather than offering any form of guarantee. The first question in the exam was 'Discuss the role of the chemist in the Wine Trade today. Pioneering then; essential now.

One of the perks of passing these exams was the possibility of a scholarship, and I was fortunate to be summoned to Jerez under the Williams & Humbert (W&H) umbrella. Ironically, in my career at this time I was also on the point of joining Croft as export manager. When I arrived in Jerez, it became immediately apparent that communications with London had somehow broken down. No one at W&H quite knew why I was there. I was given a deckchair in their beautiful garden, a bottle of Pando and the previous day's edition of *The Times*. After the third such day of tranquil bliss, but nil learning, I hopped over to see John Lockwood of Sandeman. Over the next two days, John both inspired me to love sherry and also enlightened me as to the intricacies of this great wine. To this day, I honour his kindness.

Second enlightenment: producers who offer awards or scholarships should prepare well and make sure they take full advantage of the student visiting. You never know what memories they will take back with them, or what power and influence they may one day yield. I recall that Sarah Ahmed, the 2014

Vintners' Scholar, once told me that Jerez was no longer a 'must visit' wine region. When, I wonder, will we again get to appreciate the wonders of *manzanilla, fino* and *dry olorosos?*

In the early 1970s, spurred on by the formation of the Wine and Spirits Education Trust (WSET), my employers at the time, IDV, opened their Gilbey Vintners School of Wine near their Regent's Park offices under the tutelage of Clive Williams MW. Clive was a scholarly, no-panic sort of chap. I note that I was first asked to lecture on port on November 1st 1972 with a reminder that 'Lunch will be immediately before, at 1.15pm, and we should be pleased if you would care to join us.' In those days any IDV lunch would have included several gin and tonics as well as wine and port. Nevertheless, it was at just such a lecture that I met a tall, likeable American who was studying for his MW exam. Twenty years later, that same person became the importer for Royal Tokaji in the USA and as such, an extremely important figure in my commercial life.

Third enlightenment: more often than not, what we perceive as luck is simply a matter of seizing the right opportunity at the right time.

From 1972 to 1975, or perhaps a little later, I gave the port lecture to successive intakes of WSET Higher Certificate students. Colin Gurteen was the assistant education officer at the time – a wonderfully enthusiastic and helpful individual who remained so even after he suffered a terrible motorbike accident. Samples and slides were the order of the day. In the early years, I also gave the Madeira lecture – until someone spotted that I had never actually been to Madeira and had me removed from the roster. In fact, it wasn't until 2014 that I first visited the island, and that was on a golfing holiday. WSET lectures in those days were most definitely taken seriously, but they were also great social occasions long before the word 'networking' was in vogue.

I thought it would be amusing at this stage to try out my lecturing skills on The Organization of Wine Butlers, which five years later would become the Court of Master Sommeliers. My letter of May 12th 1972 has them at 68½ Upper Thames Street, near Vintners' Hall in the City. Geoff Armstrong, a quasi-imposing sort of fellow, was the National Secretary, but it was Guy Gordon Clark, via George Bull, who kindly proposed me to lecture on port to the organization's 80 or so members. I honestly don't remember much about the occasion, other than that the students clearly exhibited a great fondness for the subject matter. It is a credit to their successors that the Court of Master Sommeliers evolved into the much-respected organization it is today.

* *

Fast forward to 2000, when I was asked to represent The Vintners' Company as a Trustee of WSET. By this time, the somewhat closed old boys' network that had characterized the London wine trade of the 1960s and '70s had morphed into the thriving global lifestyle business of the 1980s and '90s. A former prime minister had recently proclaimed 'educashun, educashun, educashun' to be the way forward. I was more than happy to play my part.

At the time of my appointment, though, the organization was floundering a bit. It seemed to me that there were one too many brigadiers in charge, which may have gone down well with Vintners' Hall, but left the organization in dire need of more commercial experience. A year later, enter Ian Harris, ex-Seagrams. WSET's deft Chairman, Keith Garrard, made the introductions as we were lined up to greet our new chief executive. 'I don't suppose you have met Ben Howkins?' Keith inquired. Quick as a flash, Ian smiled and replied: 'Oh yes I have.' Bemused, I had no recollection whatsoever of this new *wunderkind*. 'Ben once turned me down for a job at Morgan Furze,' added Ian. 'Best thing that ever happened.' There was laughter all round, although to this day I am not entirely sure what Ian meant by that. It is true that faces are often forgotten in such circumstances – yet another potential pitfall among life's rich pageant.

Among Ian's biggest achievements as CEO was to change people's perception of wine education from being a 'cost centre' into a 'profit centre'. Proof of the value of wine education came from high street retailers, who quickly discovered that managers and staff who had attended WSET courses made more money than those who hadn't. Almost overnight, we zoomed into profit, with better defined courses, a truly global approach and a host of willing sponsors.

During my four years as trustee, we also moved from the stylish, but cramped, Five Kings House adjacent to Vintners' Hall to a freehold building in Bermondsey Street, SE1. This was a brave, but brilliant, decision that enabled WSET to grow from an annual 10,000 students to 10 times that amount in just 20 years (and to which the Oscars-like Annual Prize Giving Ceremony at the Guildhall serves as a wonderful testament). The one battle that we failed to win was to align the Institute of Masters of Wine (IMW) more closely to WSET. To most intelligent people, it seemed entirely logical that the two most prestigious UK wine education bodies should enjoy a close relationship. We tried, oh we tried… but a faction of MWs remained steadfastly against the idea, or even that we share our splendid new building.

Recently, Ian Harris kindly acknowledged the help that I continue to give WSET during my regular business visits to the US and other parts of the world. What he really meant, I think, is that in my present globetrotting role I contribute more than I ever did as trustee. Today, WSET is not only a great brand but a truly global one and I am proud to be part of it. True, the Court of Sommeliers and other educational bodies all contribute hugely to a greater understanding, appreciation and knowledge of wine, but from a professional perspective, WSET is the unquestioned world leader.

To my mind, this success can be traced back to the very earliest days of the organization, when 'management, marketing and salesmanship' were included in the syllabus. This commercial thread, which has been part of WSET's rationale ever since, acknowledges the fact that while wine is a product that inspires great passion in the trade, to be successful and ahead of the game we must never forget that we are first and foremost in business. WSET fosters a culture of 'givers' rather than 'takers' – a tradition rooted in the formation of the Worshipful Company of Vintners more than 600 years ago. In those days London was the centre of the wine trade. Arguably it still is – the big difference being that the rest of the civilized world has since joined in the fun.

CHAPTER FIVE

From Gin Palace to Quinta

A corporate reshuffle had resulted in International Distillers and Vintners (IDV) taking over the wine and spirits interests of Watney Mann, brewers of the infamous Red Barrel, which included Brown & Pank. IDV had originally been the target of Showerings, the Babycham people, but was rescued by Watney Mann, which was then taken over itself by Grand Met, which had just acquired Truman's, the smart East End brewers. Over time, both Guinness and Distillers joined the party, creating today's conglomerate Diageo. All good, straightforward corporate stuff.

Created in 1962 and led by Jasper Gibbons Grinling who, like many in his family before him, had a flair for design, IDV was the brainchild of some true wine trade visionaries, equally steeped in wine trade lore. Jasper was the half brother of Hugh Johnson's wife Judy, and IDV's prestigious headquarters in Regents Park, London NW1 was the envy of many competitors.

Among the other founding directors were characters such as Walter Gilbey, who loved driving the traditional Gilbey Coach and Four, the irrepressible Bobby Gold, and Geoffrey Hallowes, who was married to the wartime heroine Odette Churchill.

IDV already had an enviable reputation among the wine and press fraternities for being a bit different. The company was an amalgam of high-end wine merchants including the Royal Warrant holders Justerini & Brooks, who owned J&B, the lead whisky brand in the USA; Gilbey's, which included Gilbey's Gin, the world's number two brand after Gordon's; and Twiss Browning & Hallowes, which held the Hennessy Cognac and Heidsieck champagne agencies for the UK.

Monies flowing in from these international brands were to be profitably diverted into new product development, resulting in a further crop of global successes including Bailey's Irish Cream, Malibu, Croft Original and Piat d'Or. But even before the reshuffle, I had singled out IDV as the one company I would like to join: it had prestige, it was global in outlook and it was innovative. In my mind's eye IDV offered an escape from brewing and wholesaling to an altogether more adventurous arena – and, as luck would have it, this happened without me doing anything at all. One day, out of the blue, I received a memo (or it may have been phone call) in my spartan Stockwell office inviting me for an interview at IDV's imposing and supremely elegant Regency headquarters in No 1 York Gate.

'I would like you to join our young team as a brand manager in our marketing department' was the upshot, delivered by that leader among leaders, George Bull. George went on to become a director of IDV, chairman of Grand Met and co-chairman of its successor, Diageo. As a 'grand fromage' of the wine and spirit industry, George was duly knighted, and we still meet for lunch twice a year at the Pickwick Club. Back then, though, he was a charismatic ex-Guards officer who, as marketing manager of IDV, pioneered the art of brand management in the UK's wine and spirit trade – possibly the world's.

Before IDV, the wine trade had no real concept of marketing. Wines were imported, tasted and sold. Lunches took the place of business meetings. Relationships with suppliers were as important as those with customers. Loyalty was all. The whisky and gin producers were, almost unwittingly, label-builders rather than marketeers. They were upmarket salesmen who happened to have advertising departments; few, if any, cared about marketing, which at the time was thought to be the province of fast-moving consumer goods, or 'FMCG' as they were somewhat dismissively known.

The genius of IDV was to recognize that brands were themselves valuable assets, be they Heinz, Hoover or Hennessy, and in due course serious market-eers with an FMCG background were recruited to pave the way – along with a smattering of home-grown talent, me included. The immediate fruits of their labours included Smirnoff vodka, which had just been introduced to the UK.

In my new role I became the brand manager for Piat de Beaujolais, Croft port and Château Loudenne, along with a few spirits that included Gilbey's Gin. George Bull also asked me to take on Brown Gore & Welch, a wonderful agency importer that had been recently acquired by IDV and which brought with it Bouchard Père burgundies and Bols Advocaat among other delicacies.

George was a brilliant delegator. His recipe for success was to produce a current appreciation of the marketplace, add a three-year sales and marketing plan, and then discuss it with the producer or supplier while persuading them to stump up as large an advertising and PR budget as possible to supplement IDV's own contribution. The trouble was, most of our producers had never been involved in this way before and at first, they were completely bamboozled. Early on, George and I went to visit Bols in Amsterdam – founded in 1575, the world's oldest distilled spirits brand. Ours was the first marketing plan they had seen in nearly 400 years. It was a defining moment for both parties.

Gilbey's Gin was, of course, an 'in house brand', meaning that we had to discuss and negotiate with our colleagues. Since spirits could not be advertised on TV, our advertising and PR agency PPR proposed that we link our 1968–69 activities with the Hon John Gilbey, the charming senior member of the Gilbey family, thereby obtaining both publicity and prestige for the brand.

The result was Gilbey's Floating Gin Palace – not any old gin palace, but a converted paddle steamer, the PS *Ryde*, which at the time was owned by British Rail and resided on the Solent. This venerable sea-going vessel was to be leased from its owners for an eight-day trip along the south coast to Tower Pier in London and back, during which there would be four days of festivities featuring Gilbey's Gin. The total cost was estimated at £7,430 – quite a daunting sum for a brand manager earning £1,600 per annum.

Tony Garrett Anderson, a larger-than-life character from PPR, presented the plan to us in April for implementation that September. It turned out to be a massive undertaking and took over my life for the next six months. Tony's preferred meeting place was the Savile Club, glass in hand, rather than the office. He always had a twinkle in his eye, was a fine toper, and was equally generous with his cigars. He was also a master at creating events and I learned a lot from him. For Tony, nothing was impossible, especially if you wore a bow tie and oozed Irish blarney. I even received an invitation to join him and his wife for a short holiday in their villa in Minorca after it was all over. His 'thank you' present to me was an original 1847 framed set of eight engravings of 'The Bottle' by George Cruikshank – a brilliant, if terrifying, reminder of what drink can do to a family. I took it in good spirit, as it were.

Right from the start, it was clear that this was no run-of-the-mill, airy-fairy, PR event. The timetable was organized with military precision, with every second of every day accounted for. The guest list was equally impressive. The Hon John Gilbey and his elegant wife, Chippy, were the principal hosts, aided and abetted by the senior directors and managers of IDV. Gilbey secretaries, dressed in Gilbey jerseys, acted as eye-catching guides. George Bull was closely involved, as was that other great entrepreneurial spirit, Tom Jago, who at the time was busily experimenting with the ingredients that would eventually become Bailey's Irish Cream.

We invited ambassadors from the 35 countries in which Gilbey's Gin was distilled, and members of parliament representing the constituencies in which the ship's crew lived, including one Margaret Thatcher from Finchley. Also on the guest list were the mayor of Tower Hamlets and the local Pearly Queen. The amount of thought, ingenuity and planning that went into the event was staggering, as was the attention to detail. The fact that it was international made it all the more interesting, as well as bringing me into contact with countless IDV colleagues who I would not otherwise have met.

We held two black tie dinner-dances while sailing down the Thames. One, organized in conjunction with the RNLI, was the Thames Lifeboat Ball at £3 per double ticket with Humphrey Lyttleton and his band. The other was the Gilbey Ball, complete 'with a licensed bar and free Edwardian buffet', for which we engaged the services of Acker 'Stranger on the Shore' Bilk and his Paramount Jazz Band. The Gloucester City Police Band was there to welcome 30 war veterans who had once served on PS *Ryde* and who we had tracked down, along with the city editors of the national newspapers, Pathé Pictorial, the wine trade press, ship's stores customers, and assorted restaurateurs, hoteliers and publicans. The UK Bartenders Guild ran a cocktail competition with the Pearly Queen in attendance while Angus McGill of the *Evening Standard* ran another for Gilbey's Gin linked to the paper's 'Pub of the Year' competition that attracted over 1,000 entries.

Throughout it all, professionalism was key – except perhaps on the final day when, after lunch, the *Ryde's* Captain – a cheerful Cornishman by the name of Yealland – possibly enjoyed a glass or two more of gin than he should have done and the Floating Palace appeared temporarily to lose its bearings. We subsequently found ourselves continuing downstream past Tilbury when we should have turned about – a crisis that necessitated putting ashore at Tilbury docks for a Chinese takeaway to sober up the crew. In the end, we catered for more than 600 people, accompanied by changes of scenery so frequent that they would not have been out of place in a West End theatre. Gilbey's Floating Gin Palace was judged to be a huge success and became a benchmark for extracting optimum value from PR events. On a personal level, it garnered me unprecedented prestige, both internally and externally, and led to an unexpected bonus. No one, it seemed, wanted the piano that had recently been played by some of the country's finest jazz musicians, so I had it shipped to my ground floor flat in Cadogan Gardens. I subsequently mastered 'Chopsticks', but that was my limit.

* *

Another brand that proved to be an amusing vehicle for fun and games was Le Piat de Beaujolais. Charles Piat was the extrovert owner of this celebrated

Mâcon-based producer and both he and his elegant aristocratic Russian companion, the Princess Lieven, were great promoters. The princess owned Château de Bellevue in Morgon – a lovely property – while Charles, a self-confessed golf addict, had built his own course on the outskirts of Mâcon. With this in mind, we dreamed up the idea of holding a contest to hit a golf ball across the River Thames at Mortlake. Nine three-men teams took part, and although there were more plops than thuds, our little stunt nevertheless made the headlines.

Charles and I also ventured to Belfast one day, shortly after the start of the Troubles. Such was the reputation of Piat in Northern Ireland that the indomitable general manager of W & A Gilbey there laid on an airport welcome consisting of scantily clad cheerleaders swirling batons and such like. We repaired to his office mid-morning only to find the Lord Mayor of Belfast asleep on a sofa, looking for all the world like Father Jack in the priceless television comedy *Father Ted*.

A few years later, I happened to be in one of Grand Met's hotels in Paris, the Hotel Lotti, when I learned that Charles's father, André, had died. I had just sat down to write a letter of condolence, when who should I spy walking through hotel's foyer, but Charles Piat himself. He saw me and came over to chat, causing me to hastily cover up my partly written letter with what must have been a guilty look on my face. "allo Ben,' he said with a wry smile: 'I see you are writing love letters again!' It so happened that Charles had met my then girlfriend and had taken a bit of a fancy to her. I muttered something totally inadequate and blushed.

Le Piat de Beaujolais, the forerunner of that runaway brand success Le Piat d'Or, was packaged in a special bottle resembling a bowling pin. We had just introduced magnums of the 1967 vintage, of which Fortnum & Mason were so keen to be the first stockist that I drove to Mâcon, collected the first six examples, then drove back to London and delivered them to their door. The customer is always right.

We launched Le Piat de Beaujolais at Le Gavroche – a new start-up by the

Roux Brothers in Lower Sloane Street. Albert and Michel had chosen to offer a soufflé as the first course, but at the time they had never produced one for 40 guests in one go. An hour went by, with magnums of Le Piat being enjoyed on visibly empty stomachs. Clement Freud took to telling stories while standing on the table, while Raymond Postgate looked on impassively and Pamela Vandyke Price shrilled with laughter. A good start. We subsequently celebrated the wine's first anniversary with a dinner at the London Hilton on December 11*th* 1968, where *quenelles de brochet, soufflé de fromage, perdreau rôti* and *cerises flambées au marc* were all appreciatively washed down with the aforementioned magnums, along with the princess's Château Bellevue, Heidsieck Red Top and Hennessy XO.

* *

One of my favourite places to visit then, and for many happy years afterwards, was Gilbey's prettily pink property in Bordeaux, Château Loudenne. Martin Bamford MW, absolutely one of a kind, was despatched from London to sort out the building after years of semi-neglect at precisely the same time I joined the IDV marketing team in 1968. Situated on the bank of the River Garonne in the northern Médoc, Loudenne had originally been bought by the Gilbey family in 1875 as a staging post from which to ship their extensive purchases of claret back to the UK. Martin, who had started at Harvey's before being head-hunted by IDV, had a very clear idea of what the Château should be doing now – indeed, he had clear ideas about almost everything. His forceful views even extended to the budget that he had been given to restore this undeniably picturesque property, with its rolling meadows stretching down to the river – he simply ignored it.

The happy result was that Loudenne ended up punching far above its weight as a Cru Bourgeois. It remained a staging post par excellence, but instead of loading barrels onto waiting ships, Martin used it to launch both Château Loudenne and himself onto the burgeoning US market. By the early 1970s, Americans were beginning to appreciate fine wine en masse. Martin astutely welcomed these new converts to dine and to stay at Loudenne whenever they were in Bordeaux. Word soon got round and, almost overnight, Loudenne became a 'must stay' destination for top wine buyers from around the world.

One of the more extrovert customers was Max Zimmermann, who had recently created a mega-wine store in Chicago that turned over $12 million a year – a colossal amount in those days. Max, who was never without his gangster-style hat, was a frequent visitor at Loudenne. On his return to the States he would always send a most welcome purchase order from 'Max the Hat'.

There could be no more genial host than Martin. He installed a charming couple, Sylvain and Josette, as butler and chef respectively and served the very finest Bordeaux wines while the orders flooded in. To optimize margins, Martin secured exclusive global deals with Châteaux Giscours and de Pez. He also set about creating his own Bordeaux brand to rival the well-known Mouton Cadet – which is where I came in. I was responsible for the first back label of our new brand, 'La Tour Pavilion'. As it turned out, this lasted considerably longer than the front label, which incurred the wrath of Château Latour and was hastily changed to La Cour Pavilion.

Ever the bon viveur, it was not long before Martin found two like-minded souls in Bordeaux. Nicknamed '*Les Trois Cochons*', Martin, John Salvi MW and John Davies MW liked nothing better than to lunch or dine in France's three-star Michelin restaurants as often as they could – preferably twice in the same day.

Once, I led a film crew to Loudenne, intent on capturing the unique atmosphere. Unfortunately, the cameraman got so excited about the sunsets over the dunes, which were not part of the brief, that he ran out of film for the main event: the Fête de la Fleur, which, needless to say, involved a gastronomic feast followed by dancing in the courtyard.

Martin also kept a black cat called… Cat. There was always a keen sense of anticipation whenever we were called into dinner. Cat would stroll into the drawing room first, followed by Martin, who would quizzically announce 'Dinner meal is served'. It seemed that Pétrus was almost on tap – at least, for those of us he considered true friends. At one time, I took an eager Michel

Roux to visit Loudenne. Albert, the chateau's handyman-cum-chauffeur, was deputized to drive us back to the airport but unfortunately forgot to take his morning pills. Our car was soon veering all over the road, very nearly tipping us over, and we managed to arrive at the wrong terminal. Maxwell Joseph, the head of Grand Met and thus Martin's ultimate boss, was so in love with Loudenne that he kept his Rolls Royce there. During one of his visits, the gallant Albert was again despatched to fetch 'MJ', as he was fondly known, from the airport. Again, the pills must have been forgotten, since Albert crashed the Rolls en route. Asked to explain himself later, he could only mutter: '*Je m'excuse. C'était dans un moment d'inattention, Monsieur.*'

The irrepressible Martin died too young, aged 42, on the eve of the great 1982 vintage – a great loss to the world of wine. Edmund Penning-Rowsell, fabled wine writer for the FT, and I created a 'Martin Bamford Loudenne Award' for the wine student or journalist who wrote the best piece on Bordeaux. Regrettably, this was not followed up by IDV after the first few years, but later two of Martin's closest friends, Robin Don MW and Ronnie Hicks MW, secured a cask of Loudenne 1982 which they had bottled into halves, bottles, magnums, jereboams and imperials. The 10-year plan was to enjoy and compare the different sized bottles as they matured. Our inaugural dinner was held at the Dorchester on November 9th 1992, when a galaxy of Martin's friends drank to his memory. Martin was a classic visionary, arguably the most influential driver of the US wine market in the 1970s, the decade in which Americans consummated their love affair with Bordeaux. The 1970 vintage was actually a watershed in terms of investment – and all this long before Mr Parker came along.

✳✳✳✳✳✳✳✳✳✳✳✳✳✳✳✳✳✳✳✳✳✳✳✳

From Bordeaux to Burgundy. As previously mentioned, the much-loved wine shipper Brown Gore & Welch (BGW) was UK agent for one of the region's most trusted and sought-after producers, Bouchard Père.

BGW had splendid offices in Seething Lane in the City, where all the grown-up shippers were – originally so that barrels of wine could be rolled off ships moored on the Thames and into their cellars for bottling. The directors of BGW, led by Bob Derouet and Tim Derouet, were both delightful and charming, and really knew their wines. Lunch was the main focus of the day, for obvious reasons; without a chance to taste and evaluate, how could one buy? My allotted task was to request from these senior gents a three-year forecast of their expected sales. You would have thought I was asking them to commit hara-kari. 'What do you mean, forecast?' came the reply. 'We sell what we buy.' Undeterred, I reckoned that if I arrived at their offices at around 9.45am, I would have just over half an hour of their full attention – that is, from their arrival at the office to the first glass of Fino Nilo, which was always offered at precisely 10.30 am.

That became essentially my working day in Seething Lane. Lunch was always with customers and often lasted well into the afternoon, by which there was just time to catch the train home. One day, a big retail buyer came to lunch. All went well until we started playing Hampshire Hog – a card game beloved of BGW's directors and staff alike. Our guest, who was desperate to place an order for several hundred cases of Bols Advoccat, but was also pressed for time, was blithely ignored by everyone in the room. 'Will no one take my effing order?' he eventually blurted out. No-one batted an eyelid, play continued, and the customer left without ever placing his order. Under such circumstances, forecasting was quite difficult. Eventually, though, the management of BGW was 'streamlined' in the interests of efficiency. It was at that point I realized that it was more fun working for a company that took over other companies, rather than being on the receiving end.

By the beginning of 1970, it was time to move on from managing brands. Perhaps I was having too much fun? Within the space of a few months, I was offered no less than four internal roles within IDV – possibly due to the fact that there were two separate personnel offices, one in York Gate, and one at the company's distribution hub in Harlow, Essex. Two of the job offers were in Harlow. I lost no time in politely refusing them. Of the York Gate posts, both were for international marketing managers – one at Croft port, the other at Croft sherry. Croft port had been around for 300 years, while Croft sherry, via its new brand, Croft Original, was less than 12 months old. Each was under separate management and both seemed eager to hire me. In the end, I chose the established port brand under Peter Jackson Cousin over the innovative sherry brand under Manuel Zarraluqui, but Manuel had other ideas – which is how I ended up being International Marketing Director for both.

CHAPTER SIX

A World of Wine Beckons

On my first day with Croft port, Peter Jackson Cousin and I took a flight to Frankfurt to meet our German distributor, a Dr Reiss, at Cinzano. Peter had learned his management skills in the fashion industry and had a great sense of style. He did, however, have one strange habit, which was to stand up in the middle of a business discussion and play a game of pocket billiards as if he were in some a sort of trance. This manoeuvre served as a distraction even at the most intense of meetings, although I never had the nerve to ask him about it. After a jolly lunch, and a further chat with our hosts, we were driven back to the airport for our flight home. 'I have joined the jet set,' I mused on my way home from Heathrow, just in time for dinner.

To prepare me for such exotic adventures, I had been enrolled on a Marketing Centre Europe (MCE) course in Paris entitled 'Marketing through Distributors.' I was joined there by participants from all over Europe, including market leaders such as Johnson & Johnson from Belgium and Colgate Palmolive from France.

The use of the word 'through' rather than 'to' said it all. For many years, the default approach of exporters had been to sell the importer/distributor as much product as possible, with the result that the latter frequently became overstocked and had to sell the product at a discount. As I was to learn, by planning a marketing and sales strategy in conjunction with the importer

PHIPPS NORTHAMPTON BREWERY COMPANY LIMITED

REGISTERED OFFICE : **THE BREWERY · BRIDGE STREET · NORTHAMPTON**

OUR REF   SFF/EDP   TELEPHONE: Nᵒ 2943 (6 LINES)
YOUR REF   796 (3 LINES)

Mr. E.Howkins,   20th June,1961.
Moulton Lane,
BOUGHTON,
Northampton.

Dear Sir,

      Further to your recent interview, I have pleasure in offering you an appointment as trainee in our Wine & Spirit Department, on the following terms :-

(1) Commencing salary at the rate of £500 per annum payable by bank credit monthly on the last day of each month.

(2) You will be eligible to participate in our Cost of Living Bonus Scheme and Profit Sharing Bonus Scheme in accordance with the rules governing these schemes.

(3) You will be required to join our Staff Contributory Pension and Life Assurance Scheme when eligible in accordance with the rules.

(4) Your appointment will be determined by one month's notice on either side, to expire at the end of any month.

      Will you please let me know whether you are prepared to accept this offer on the terms stated above, and confirm that you will be able to commence your duties on Monday, 26th June, on which date you should report to the undersigned at 9 a.m.

                        Yours faithfully,
          For Phipps Northampton Brewery Company Limited

                        Director & Secretary

Left: The author (far right) with fellow officers of the Northamptonshire Yeomanry – Lt Harry Cazenove, Capt Peter Symington, Major Dick Ensor and Capt Paddy Hartigan.

Right: A sight long gone in Jerez – treading the grapes at vintage time, González Byass 1963.

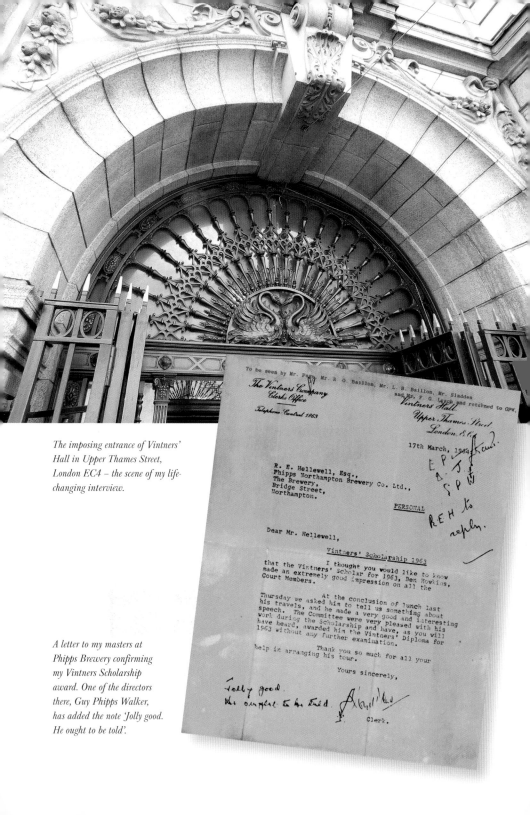

The imposing entrance of Vintners' Hall in Upper Thames Street, London EC4 – the scene of my life-changing interview.

A letter to my masters at Phipps Brewery confirming my Vintners Scholarship award. One of the directors there, Guy Phipps Walker, has added the note 'Jolly good. He ought to be told'.

To be seen by Mr. Page, Mr. R O. Baillon, Mr. L. B. Baillon, Mr. Sladden and Mr. F. G. Lynch and returned to GPW.

The Vintners Company
Clerks Office

Telephone Central 1863

Vintners' Hall
Upper Thames Street
London, E.C4.

17th March, 1964

R. E. Hellewell, Esq.,
Phipps Northampton Brewery Co. Ltd.,
The Brewery,
Bridge Street,
Northampton.

PERSONAL

Dear Mr. Hellewell,

Vintners' Scholarship 1963

I thought you would like to know that the Vintners' Scholar for 1963, Ben Howkins, made an extremely good impression on all the Court Members.

At the conclusion of lunch last Thursday we asked him to tell us something about his travels, and he made a very good and interesting speech. The Committee were very pleased with his work during the Scholarship and have, as you will have heard, awarded him the Vintners' Diploma for 1963 without any further examination.

Thank you so much for all your help in arranging his tour.

Yours sincerely,

Clerk.

Jolly good.
He ought to be told.

In 1967, it was proposed that I should have a professional photo taken for my monthly wine column in the
Northamptonshire Independent *for which I was paid £1 per piece.*

Top: On board the Gilbey's Gin Palace, the Captain and Mrs Yealland chatting to Acker Bilk, creator of the 1962 top 10 hit 'Strangers on the Shore'.

Above: The author with George (later Sir George) Bull aboard the PS Ryde.

Left: The author manfully attempts to drive a golf ball across the River Thames at Mortlake during a Piat de Beaujolais promotion.

Above: David Dand, MD of Baileys Irish Cream (on the author's left), during a lighthearted moment at the IDV conference in Phoenix, Arizona.

Below: the author and Robin Byers toasting their arrival back in Covent Garden after the Beaujolais Nouveau run.

Above: Château Loudenne in the Medoc, Bordeaux. It was bought by the Gilbey family in 1875 and from the late 1960s was superbly run by Martin Bamford MW.

Right: The magnificent ballroom at the Factory House in Oporto.

Below: Quinta da Roeda, the delightful tea planter's bungalow owned by Croft where Robin and Elsa Reid entertained so many friends from around the world with their renowned hospitality.

Above: The author being presented with his long service award by James Espey then MD of IDV Home Trade, who became a good friend and founder of the Last Drop brand.

Right: The author wields a traditional Jerezano valencia for pouring sherry.

Below: A happy and gently pregnant Clarissa in Jerez between Juan Manuel Lopes de Carrrizosa, a fellow director of Croft Jerez, and the author

Above: The author being intronised into the Confraria do Vinho do Porto in Oporto by Robin Reid

Left: the author after being intronised into the Confrerie des Chevaliers du Tastevin in Bordeaux, flanked by Bernard de Nonancourt, President of Laurent Perrier (left) and a director of the Confrerie (right)

Right: the author's certificate of the Confrérie des Chevaliers du Tastevin, Burgundy which he received at the same time as Giles Townsend in 1974.

or distributor, better profits could be achieved by both – though this was, of course, before the days of 'through profitability' when you, as the producer, owned your importer/distributor and thus stood to benefit from two sets of profits. Again, it was IDV that led the way.

Although Croft had been producing port for three centuries and had been bought by the Gilbey family several generations ago, its main business – as with all port shippers – was to export the blended wine in barrels to selected importers in Europe. Peter and I had the objective of persuading our key customers to switch from importing in bulk to importing by the bottle, which would give us more control over the bottling process itself, as well as the labelling and the presentation of the product in general. It would also give us the necessary margins to reinvest in the brand.

Distributors outside Europe already imported Croft port bottled in Portugal, so the stage was set. In what seemed like an exciting new departure I was swapping my customer base in London and the North Midlands for one that took in some of the world's most exotic destinations, Paris and New York among them. I had my own office and my own secretary. My life was spent in a whirlwind of meetings at York Gate, regular international travel, and entertaining customers at the Factory House in Oporto or at Quinta da Roêda in the Douro.

At Roêda, on the banks of the Douro itself, Robin Reid and his lovely Portuguese wife Elsa acted as the most brilliant hosts. Robin was an indefatigable storyteller, Elsa the doyenne of châtelaines. Three hours' drive from the bustle of Oporto, Roêda was such a haven of peace and tranquility that we used to count the minutes, seldom hours, from the time when a jet-lagged visitor arrived to the moment they fell asleep, glass of chilled white port in hand, in one of the assorted deck chairs that lay about the lawn overlooking the vineyards.

By this time (1973) Great Britain had joined the EEC and bottling at source was becoming mandatory. Wine scandals were on their way out – at least, for the time being – and brands were very much the future. The trick, as always, was to find the right importer, agent or distributor for your brand in each of the major consumer markets. And then to manage expectations.

France was, and still is, the largest export market for port. Historically the French have always enjoyed the sweetness of port as an aperitif in bars in much the same way that the English used to enjoy drinking sweet sherry. Many was the time we were told that to promote port in France as an after-dinner drink was a complete waste of time, and that French people would much prefer to imbibe a 20- or 30-year-old tawny port before their meal. Who was right? The consumer, of course.

Our distributor in France was Rémy Martin, which meant that a port brand would fit comfortably into its portfolio without competing with its cognac. It was on the very morning of one of my meetings with Bernard Alvarez, our chain-smoking oppo at Rémy, that I left Steven Spurrier's apartment (where I had been staying the night) with Steven's resonant parting words still ringing in my ears: 'I've got this tasting this morning. I'm not sure how it is going to go. I have some California wines lined up to show the French that great wines are now being made in California'.

Steven, of course, had by this time (1976) moved to Paris, where he had bravely set up as a wine merchant and in his spare time founded the Académie du Vin – a series of wine appreciation courses patronized largely by expat English speakers. On this occasion, Steven's intention was to be complimentary rather than controversial, but the event to which he was referring was the famed 'Judgement of Paris': perhaps the most influential blind tasting of all time.

Our revered chairman, George Robertson, a multi-linguist himself, tipped me off that business is always helped along if one says a few words in the local language. Sagna were our distributors in Italy. One year, I was invited to speak at their annual sales conference by the shores of the majestic Lago Maggiore. Rather as at Moët, it seemed that Barone Ernesto Sagna only employed people with titles: Conte Georgio Balbo was in charge of marketing while a *marchese* was in charge of PR, and all of the 80-plus sales people were impeccably dressed. As coached by George, I duly gave my speech in fluent Italian. All were flabbergasted, especially Ernesto and Georgio, since we normally conversed in French. Questions were then raised from the floor in Italian, at which point I had to hold up my hands in surrender: I was literally stuck for words. In the end, Georgio kindly translated for me, but I had nevertheless earned a new respect and I never forgot George's advice.

In Switzerland we had inherited a charming, but awkward, agent based in Geneva, who always called me Monsieur 'Ofkins. His insistence on continuing to import from us in bulk to protect his margins became something of a thorn in our side and we eventually parted company. Even so, I still made a point of visiting him as often as possible. Any excuse to be near a ski slope.

George Robertson once decreed that he and I should visit our agent in Denmark by overnight ferry, which gave us all the more time to enjoy our smørrebrød. We then went onto Sweden, where I relived my younger travelling days by sleeping in a wine and spirits warehouse – no hotel rooms being available.

Greece was not a major market for us, but Robin Byers and I had been invited by a wine merchant friend of his to spend a week on his boat. Robin informed me that this friend, Manos, already had a port brand, and that there was no point in talking shop while we were there. Manos met us on arrival in Athens, but for some obscure bureaucratic reason we were unable to leave the airport, and instead had to sit on the dusty pavement in the boiling sun. The only liquid we could muster was a bottle of Croft 10-year-old tawny that I had brought as a present for Manos, so the three of us proceeded to share its warm contents – hardly the ideal way to woo a prospective customer. Manos, though, pronounced our bottle to be fantastic. He jettisoned his existing port supplier there and then and became our distributor in Greece.

In Australia, on landing in Sydney, I was met by a white Rolls Royce that I was assured was the only one of its kind in the country. If nothing else, it gave an insight into the profits Gilbeys Australia were making from selling gin.

Later I ventured to the French overseas territory of New Caledonia, which was a good market for us, since the inhabitants drank their share of port as good French people do. In Noumea, the capital, I was intrigued to find the most modern supermarket I had ever seen – a reminder that being a late adopter of any new innovation at least enables one to scour the world for the most up-to-date technology, placing you ahead of the game.

My first visit to Japan, in 1974, was a real eye-opener. China was of course closed to visitors at this time, and this was as 'east' as it was possible to get. My opposite number in Nikka Whisky Distillers, our distributors, was delighted to discover that we were the same age; face was saved and he visibly relaxed. We had been planning a big press reception to launch Croft Port in Japan, which turned out to consist of 20 immaculately dressed gentlemen from the media seated around the boardroom table in complete silence. How unlike the UK, I thought. Strangely, they had no notebooks.

Unfortunately, during the presentation, I got the slides in my carousel mixed up and some were missing altogether. I was seized with panic, to put it mildly: how could I have been so disorganized? It was then that my Japanese colleague uttered the immortal lines: 'Do not worry about the slides. All the gentlemen have your press release and they have already printed it. No need to show them anything else.' This, it transpired, was a courtesy meeting. Face personified.

It was on the same visit that I first became aware that Japanese whisky, as produced by Nikka, is as good as, sometimes even better, than its Scotch counterpart. In the meantime, a visit to Kyoto by bullet train revealed the beauty and tranquility for which this ancient seat of Japanese culture is famed.

On a subsequent visit, an IDV colleague and I were unexpectedly asked to a Japanese home. This, in itself, was unusual, especially as we had only met our host in Tokyo by chance. In the company of our respective minders, we were driven to a classic wooden Japanese house at the appointed hour. Our host – I never did discover his name – welcomed us with a big smile and an offer of beer, which was happily accepted. The conversation was slow, but the beers kept coming. Meanwhile, our minders, who sat on the floor behind us, seemed to be endlessly engrossed in the whisky bottles that they had bought with them.

After a few hours, we wondered whether we were going to be offered lunch – and still the beers kept coming. I think the holdup may have been due to the fact that our host's wife was busy shopping. By this advanced stage my bladder was becoming distinctly uncomfortable, but how on earth could I communicate this to my host? I muttered something and hoped he understood. He showed me to a cupboard with a basin but no loo. What to do? I held tight, re-entered the room and sat down again at the table. My colleague couldn't stop laughing, which did not help.

Eventually, I blurted out: 'I must go to the loo, the toilet, the washroom, the john, the men's room, whatever.' Slightly surprised, mine genial host queried: 'Ah, big one or small one?'

My memory is somewhat blurred after that, but his wife duly turned up at about 3.00pm, triumphantly brandishing a bottle of Mateus Rosé to have with our lunch.

As I was to discover later, while on visits to China, it is never good to have any sort of physical complaint when one hasn't the faintest idea how to communicate in the local language. Once, in Chengdu, I found myself severely constipated. I was too embarrassed to ask at the hotel, so instead I hoofed it one morning to the nearest pharmacy. Two delightful young Chinese girls greeted me, and I tried to explain. I drew an absolute blank. I then started jumping up and down, pointing to my nether regions, mouthing 'No poo poo, no poo poo.' Their hands covered their lips as they erupted into uncontrollable laughter. I was finally sorted.

Another time in Taiwan, after suffering a bout of shingles in the UK, I woke up one morning only to fear that this nasty illness had returned. I duly contacted our local importer, the lovely Flora Chang, who immediately alerted the hotel. A charming member of the hotel's staff then escorted me to the local hospital, where she queued and I sat for three hours in front of about 20 identical doors. Eventually, one of the doors opened and I was greeted by a doctor and nurse. By then it had dawned on me that I did not have shingles, but that the sheets on my bed had been so clean and stiff that they had left very similar marks on my chest. The doctor took it in good heart, but I was more fearful of what Clarissa would say about wasting medical professionals' time.

Thailand was not a big market for us, but my sole visit to Bangkok was nevertheless memorable for its demonstration of political power in action. My IDV friend, Derek Plunkett, J&B's man in the Far East, had insisted that I must stay at the Oriental Hotel, and preferably in the legendary Somerset Maugham suite. Ironically, I discovered that this had already been booked by Joseph Kagan aka 'Mr Gannex'. Somehow, we were introduced, and I got to see this remarkable room. A British-Lithuanian industrialist, Joseph Kagan was a close friend of Harold Wilson, the then prime minister, who was famously often pictured wearing a Gannex raincoat. Wilson had asked Kagan, as his special envoy, to meet up with the prime minister of Thailand to sound him out on various issues. And so it was that five of us sat down together in the hotel lobby. I have never heard, before or since, a person whose first tongue was not English ask such clear, fluent questions without ever wasting a word. Kagan said that he had spent the evening with the Wilsons on the night of the 1964 General Election, and that Wilson had subsequently gone off to see the Queen expecting not to be impressed. He came back singing her praises, very much a converted royalist.

As ever, the United States provided more business opportunities, more scope and more fun. Consumers there were just beginning to explore wine options, even though beer, dry Martinis and Scotch were still the staples of our target market. Cheapo Gallo wine from California was the first step for many. Imported wines were not exactly regarded with suspicion but were seen as a bit complicated and not very patriotic.

The chief minefield, the proverbial elephant in the room, was (and still is) the three-tiered system that dominates the wines and spirit industry in the

USA. A sop to the repeals of the Prohibition era, it enshrines in law that all producers or distributors of alcoholic drinks must sell to a wholesaler, who then sells to a retailer, who then sells to the consumer. In practice this prevents a wine producer from selling direct to a wholesaler or retailer, which is of course common practice in free markets such as the UK – although Norway, Sweden and the provinces of Canada still retain government monopolies. The system is orderly, which was doubtless a necessity post-Prohibition, and maintains margins for all, but it also means that American consumers pay proportionately more for their enjoyment of alcohol.

Croft had employed a broker, the enigmatic Freddie Seggerman, to find distributors in all the major states – a time-consuming task, since each brand needed to be separately registered in each state, added to which there was not enough margin to reinvest in the brand and coordinated marketing plans were out of the question.

Our New York distributor was Herbie Kahn. I remember we met in his office in Manhattan one winter's Friday afternoon just as the sun was about to set, heralding the Jewish Sabbath. All at once he suddenly grabbed his hat and rushed out of the room with the words 'Bye, gotta go… don't want to get caught stranded on a street corner for the weekend.'

Soon afterwards, we appointed Austin Nicholls as our sole US importer, which at least gave us control of our marketing and sales strategy so far as the consumer was concerned. At that time, New York boasted wine retailers far more impressive than one could ever hope to find in the UK. First out of the traps following Prohibition was Sherry-Lehmann, founded by brothers Sam and Jack Aaron in midtown Manhattan in 1934. The new competitor on the block was Morrell's, recently created by the charismatic Peter Morrell, who set up shop a few streets away. Everyone wanted their brands to be listed by one or other of these giants, both for credibility and prestige. By this time, Alex Bespaloff, whom I had met briefly in Bordeaux during my Vintners' Scholar visit, had established himself as the leader of the wine 'in crowd' in New York, so through him I got to know, Sam Aaron's son, Michael, and his ex-wife. Peter Morrell was very fond of vintage port and when we dined together in Alex's apartment on the Upper

East Side, he kindly brought a bottle of the famed Croft 1945 for us to enjoy. Alex taught me something that day – namely, the finer the wine, the simpler the food. We had cold roast beef followed by hard cheeses.

Alex was a self-proclaimed bachelor until his happy marriage to Cecilia in later life. He was also the consummate networker, having written one of the first American consumer-friendly wine books, *Inexpensive Wines*, in 1973, and was a regular columnist for New York magazine. He knew absolutely everyone and had the most engaging personality, coupled with a distinctly Russian-Jewish sense of humour.

We shared coffee and cigars with Frank Serpico, then the most famous cop in New York for being the man who defied the system. We dined in Chinatown with the then mayor of New York, the amiable Ed Koch, who was a keen wine lover. And we linked up with Alan Rickman of *GQ* magazine for an article on wine spitting – 'Great Expectorations', as it was headed – in which Alex confessed that although he was no *spitmeister*, 'if you don't, you'll be pickled by lunchtime.'

On occasions Alex and I used to dine at Elaine's on East 88th Street – the go-to restaurant for the city's writers and other prominent New Yorkers. One evening, Woody Allen was dining at the next table. His choice of wine was Château Lafite, for which he is to be commended, but I do seem to remember that he also had a bottle of Coca Cola nearby…

Many days and weeks were spent on these Transatlantic visits, criss-crossing the States to meet with customers. Michael Longhurst, who was responsible for the sales of Château Loudenne in the US, did the same. We used to call each other before our trips to see if we could meet somewhere for the weekend. Michael was a great sport and one weekend we checked into the MGM Grand in Las Vegas.

With 3,000 rooms, the MGM Grand, before it was burned down in 1980, was the largest hotel in the world. I have always enjoyed roulette and have a little number sequence that has helped me on this and on many subsequent visits to Las Vegas to win against the house. Even so, we could not believe that all drinks were free; the IDV house brand, J&B whisky, took a gentle hammering that first weekend.

Michael and I met coincidentally on several occasions. One time I was waiting patiently, very patiently, for an appointment in Los Angeles when who should stroll out of the buyer's office but Michael, who had evidently been working overtime. The one time we flew together was a mistake. I was queuing for a flight to Washington DC while Michael was waiting for one to nearby Baltimore. We both became so deeply engaged in conversation that we ended up getting on the same plane – to Baltimore. Oblivious, we were still chatting as we went through the airport arrival lounge, and when I asked the cab driver to take me to an office address he greeted me with a blank look. 'This is Washington DC isn't it?' I asked him somewhat shirtily. Collapse of stout party. I was in the wrong city.

On another occasion, in Boston, I met up with David Dand, managing director of a new brand that IDV had created named Bailey's Irish Cream. David was normally the most exuberant of colleagues, but on this occasion he was a touch morose: try as he might, he could not find a distributor to take on Bailey's. To claw back sufficient margin to reinvest in the brand, he needed a bottle to retail for $8, but only a few months before, Heublein had introduced a similar product, the strangely named Hereford Cows, for around half that. No one wanted Bailey's. Fortunately, I had just had a very positive meeting with Ken Bray at Austin Nicholls and though David said that he had already called on him, I suggested that perhaps he might care to try again. He did, after which Ken ordered 90,000 cases to be shipped by the end of the year. In the end, Austin Nicholls shipped 500,000 cases of Bailey's that first year. Bailey's current annual global sales are around eight million cases.

Forecasting, let alone budgeting, is always difficult. The only certainty is that you will never be wholly accurate. When we created Croft Distinction, a 10-year-old tawny, we had no idea what volume to budget for, since this was an unusual style of wine that had never been promoted before. Finger to the wind, we set a modest 1,000-case target for the year. After the IDV annual Christmas party, which was held in typically quirky IDV style in mid-summer, when no one was too busy, the somewhat over-indulged Brian Barnett of Augustus Barnett, our biggest UK retailer, said: 'Put me down for 1,000 cases.' Naturally, he had no idea what our annual budget was. This was swiftly followed by the UK's second largest retailer, Ahmed Pochee, founder of Oddbins, who, not to be outdone, said 'I will take 500 cases'. Job done, though such good fortune is rare.

In between my excursions abroad, IDV organized global conferences for senior managers to bring everyone together. One such took place in York in 1978 and was attended by the then virtually unknown Marvin Shanken, who had just launched a new wine magazine, *Wine Spectator*. In a way, it was Anthony Tennant, then chairman of IDV, who gave Marvin the supranational platform he craved. Today, *Wine Spectator* is a global phenomenon.

Behind the scenes at York Gate and at IDV's Harlow production centre, scientists and what today would be termed 'blue sky thinkers' were hard at work dreaming up a myriad of new concoctions. Some of these were wine-based, others spirit-based, but all had a target consumer in mind – something of a revolution in corporate thinking. Looking again at the summary of a New Product Development conference, I am struck by the sheer amount of background work that was carried out. For one aperitif project, no less than 15 names and flavours were studied that were then narrowed down to five – 'Belle Île,' 'Caporal,' 'Julep,' 'Miura' and 'Barbuda' –before being rechristened 'Lymbo'. 'Holy Spirit' was the overarching code name for potential spirit brands. Among the concepts being progressed were 'Sega Réale,' a clean, fresh spirit flavoured with either a lemon or lime, and 'Peacemaker,' a fruit-flavoured spirit containing Canadian whisky and Mao Tai, China's most prestigious spirit, which was suitably watered-down for Western requirements. Needless-to-say, none saw the light of day. Many of these ideas were intended to utilize IDV's existing global production capacity, such as Black Velvet whisky in Canada, but most of the fruit tastes emerged from early morning discussions with purveyors in Covent Garden Market, who were well placed to identify the latest trends – for example. kiwi fruit in the UK.

Even so, just as Showering's had done with the successful launch of Baby-cham 20 years earlier by using the excess apples on their farms, IDV hit upon a winning formula by employing liquid assets that had hitherto been surplus to requirements. At the time, Express Dairies, a sister company in Ireland, was producing far more cream than the market could cope with, while sales of IDV's Redbreast Irish Whiskey were similarly compromised, resulting in a glut of both products. Add a little flavouring, plus a hefty dose of consumer research, research and yet more research… and bingo!

Bailey's Original Irish Cream would go on to become a ground-breaking success for the whole industry, yet at this conference we were still debating whether to leave it as a single brand or create a line extension. Fortunately for Bailey's at this stage in its history, we decided on the former. Now the extended brand works superbly.

Another abiding memory I have of this conference is playing darts in a nearby pub on the final evening. For the past three days we had been swept up in an international alcoholic whirlwind that had transported us from continent to continent. Our fantasies of conquering the world were quickly brought back down to earth by the pub's landlord, who confessed that his biggest worry was whether to join the city or the regional darts championships, both of which required different boards. So much for our high falutin' ideas.

Another conference, the brainchild of my friend James Espey and billed as an International Marketing Seminar, took place a few years later in Nassau. I presented a report on Europe. My opening remarks began thus: 'An area of 31 countries, speaking 19 languages and with 290 million inhabitants, Europe is clearly diverse. Since 1945, our industry in Europe may be divided into three eras: 1945–60 – that of the manufacturer; 1960–75 – that of brands, marketing and consumerism; and 1975–present – the era of distribution. Despite the Common Market, Europe cannot be regarded as a single unit. Chauvinism is alive and kicking…'

Well, I was right about one thing.

Later in the programme, I banged on about Croft Original sherry, stating: 'Launched in 1965, Croft Original took some time to establish itself, selling a mere 25,000 cases after five years; but 10 years later this had risen to 525,000 cases. This success has been based upon a brand which gave a new dimension to the sherry market and was conceived with the consumer in mind.'

At a conference in Phoenix, Arizona, the keynote speaker was Scott Carpenter, one of the original Mercury Seven US astronauts. Thinking of the amazing views he must have experienced orbiting the Earth, I asked him at the bar if he had ever been to England – and if so, what was his favourite place. 'Yes, I have', came the reply, 'and I love Esher.'

This was not my only astronaut encounter. Back when I was at Amherst, I spent the Easter vacation with my father in Florida. At lunch one day I found myself sitting directly opposite Alan Shepard, the first American in space and the man who, as commander of Apollo 14, had famously hit two golf balls on the Moon. I recall that he was entertaining company but was annoyed that he had just been told to give up one of his favourite sports – go-karting – for safety reasons. He also told me that the worst of his training sessions had involved being spun round in a centrifuge. I could only imagine.

It was during this time that I finally bought my first house – in Fulham – after 10 or more spent years sharing flats and houses with assorted friends. Two of those houses were owned by Chief Whips in the House of Lords, one was jointly owned by two members of Parliament, and another was let out to *Mayfair* magazine, by which it was used for centrefold photo-shoots. My bachelor flats in South Kensington and Sloane Square were both shared with an assortment of friends.

London at the time was the centre of the universe, or so we believed. Restaurants such as Bistro d'Agran and the Stockpot and were perpetually full of boys taking out girls, many of whom had met at the same cocktail parties. Wine bars, such as Bill Bentley's, were just beginning to vie for popularity with pubs like The Antelope, The Denmark or the Admiral Codrington as 'in' places to go. Nightclubs, such as Raffles and the Blue Angel, were full of people behaving badly.

At one time when I found myself flat-less, Lord Denham (Mitty to his friends, Bertie in the House of Lords) and his wife Jean kindly invited me to live in their old farmhouse in Clapham. Mitty and I had met through the one and only Paddy Hartigan, when we both soldiered together in the Northamptonshire Yeomanry. Mitty loved port. One evening at his house in North Buckinghamshire, he very generously gave me my first taste of Taylor's 1927.

Mitty at the time was Chief Whip in the House of Lords and was renowned for making the best Bloody Marys in the world, which doubtless helped him win over many political waverers. He once asked my advice on what port he could bring in to share with another devotee, Christopher Soames, Leader of the Lords under Margaret Thatcher. We agreed on Croft 20-year-old tawny. Thereafter, every month or so, I would park right outside the Peers' Entrance, acknowledge the salute from the commissionaire, and carry the 20-year-old up the stairs to Mitty's rather grand office. Once, I also brought a magnum of Croft Distinction 10-year-old to give to my old Bangkok chum, who by this time had become Lord Kagan.

Much has changed since then, but apart from the odd private sale I never liked nor wished to sell wine to friends. It was my way of keeping some distance between my private life and my business life, which is never easy in the world of wine. Even so, people sometimes asked me about the wines in their own cellars. On one such occasion, a friend had inherited a stash of the extremely rare vintage port, Rabello Valente 1931, of which only two pipes had ever been shipped – one to the Bishop of Birmingham, the other to my friend's grandfather. Unfortunately, my friend's butler, a man by the name of Travers, took rather a liking to this particular tipple and managed to empty half the cellar by cunningly removing the back stack of bottles. Travers was duly asked to hand over the keys to the cellar.

In 1976, I met and married my wife, Clarissa. We first ran across one another that March during a skiing holiday in Val d'Isère, where she was enjoying a short sabbatical from nursing as a chalet girl. Love was undeniably in the air and bingo... we married in November. Magnums of La Cour Pavillon 1970 carried us blissfully through our wedding lunch at Crissie's parents' home in Cambridge. It was about time that I settled down, or so I was told by my friends. Thank goodness I had bought my house in Fulham.

A few years later, I initiated and organized the tercentenary of Croft & Co 1678–1978. By this time, Croft Port and Sherry had been merged into a single company, so we divided the event into two parts – the first in Oporto, the second in London. For the Oporto extravaganza, we invited all our agents and importers – and to our delight, they flew in from every corner of the globe, including Japan, Hong Kong and the USA. The days were spent conferencing, dining and relaxing amid the splendid surroundings of the Douro, enabling us to present a cohesive marketing strategy to our key markets. The Factory House in Oporto and the lawns of Quinta da Roêda provided the perfect backdrops – a reminder that the wine industry is so fortunate in having such glorious locations to entertain customers. There may be more margin in spirit brands, but geography and provenance have always been on the side of wine.

The second event took place at Apsley House, former London home of the Duke of Wellington, the connection being that Sir John Croft and the Iron Duke had known each other during the Peninsula War of 1807–14. John Croft had ensured that his commander's cellar was well stocked, and they had occasionally enjoyed a glass of port together. The event took the form of a magnificent dinner, to which the great and the good of the wine world were invited. Among the guests were the Portuguese and Spanish ambassadors, who were there to officially represent port and sherry respectively. We also invited the Belgian ambassador, who was godfather to one of the Wellesley offspring, but in a private capacity. Unfortunately, our Belgian friend subsequently took umbrage at not being accorded the same status as his fellow ambassadors, and the following morning George Robertson and I were summoned to the Belgian Embassy. George, who knew a thing or two about such awkward situations, counselled that we should arrive early. We did, and although we were kept waiting the regulation 20 minutes, we were then received by a smiling ambassador and no more was said about it. Lesson learned. When faced with a diplomatic incident, act swiftly and decisively.

CHAPTER SEVEN

Mayfair Wine Merchant

From brand management to company management was my next logical move. IDV was racing forwards with exciting new brands like Bailey's and Malibu, and J&B Rare whisky was powering ahead in the US. Our distributors, many of which were family concerns, were being devoured on a regular basis, all the better to control IDV's brand distribution in key markets. In 1981, IDV concluded that it needed a 'look out' man in the US, since Grand Met, our parent company, had just acquired the Liggett (tobacco) Group, which in turn owned three valuable American drink import businesses: Paddington, Carillon and Austin Nichols. IDV needed to flex its own muscles. George Bull suggested that I might be the man to make it happen.

By this time, our son Jamie and daughter Lucy had been born in our new home in Wandsworth. Clarissa and I looked at each other, nodded, and silently agreed that we were up to the challenge of taking two young children across The Pond, to begin a new life in Manhattan. George Bull duly Concorded to New York for further discussions, while we waited with bated breath. In the space of just a few days, our hopes and plans were dashed: George had been assured that there was no need for such an IDV role in the US, so my presence was not required after all. During the following frantic few months, I was sent instead to understudy the delightful Peter Willis Fleming, managing director of Morgan Furze, London's leading wine and spirit wholesaler. Peter was tragically dying of cancer and I was earmarked to succeed him, which I did the following year.

The 1980s was the Thatcher decade, and like so many businesses Morgan Furze's fortunes were closely tied to the fluctuating state of the economy: when it was healthy, people celebrated with champagne; when the straits were dire, house wine was the norm. Our main income streams were from London hotels and restaurants. Champagne was more profitable than house wine, so by the boom years of the late '80s, Morgan Furze was reporting a healthy bottom line. Once again, I was fortunate to be in the right place at the right time.

To help my transition, I was enrolled on an Ashridge Management Course in Buckinghamshire, where the constant message was 'Marketing begins and ends with the consumer'. A few years later, I was again dispatched to brush up on my management skills, this time to Ware for an Effective Negotiating course based on the philosophy of the formidable Dr Chester L Karrass. I recall that there were 25 sections in all, including the 'Good Guy and Bad Guy Technique', 'Syndicating the Risk' and the 'Bogey Tactic', which I never quite fathomed.

Our prestigious offices, which were just behind Park Lane in Mayfair, had once been a milliner's shop and were later the studios of the famous society photographer Baron, where Tony Armstrong-Jones, later Lord Snowden, began his career as an assistant. The address was 12 Brick Street, not to be confused with Brick Lane in London's East End, where several confused guests turned up for what proved to be a much-delayed lunch.

One day, I picked up my phone only to hear a slightly querulous voice insisting he speak to the MD. 'Tis me' quoth I, 'Ben Howkins. Who are you?' 'Alan Johnson-Hill' said he. 'I live in Chelsea and all my neighbouring restaurants tell me they buy their wine from you'. 'Sorry, what was your name?' I asked the caller. He repeated it and I recalled that Alan and I had known each other a bit at Rugby. We swiftly moved onto firmer ground and it transpired that he had just bought a vineyard in Bordeaux called Château Meaume.

Would we like to buy some? Alan also owned a slice of the wine retailer Majestic, so he did not get carried away with his pricing as some of the more prestigious Bordeaux châteaux were wont to do. His wine also handily filled a gap in our portfolio and in due course we bought the first 1,000 cases to be imported into the UK. Since then, Alan and his wife Sue have welcomed many UK wine trade visitors to their home, probably learning more about the Bordeaux market from them than from their fellow château owners.

Lunch at Morgan Furze was very important. I'll repeat that. Lunch was very important; the day revolved around it. On my arrival in the office, following a leisurely drive from Wandsworth in my BMW to my reserved parking place in the garage opposite, almost the first question my secretary would ask was: 'Which wines would you like served for lunch today?' I find such decisions difficult at the best of times – and with a raging hangover, almost impossible.

Our dining room was in the basement and featured a splendid round table. Our cook was the comely Belinda, who was admired as much for her charm and mini-skirts as for her unquestioned culinary skills. The wine cellar was adjacent to the kitchen, so once you had installed yourself in this atmospherically charged suite of rooms, you tended to remain there for the duration.

Our guests were drawn from London's top hotels, restaurants and retailers, City institutions with serious dining rooms, and those Oxbridge dons fortunate enough to oversee their Colleges' fabled wine cellars. An invitation to lunch at Morgan Furze was much sought-after: you never knew who you might encounter or what deals you might do. Afterwards, guests could meander back to their West End Clubs, take a stroll through picturesque Shepherd's Market, or taxi back to the City.

Of course, the main purpose of lunching was to sell wine, which was encouraged, though sometimes forgotten. Morgan Furze was the *de facto* London agent for Château Lafite Rothschild, along with their second-tier wine, Carruades, and their fourth growth Château Duhart-Milon. These days Carruades fetches hundreds of pounds per bottle, largely due to its popularity in China. Back then, as Lafite's winemaker once confessed to me, it was thought to lack character.

We often served all three wines with gay abandon. Our claret was always decanted and one day, early on, I managed to muddle up the decanters. In a beady sweat, I continued pouring, praying that I could keep this ghastly cock-up to myself (I did). Thereafter, we affixed colour codes to the base of each decanter.

Michel Roux Sr was a regular guest, as he bought many of the wines for Le Gavroche from us, and we became good friends. In 1986, as an excuse to host a dinner for our best customers, we latched on to the fact that Morgan Furze would be celebrating its 30th anniversary. I asked Michel to be our guest speaker, and he was delighted to accept – although when I told one of my stuffier directors, he exclaimed in horror: 'But Michel is a chef!' In his opinion, we should have had a City grandee or a senior don.

There were 19 tables of 12 guests each. Baron Eric de Rothschild sat between George Bull and me. Michel Roux sat between Sir John Tooley and George Walker. We feasted on sole and venison; we drank Lafite 1957 en magnum and Croft 1955. From Gilbey's Gin Palace to Croft's Tercentenary… I was getting to rather enjoy these events, and looked forward to creating more.

In fact, we had a grandee of our own – Major General Sir Philip Ward, who had been appointed IDV Corporate Affairs director and given an office in Brick Street. Among his many other roles, Philip had been Commandant of the Royal Military Academy, Sandhurst, commanded the Welsh Guards, served as General Officer Commanding, London District and later become Lord Lieutenant of West Sussex. The Army's mandatory retirement age of 64 was indeed our gain.

He nominally reported to me, which, at first, I must admit I found a bit unnerving: how could a general report to a mere lieutenant? But Philip was nothing if not diplomatic, and we had much fun together over the years. His brief was to lunch as many influential people as he could muster, then indoctrinate them with three main IDV brands, Hennessy cognac, J&B Rare whisky and Smirnoff vodka, so that they would spread the word. Some remembered; others forgot shortly after leaving.

Philip was the most generous and lovely man. He was astounded to learn that Grand Met employed more people than the British Army, and must have invited at least half of the latter's senior officers to lunch at Brick Street.

We had also started doing business with Paul Raymond of Raymond's Revue Bar fame. I asked Philip to invite him to lunch, which Philip always preceded by chatting up the invitee's secretary or PA. Paul duly arrived in his white Rolls Royce and during lunch informed us that he had once been in the army himself – more specifically, a corporal during his stint of National Service. Things went from strength to strength. By 4.00pm, Philip and Paul could be seen marching around the luncheon table saluting each other – the General and the Corporal. Paul eventually left at 6.00pm in his chauffeur-driven Rolls, which reappeared an hour later with a hand-delivered letter of thanks. I call that style.

In a similar vein, among our more profitable accounts was the nightclub Stringfellows. Clarissa and I were always asked to Peter Stringfellow's birthday parties, where we were warmly welcomed by Peter himself before being ushered to our own 'VIP box', fully equipped with a bottle of Krug. Once, while I was there, I went to the gents, amused that I had left Clarissa at the bar chatting to a transvestite. I was completely gobsmacked when two tall, elegant 'ladies' joined me at the urinal ' 'allo Fred,' said one. ''ave you seen George yet?'

For some unfathomable reason, Clarissa and I often rowed in our taxi home from Stringfellows. We eventually came to the conclusion that it was the excruciatingly loud music, and I remain convinced that loud music played in cars late at night can be just as much of a hazard as drink-driving or mobile phone calls.

* *

George Walker, creator of the Brent Walker leisure conglomerate, was another regular at lunch. Every season George hosted a special weekend at his chalet in Zermatt. Tim, one of his inner circle, told me that I ought to get 'on the list'. Eventually I did and it was fascinating. The first morning, I skied past George and waited at the finish. Big mistake. No one skis past George Walker. On all subsequent runs, I diplomatically stopped a hundred yards or so from the end and waited for this charismatic, but deeply competitive man to pass me.

Possibly our largest single account was the nearby Intercontinental Hotel at Hyde Park Corner. Intercontinental Hotels was another of our sister companies – not that that made life any easier. One bone of contention was our delivery service, which was reckoned to be about 95 percent efficient. Our elegant hotels director, Tim Hanbury, and I were duly summoned to a meeting with the Intercontinental's robust general manager, Graham Jeffrey. After a rather frosty meeting, at which we were told in no uncertain terms that the hotel operated at service levels of nothing less than 100 percent, we were offered lunch. In true smart hotel fashion, the main course was served under cloches, which Graham proudly informed us were brand new. Once we had all been served, the nod was given for the waiters to remove our cloches in sync – only for them to find, try as they might, that the cloches would not budge. The home team were aghast, while we allowed ourselves a wry grin. I could not stop myself: turning to Graham, I smiled '100 percent service?'

Graham and I became firm friends after that and still see each other regularly after nearly 40 years. It is friendships such as these, whether formed among the vineyards and cellars, or in restaurants and hotels, that bind so many of us together. The wine vein runs deep: sharing and comparing is what we do, and hosting and entertaining are our bread and butter. There is little room for selfishness or for ego trips.

One trip that still makes me chuckle was in a private jet to Armagnac. For some obscure reason, Harold Brooks Baker, editor of *Burke's Peerage*, the royal photographer Sir Geoffrey Shakerley, Douglas Sutherland, the author of Debrett's *The English Gentleman* series and yours truly were all invited to stay by Olivier de Montal, producer of the well-known Armagnac brand of the same name. It was the first time that Clarissa had had her suitcase unpacked for her by the butler in Olivier's sumptuous home, Château de Rieutort in Gascony. I recall visiting a well-run *foie gras* farm by helicopter, feasting well and enjoying much fine Armagnac, but I cannot for the life of me remember why we were there. I think it may have had something to do with a book.

IDV had just taken on, by accident really, a then little-known brand of gin by the name of Bombay. Could we find it a sport to sponsor? I have always enjoyed croquet in the languid summer months, and in 1981, *The Sunday Times* did a feature on croquet as a potential spectator sport. I thought it might become a TV sport. The ingredients were there. Coloured balls, crafty play, viciously competitive. I got in touch with Channel Four, but rather haughtily they turned down my suggestion. More fool them. Today, Bombay Sapphire is now one of the most sought-after gin brands in the world.

Lunches at Morgan Furze took place almost every day, since each sales division hosted their own for customers. It was more or less understood that you were not really expected back in the office after one of these lunches, particularly since guests from the hotel and restaurant trades had the afternoon off anyway. I made it a rule, however, that if I was 'invited' to one of these divisional bashes, I would make my excuses and run at 3.00pm. I also made a mental note that at any business lunch, whether on home ground or elsewhere, I would give myself at least two action points to follow up – a maxim I have followed to the present day. It was too easy simply to eat, drink and make merry: if one was fortunate enough to be in this game, I concluded, then a modicum of respect was not only due but kept one sane.

We always printed our menus on a small card that, when folded, tucked easily into breast pocket. On the inside were the courses and the accompanying wines; on the back were the names of the guests. We encouraged everyone to write tasting notes against the wines and to take the menus away with them – such a simple gesture, yet how many times have we all been somewhere, eaten well and drunk even better without actually remembering what or who with?

How else would I remember that on May 7th 1981, Philip Ward and I had enjoyed a double magnum of Château Giscours 1971 with Cyril Ray, Martin Bamford and Major General Derek Boorman among others… that on February 9th 1984, Lord Chalfont was among the lucky guests to partake of a Château Margaux 1945 and Croft 1960... that on July 21st 1987, General Sir David Fraser joined us to share both a Château Lafite 1976 and a Lafite Très Vieille cognac... or that on April 12th 1988, Paolo Zago, MD of The Connaught, Martin Skan, the owner of Chewton Glen, and David Levin, the owner of The Capital, were among the guests who joined us to sample Château Haut-Bailly 1966 and Graham's 1945 vintage port.

Most days I lunched on home ground, either at Morgan Furze or at the Guards and Cavalry Club, thanks to the munificence of Philip Ward, who by then had become chairman. It was home ground in the truest sense, since the basements of both buildings met in the middle.

As I recounted in Chapter 4, it was around this time that The Wine & Spirit Association asked me to head up the Wine Development Board to promote wine drinking in the UK. Meanwhile, as MD of Morgan Furze, I was enrolled into the Confrérie de Bordeaux, the Confreria de Vinho de Porto and the Chevaliers du Tastevin in Burgundy. Countless invitations to tastings, lunches, dinners and gala dinners followed, along with trips to Ascot, Goodwood, Gatcombe Park and polo at Windsor. Farther afield, lunches at Château Latour and Château Lafite Rothschild in Bordeaux and at the Factory House in Oporto regularly tumbled my way. Strange as it may seem, I could not bring myself to refuse any of them.

So far, I have refrained from going into much detail about the wines that we enjoyed during this unforgettable decade. I have kept literally hundreds of tasting notes and menu cards, which together would fill a book in themselves. However, it would be remiss of me not mention some of the vinous highlights of our various tastings, lunches and dinners.

Château Lafite Rothschild has a splendid tradition of offering exalted guests the Lafite of either their birth year or their wedding year. On a visit with Clarissa in 1982, they kindly suggested opening the latter, 1976, my 'war baby' year presumably being off-limits. We began the meal with foie gras accompanied by a deliciously memorable Château Suduiraut 1970. On my next visit a year later, this time in the company of Giles Shepherd, MD of the Savoy Group, we enjoyed 'my' Lafite 1976 again, along with Giles's birth year of 1937, followed by Lafite 1919. Who, I wonder, was the mystery 63-year-old?

In March of the same year, this time at Château Loudenne, we kicked off with Château Laville Haut-Brion 1976 followed by Châteaux Pichon Lalande Pauillac and Latour 1955, a Château d'Yquem 1962 and a Croft 1945.

There is something both deeply satisfying and profoundly sensual about lunching or dining in a Bordeaux château. You are linked forever with that wine. Wines do tend to taste better in their home environment, perhaps because they are a natural match with the local produce, or perhaps because they have not travelled far. Whatever the reason, the experience binds us to that particular *terroir* and we are all the better for it. A Bollinger 1952 at Bollinger's lunch table in September 1982 did just that.

On November 27th1984, Luc Lacerre et Fils, the self-styled 'quality wine merchants of Wales', kindly invited 30 of us assorted winos to a tasting of 'the outstanding post-war vintages of Château Latour and Château Lafite.' On arrival, we solemnly worked our way through no fewer that 22 vintages, from 1945 to 1981, of two of the most famous wines in the world. As Jancis Robinson MW subsequently noted in her write-up in the *Financial Times*: 'In two hours, these stocks were depleted by 88 bottles of First Growth claret – some worth hundreds of pounds each'.

My own notes focused mainly on colour, which is often a clue as to how well the wine has been made and how well it has aged:

1945: *Colours together. Latour beautifully balanced; Lafite sensational in all respects.*
1955: *Colours moving away again. Latour has a big yet soft aftertaste; Lafite is beautifully balanced, delicate.*
1973: *Latour more youthful in colour.*
1976: *Lafite more youthful in colour.*

As David Peppercorn MW once noted: 'It was striking that Latour had the edge over Lafite from 1953 to 1975. Lafite's premium reputation was only restored when Baron Eric de Rothschild took over from his uncle Baron Elie in 1974.'

It was a fascinating, if bizarre, experience. I have no idea who Luc Lacerre et Fils were or what became of them, and I cannot even remember where this 'tasting of a lifetime' took place. All I can say is that a massive 'thank you' to someone is in order.

Some 10 years later, I have a record of a similar tasting where I sampled no fewer than 14 different champagnes. The youngest was a Krug 1976, the oldest a Pommery 1837. Somewhere in between were a Delamotte 1874, the last year of Gladstone's first government, and a Sillery 1865, the year of Lord Palmerston's death. The latter was absolutely fantastic – in perfect balance. Again, I have no idea who set this up – but once more, a huge 'thank you'.

* *

Another of our sister companies, Gilbey's Wholesale, had for some time been running awards for the best UK restaurant wine lists. I wondered if we might link up with the *Wine Spectator*, which was doing the same thing on a grander scale in the US. Marvin Shanken wrote back to say that they were looking to expand into Europe, and that he would be very grateful for any suggestions or recommendations we might be able to make. In the end, though, Gilbey's saw fit to downsize their awards, while the *Wine Spectator's* went from strength to strength.

Interspersed with my desk job of managing 20-odd souls and driving up sales came the blatant necessity to entertain, which, as we have already seen, took many twists and turns. Building relationships was everything. London by this time was awash with companies and people supplying wine, most of which was interchangeable on any restaurant's wine list. Customers tended to buy from the companies and people they trusted and liked, which meant being seen at the top tables, hosting ever more extravagant lunches and dinners, and organizing more and more vineyards visits.

Clarissa was always a fantastic help on such occasions – ready to chat to complete strangers; happy to entertain, and be entertained by, 'the trade'. Sometimes this involved trotting off to jaunts at Epsom with Moët, to Goodwood with Lanson, or to Apsley House with Laurent-Perrier, the champagne houses' margins giving them the budgets them to spend lavishly on PR events. At other times we entertained trade friends at home. I had met Jennifer Patterson, later to become one of the Two Fat Ladies, when she was the cook for *The Spectator*. One evening she arrived for dinner at our house in Wandsworth riding a scooter. She left on it too, decidedly wobblier and waving her arms in the air.

By this time, our two children, Jamie and Lucy, were growing up fast. Pre-prep in London was followed by boarding school outside, and school runs duly turned into cross-country marathons. Clarissa also had to juggle her nursing responsibilities with our crowded social diary, which often meant lightning changes of clothing. Late hours were normal, and I was often travelling for two or three months a year. How very fortunate I was – and still am – to have the support of a wife who understands that such commitments were necessary in order to enjoy many benefits the wine world confers.

The same goes for my children, who quickly learned that knowing about wine gave them an edge over those not similarly blessed. They were able to taste some amazing wines – including a memorable 100-year-old tawny port that Jamie and a friend happened to 'discover' in my cellar after Jamie's 21st birthday party.

For many years, no Christmas dinner was complete without our treasured Giscours 1982.

Later, their knowledge and appreciation for wine enabled Jamie and Lucy to enjoy being grown-up at dinner parties, as well as hosting their own. They felt equally confident at multi-generational gatherings. My constant travels gave them an appetite for exploring worlds beyond their comfort zones and they could see the pleasure in meeting so many fascinating people from so many different parts of the globe. Latterly, it has been incredibly rewarding to share wine lore and glasses in equal measure with them and their many friends.

Now that they both have children of their own, I can already sense that the 'gene' is being passed on. The wicked gleam in our grandchildren's eyes when they hold a glass of wine says it all.

* *

Back in the world of Morgan Furze, one sunny evening in June 1987, at Hampton Court, I found myself on Princess Anne's table, sitting next to the Duchess of Gloucester. The occasion was a Summer Banquet to celebrate the centenary of St John Ambulance Brigade, for which we had partnered with the magazine *Harpers & Queen*. While we were sipping our old friend, La Cour Pavillion 1983, the Duchess asked me if I could advise on her late father's wine cellar, which appeared to consist mainly of half bottles of claret. She then drew a list of the wines from her handbag, which promptly fell under the table. After several embarrassing moments searching for it, cheeks somewhat reddened, I ventured to suggest that since her husband was teetotal, she would be best advised to drink the wines herself.

For obvious reasons we were always keen to support our customers, and the hotel and catering industries were full of characters prepared to drive their brethren on to greater heights. The Académie Culinaire de France Filiale de Grande Bretagne held annual gala dinners hosted by the top chefs of the day, including Albert Roux of Le Gavroche, Michel Bourdin of the Connaught and Herbert Berger of the Mirabelle. These charity events required both our wines and our presence. In truth, though, it was not much of a hardship sipping Château Malescot-Saint-Exupéry 1983 or Croft 20-year-old tawny port safe in the knowledge that you were doing 'good business'.

We were also fortunate in that the majority of our customers were inherently solvent: Oxbridge colleges, West End clubs, Livery companies and City institutions alike required little in the way of chasing for payment. The established restaurants, too, paid regularly, if sometimes belatedly. The excitement came with the newer, trendier restaurants that everyone said we must secure and supply before our competitors got there first. This provoked ongoing heated discussions between our eager-beaver but very much London-centric sales people and the remotely based credit control department in Harlow. In those pre-internet days, the most effective credit checks were made via other wine and spirit suppliers. Through various formal bodies, such as WSET, as well as informal trade associations and clubs such as the Under 40, we soon all got to know each other and exchanged helpful information. We even formed a 'Two O'Clock Club, so-called because that was the time when hoteliers and restaurant owners took a break from their hosting duties and had lunch themselves. The rule was that we, the wine merchants, would supply the wines while the restaurateurs supplied the food. No money changed hands, apart from cash tips to the waiters. The wine merchants were led by the irrepressible Val Brown. The restaurateurs included Patrick Gwynne Jones of Pomegranates, Dan Whitehead of Dan's, Michael Proudlock and Rex Leyland of Foxtrot Oscar, Tom Benham of Monkey's, Brian Turner of Turner's and Patrick Board at the Mayfair Hotel. All became firm friends. It was by such means that we got to hear the word on the street while enjoying ourselves into the bargain. At the same time, rather like forging loyal bonds for life in the vineyard, going to a restaurant where you knew the owner gave one a special feeling of loyalty and inclusiveness.

Two different lunches, both featuring the Chevalier de l'Ordre, deserve special mention. The first, in 1987, was a gargantuan affair given by Moët & Chandon in honour of Patrick Forbes, who had just retired as Moët's UK managing director. The location was Knebworth House, the Comte Ghislain de Vogüé and Viscount Marchwood were hosting, and the guests numbered between 700 and 800 people. Afterwards Patrick made an eloquent, though very long, speech before being invested with the *Chevalier de l'Ordre de la Légion d'Honneur* by the French Ambassador.

The other occasion, which took place a few years later, was a more select lunch given by Michel Roux at the Waterside Inn for 70–80 friends to celebrate his award of the *Chevalier de l'Ordre National du Mérite*. This was a lesser award than the *Légion d'Honneur*, but the fact that it was bestowed on him by President Valéry Giscard d'Estaing in person more than made up for it.

Two further royal wine stories. At a Morgan Furze lunch in May 1982, I got talking to Patrick O'Connor, who was about to write a series of features for *Harpers & Queen* on people who keep interesting wine cellars. Could I help? It just so happened that Clarissa and I had recently visited Althorp, home of the Spencer family, as I had grown up in a neighbouring Northamptonshire village. Johnny, Earl Spencer, was showing us around the house when I mentioned my interest in wine; we were promptly ushered to the wine cellar. It turned out to be a bit of an Aladdin's cave, with old cognacs around every corner. The Earl had confided in me that he had far more faith in wine merchants than in stockbrokers, so when Patrick raised the subject of wine cellars, it immediately struck me that Johnny Spencer would be the perfect person to kick off the series. It was not long, of course, since Diana, the Earl's daughter, had married Prince Charles, and I felt that the Spencers could do with a little positive PR to offset the somewhat negative reputation of Diana's stepmother, the notoriously prickly Countess 'acid' Raine. To my mind, it would give the Earl a welcome opportunity to talk about something relatively uncontroversial in which he was genuinely interested.

I wrote to him on June 3rd. On June 11th, by way of a reply, I received a postcard from Raine:

'My husband has asked me to thank you for your most kind thought, but we are not giving interviews to the press at present, as frankly we have had too much of these!' He was silenced. Such a pity.

In 1984 I received an invitation, along with Giles Townsend – a great friend and colleague from Morgan Furze days who had just joined the Savoy Group as wine buyer – to be enrolled in the Confrérie des Chevaliers du Tastevin in Burgundy. That November, we set off with our wives to attend the ceremony, to be followed by dinner at the legendary Clos Vougeot. These events are full of vinous pomp and ceremony, coupled with much camaraderie, a feast beyond feasts, and endless glasses of delicious Hautes Côtes de Nuits – an evening of fun shared with 700 people of whom you probably know fewer than seven. Giles and I sat next to each other, waiting to be called upon accompanied by the traditional fanfare of trumpets. My meagre citation of wine achievements was read out and I was duly gonged. Then it was Giles's turn. Despite the fact that his list of achievements was no longer than mine, his citation went on and on, causing my self-effacing friend to get redder and redder. La Confrérie had evidently tumbled to the fact that Giles's father was Group Captain Peter Townsend, who had nearly married Princess Margaret. Their excitement was palpable: could it be that I was sitting next to the illegitimate son of the Queen of England's sister?

CHAPTER EIGHT

Happy Consulting

In the late 1980s, I found myself being wooed by the wine trade's leading headhunter, Richard Novis. The suitor was none other than the unashamedly upmarket Taylor's Port – still a family company and headed by the debonair Alistair Robertson. About the same time, I was made redundant. No sooner had this happened than IDV's HR director himself was made redundant, at which point I was asked to become un-redundant. 'Too late!' I cried. Amid the confusion I was also asked to run another of London's top wine merchants – a job I regretfully declined, as I was on the point of signing with Taylor's. It was the right decision: the person who took my place is still doing a far better job than I could ever have done.

And so I joined Taylor's, my primary task being to grow the brands of Taylor's and Fonseca internationally. Thanks to my old friend Robin Byers, I set up shop in an über-elegant townhouse in Grosvenor Crescent Mews, immediately adjacent to Hyde Park Corner. Taylor's premises in Portugal were even more impressive. Overseas visitors never failed to be wowed when given a tour of the company's extensive lodges in Vila Nova de Gaia, or the family's enchanting Quinta de Vargellas in the Douro Valley.

The US market, as always, was a source of endless fascination. During my several visits to the United States for Taylor's, two events stand out. On the back of my recently published book on port, *Rich Rare & Red* (*see* Chapter 11), our much-respected US importers, Kobrand, had managed to persuade Marvin Shanken's *Wine Spectator* to include a 'Port Panel' at its annual New York Wine Experience event. This heady extravaganza always takes place in October in the Marriott Marquis at 1535 Broadway, right on Times Square, and I have been fortunate enough to attend most of them over the years. Imagine 1,000 guests sitting down with 10,000 wine glasses in front of them, 10 for each participant. A tsunami of waiters then swept down the aisles, carefully pouring each of the nine ports to be tasted at the appropriate intervals, while in front of them sat a panel of three experts holding forth – swirling... tasting... pontificating. That is what James Suckling, then European bureau chief of the *Wine Spectator*, Marvin Overton, a collector from Texas, and I did for an hour and a half one Saturday afternoon in October 1989.

We kicked off with a brand creation from my Croft days, Croft Distinction aged tawny, and ended with the magnificent Fonseca 1963. I was racking my brains for how best to end the session, since I knew that all my port rivals were sitting in the front row, more than ready to throw buns at us. As James Symington remarked afterwards: 'We told them we'd throw bread if they displeased us; but the wines were very, very good.'

All of a sudden, my roving eye hit upon the unmistakable bulk of my larger-than-life friend and colleague, Bruce Guimaraens, a member of the family who owned Fonseca, sitting some dozen rows back. I looked at Bruce, I looked at my glass of Fonseca, and swiftly concluded they were identical. Having described the Fonseca 1963 as having 'plenty of body, great structure, rounded and harmonious, full of character, giving huge pleasure,' I ended with 'Never has a wine been created so clearly in the image of its maker.' After a brief pause, I nodded to where Bruce was sitting and announced: 'Please stand up Bruce Guimaraens.' Heads turned, eyes swivelled. The ensuing standing ovation for Bruce set the seal on a very happy occasion.

Part of a producer's remit is to visit overseas customers with the importer. When challenged by American restaurateurs as to what was the best food to pair with port, I rather naively suggested hard cheeses, as in the classic pairing of port and Stilton. In New Orleans, one frustrated restaurateur informed me that 'Americans don't eat cheese,' which I discovered to be largely true. Somewhat panicked, I asked him what desserts most tickled the American palate? After a discussion of blueberry pies, apple pies and ice cream, none of which got me remotely excited, he confessed that his best-sellers were those containing chocolate. Fair enough, I thought: port and chocolate it is. Pairing your wine with a best-selling dessert means that you can hardly fail to sell more product. In my book, it's marketing at its most pragmatic.

At Taylor's we were always open to PR opportunities. A good friend of mine, restaurateur Nicky Kerman, had just bought Scott's in Mayfair. Business was good, but not great. We got talking about port tongs – those mysterious and little-known implements that are clamped around the neck of a bottle of vintage port, thereby enabling the top part of the bottle, with the cork still in place, to be severed cleanly so as to avoid any potential contamination of the precious contents. Nicky roped in Ross Benson, famed gossip columnist with the *Daily Express*, for a masterclass in this ancient art and a date was duly set for the three of us to meet up.

The week before I got in some practice in Oporto with Alistair Robertson, who as I recall was as bemused by the whole idea as I was. Nevertheless, at 6.00pm on the appointed day, I brought along two bottles of Taylor's 1970, while Nicky, for some reason best known to himself, turned up with a feather that he claimed came from a Chinese pheasant. All seemed to go according to plan, after which Nicky fell into a post-prandial slumber while Ross and I continued to explore the delights of what was a very fine port indeed. 'Gosh, I rather like drinking port at this hour,' the columnist confessed – more than once, as I remember. We finally sashayed out of Scott's just as the dinner crowd were coming in.

Ross's piece in the *Express* the next day was headed 'The Good Life', so imagine my horror when I read the first lines: 'Drank too much port; got an almighty hangover'. So much for my brilliant PR idea. Fortunately, the rest of the article was a good deal more complimentary and all was well – a reminder, though, that editorial coverage can be a double-edged sword.

My other, more challenging, task during my time at Taylor's was to sort out the company's all-important UK distribution – an undertaking that occupied a great deal of my time, involved endless discussions and was not without acrimony, although to be fair, many producers at the time found themselves in similar situations.

As I have said before, a brand only thrives when the producer and importer are in alignment and can jointly manage expectations. It has become something of a mantra of mine. The fact was, the demographics of drinking in the UK were changing. The success of Taylor's long-established presence in the UK market had been in large part due to the strength of its importers, the renowned German producer Deinhard. But now German white wines were going out of fashion, which meant that Deinhard's customer base was much diminished and it was losing market share. Expectations were very definitely being neither managed nor met.

Since I had a close relationship with Laurent-Perrier which, like most champagne houses, not only made good margins but had what I saw as a complementary customer base, I proposed that Taylor's join forces with this company instead.

It was at that point that I learned an important lesson about working with a family firm: you may be a director, you may be valued, but you are never family. For Taylor's, there was more to life than year-end results. After a couple of years, the company was still with Deinhard and I was asked to relocate to Oporto. I declined, and we said our farewells.

My parting shot was that Taylor's should steel themselves, part company with Deinhard and negotiate a 20 percent shareholding in the charismatic UK distributor, Mentzendorff – owned by the equally charismatic Bollinger champagne house. Following my departure, the deal was done, and I am happy to say that it remains in place to this day.

* *

The themes of my career so far had consisted largely of managing up-market brands and streamlining the relationships between producers and merchants, as well as accumulating an enviable list of trade and media contacts. But by now, the somewhat closeted wine trade of yore was giving way to an altogether more expansive international business with a correspondingly broad range of opportunities. Whither should I go? What should I do?

I have always been a sucker for taking on new roles, whether paid or unpaid, so while my departure from Taylor's led to some fascinating consultancy work for Moët & Chandon, Ruinart, Laurent-Perrier and Nicolas, I also became deeply involved in a raft of honorary positions within the wine industry.

Back in the mid-1980s, I had been asked by my good friend Robin Kernick, ex-MD of IDV and then the chairman of Corney & Barrow, if I would like to join him on the prestigious Royal Household Wine Committee. Trepidation, rather than alacrity, best described my feelings at the time. This was the ultimate in wine selection – choosing wines for Her Majesty Queen Elizabeth II to drink and offer her guests in each of her four homes. Tradition held that such wines should only be sourced from wine merchants holding the Royal Warrant, namely, Berry Bros & Rudd, Corney & Barrow, Harveys of Bristol, Findlaters and Justerini & Brooks. All the wines were tasted blind by all the members of the Committee.

There were six of us on the Committee and we were convened by the Keeper of the Privy Purse. The other members consisted of the Master of the Household along with senior directors of the aforementioned wine merchants. We usually met in the wine cellars of Buckingham Palace twice a year, though latterly we held our AGM, followed by a lunch, in one of the palace dining rooms where we were joined by other courtiers. On other occasions, we took it in turns to host the Committee in the splendid dining rooms of Berry Bros, Corney & Barrow or Justerini & Brooks.

Our main task was to ensure that we bought enough stock to allow sufficient maturation before consumption. For vintage port this was 15 years, for claret 12 and for red burgundy six – a good yardstick by which to maintain a balance between the older and the younger vintages. When I joined, the oldest vintage port was Sandeman 1927 and the oldest claret was Château Latour 1945.

Wines offered at Royal lunches or dinners could take on a political or diplomatic dimension. It might be considered appropriate for the Queen, as Head of State, to offer a First Growth claret to another head of state or similar, but the press often took a contrary view, as in: How dare the Queen spend taxpayers' money on expensive wines?

When President Xi Jinping of China lunched at Buckingham Palace, literally months were spent determining which claret to serve. President Xi's people insisted on a wine superior to the one that had been served to the previous president, Li Keqiang. The records were consulted. Li had drunk a Rauzan-Ségla, top of the Second Growths, which meant that Xi's had be a First Growth. The trouble was that during the current president's crackdown on bribery among Chinese officialdom, Lafite, Latour and Mouton Rothschild had all been implicated. That narrowed the field somewhat. In the end we settled for a Château Haut-Brion 1989 and face was saved.

One unusual aspect of the white wines served at Buckingham Palace is that they were all German – a hand-me-down from the days of Prince Albert. The Queen was adamant. She had once been served a Chablis on the Royal Yacht *Britannia* and did not enjoy it. Eventually, the then Master of the Household, Major General Sir Simon Cooper, managed to persuade Her Majesty that her committee 'could if it wished, consider white wines from countries other than Germany'. Normal service has since been resumed.

During a lunch shortly after the tragic death of Princess Diana, a courtier next to me turned and said 'Do you know what I took Prince Charles in bed when I had heard the awful news? A cup of tea.' So wonderfully normal. I often wonder what the staff of other heads of state would have done in such circumstances.

In 2003 I was knocked off my bicycle in Chelsea while cycling home. It was felt at the time that I could have suffered sensory damage to my taste buds.

A week later, I was blind-tasting 20 or 30 wines at Buckingham Palace and, as always, I handed in my top three to Robin, the clerk. Normally, there is a consensus of opinion. Had I gone completely off-piste in my selection? Were my taste buds shattered? Fortunately, all was well and I was within the sweet spot. Phew.

Committee members were nominally appointed for life. Quite rightly, Sir Alan Reid, then Keeper of the Privy Purse, saw through this ruse and informed me that my time was up after 21 fascinating years. My final lunch was on December 5th 2007 in the Billiard Room at the Palace. Michel Roux Jr, chef patron of Le Gavroche, stepped smartly into my shoes, thus continuing the rule of six.

Among the more arduous committee roles I took on around this time was the chairmanship of the Wine Development Board (WDB). As mentioned in Chapter 4, this body had been spun off from the Wine & Spirit Association, the controlling body of the UK drinks industry. Its Articles of Association, dated September 25th 1967, stated that its objectives were 'to encourage, pro-mote and foster the knowledge, enjoyment, appreciation and consumption of wines, spirits…both in the United Kingdom and in other parts of the world'.

The wonderful Helena Harwood, based at Five Kings House, adjacent to Vintners' Hall, kept us all on our toes as executive secretary, while we attempted to plan our next objectives. By this time the WDB's role had largely been taken over by individual producer countries, and France, Italy and Australia all had their own offices in London. Since the countries were now promoting their own wines, it rather begged the question why they should continue to fund a generic body such as the WDB. We recruited leading influencers onto the Executive Committee, including Christopher Burr MW, Nicholas Hyde of IDV, Chris Murphy from Marks & Spencer and James Rogers. Robert Joseph and Denys Reed kindly agreed to represent the media, and we had a further 20 or so regional directors, plus a PR team headed up by Fiona Campbell.

Our rationale was that over the last 10 years wine consumption in the UK had grown from seven litres per head to 12 litres per head; but although we still wanted to encourage greater consumption, we were also increasingly mindful of the drink awareness lobby, which was just beginning to gain traction around this time. Our message was therefore: 'Drink less, but drink better.' Noting that the wine market had also 'developed' a great deal over the same period, we also thought it appropriate to change our name to the Wine *Promotion* Board (WPB) – a variation on the old brand manager's trick of changing the brand name or label if sales were sticking.

Wines by the glass were still a novelty in pubs, drinking better was aspirational rather than a natural next step, and wine education was still very much its infancy. By contrast both the wine and pub trades were unashamedly traditional, which placed the WPB right at the cutting edge.

We all spent many hours chatting up the trade. We held 'Wine by the Glass' seminars, produced a leaflet entitled 'Living with Wine,' initiated a National Wine Week during May of 1993 and made annual presentations to the producer countries. Arguably our most successful seminar was one entitled 'Profit from Wine.' Presenters included Dr John Rae from the recently formed Portman Group, Andrew Eliel from Egon Ronay, Gary Lipp representing Robert Mondavi and the celebrity chef Anthony Worrall Thompson. Another upcoming chef, Hwyel Jones, gave a lecture entitled 'Economic & Social Supertanker Trends: the UK Into the 21st Century'. The trade largely depended on us for trends and statistics, so it was invigorating stuff.

We also were part of the industry lobby group that tried so hard to persuade the governments of the day not to raise import duties on beers, wines and spirits. In the early 1990s we lobbied the Paymaster General, Sir John Cope, later Lord Cope. It just so happened that John had been an old flatmate of mine during my Brown & Pank days in Leicester. This made absolutely no difference whatsoever.

My time at the WPB also coincided with one of the most audacious wine projects ever to see the light of day in London – 'Wineworld,' a themed museum of wine that eventually morphed into 'Vinopolis, the City of Wine'. This was the brainchild of Duncan Vaughan Arbuckle, an extraordinarily resilient entrepreneur with whom I shared mutual friends, including Steven Spurrier. Duncan duly enlisted the aid of the WPB in support of his scheme, and I still have the original 1993 Confidential Private Placement Memorandum.

As is probably obvious by now, I have great difficulty saying no. I was also intrigued. By the light of a torch, Duncan subsequently showed Steven and me around the 2½ acre site he had found for the museum, which was beneath the arches of a railway viaduct built in 1886 close to Borough Market. We were in at the very beginning, and Duncan's enthusiasm, determination and ambition knew no bounds. I note with amusement that in the original information memorandum I am listed as Director of Public Relations – a nice thought, except that the goalposts were constantly shifting as potential investors came and went. Backers as far afield as Toronto and Shanghai were apparently on stream, and my little black book was in demand as never before. Over the next few years, as the project ebbed and flowed, I came to understand the true meaning of what we used to call 'sweat equity', although I must say I really enjoyed being involved in such a major business undertaking from the beginning, since it broadened my experience and exposed me to a fascinating array of business ploys. What became Vinopolis was indeed visionary – as it turned out, too visionary – by showing how the wine trade could happily share a broader platform with entertainment and hospitality. If nothing else, it proved that there was vinous life outside the usual mix of pubs, wine bars, restaurants and hotels.

The WPB continued to be well regarded within UK wines circles, but by 1993 the question of who would fund it had come to a head. We closed our doors late that same year, by which time, I like to think, the wine trade was in a much healthier state than when we had found it.

During this time, I also worked closely with the wine trade's equivalent of the Fraud Squad, the Wine Standards Board, which was run by Jonathan Findlay, a delightful former commander in the Royal Navy. I was particularly excited when I was called as an expert witness in a case involving fake vintage port. At that time, fake bottles were just beginning to appear; now they are everywhere. The wines in question were Taylor 1900, Taylor 1908, Cockburn

1908, Quinta do Noval 1931 and Taylor 1945 – probably the finest selection of vintage ports of the last century. It did not take a genius to confirm they were not genuine: one look at the bottles, the capsules and above all, the labels, confirmed that at least a dozen elements were counterfeit. Both Jonathan and I had a pretty fair inkling who the perpetrator was, but annoyingly the Wines Standard Board did not have the authority to prosecute, and the police declined to do so.

Another day, another 'yes'. In the mid-1990s, someone must have tapped me on the shoulder and invited me to join the Council of the Wine Guild of the United Kingdom. Lord Montagu of Beaulieu was the chancellor and I was asked to chair the Scholarship Committee. The Wine Guild had originally been set up a decade before by Edward Montagu to promote English vineyards, of which he was a pioneer at Beaulieu. In those days the Guild might just as easily have been called 'Edward's Dining Club', but it had a serious intent and was known for attracting a galaxy of interesting members. The annual programme of events included wine tastings, dinners and banquets, many of which provided welcome opportunities to dress up in our full regalia. In addition, we endorsed travel scholarships to France, Portugal and Australia, and generally contributed to the gaiety of the nation – or so we hoped. In fact, I had already met Edward Montagu – in the early 1960s in a bar in New York with my father, since they were both fanatical about vintage cars. Edward, of course, already had one of the finest collections in the world, while my father happened to own a 1928 Bentley 4½ litre.[1] When my father subsequently brought the car to England, Edward kindly found room for it at Beaulieu.

* *

Back in the real world, I still needed to earn a living. One of my largest consultancy roles during this time was for Moët & Chandon in Paris, which I completed in June 1992. As mentioned before, Moët had always relied on

---

[1] This was, of course, the same 4½ litre Bentley in which the author inadvertently froze his friend Robin Byers and his wife during the annual Beaujolais Nouveau run (see Chapter 2).

public relations (aka charm and hospitality) to promote the brand – a strategy that during the brewery-dominated era of the 1950s, '60s and '70s had successfully carried them to the number one spot in the UK, if not the world. But by the mid-1980s, Moët's market dominance was starting to slip. Not only was champagne itself under attack from the flood of cheaper sparkling wines, from Spanish Cavas and French *crémants* to Italian Proseccos, now flooding into the UK, but supermarket own-brands were also taking an increasing share of the market. At the same time, many of Moët's rival champagne houses had discovered the virtues of brand marketing and had begun to carve profitable niches for themselves. Maastrict was also on the horizon, and the idea of UK consumers being allowed to bring back 90 litres of wine duty free filled everyone with trepidation. In short, Moët's traditional market was changing; but it was not.

At the time, Moët in the UK was being run by David, Lord Marchwood (thus continuing the company's fixation with titles), but unlike other champagne brands within the over-arching LVMH (Louis Vuitton-Moët-Hennessy) corporate structure, such as Krug and Ruinart, it lacked its own offices and sales force. What was needed was a detailed analysis of the current UK sparkling wine trade, plus a realistic appraisal of where things were going so that senior management could formulate a suitable marketing strategy.

My 47-page report rather pompously declared that 'Partnership, in its broadest form, is superseding confrontation,' by which I imagine I meant that LVMH's champagne brands needed to co-operate, taking advantage of their parent organization's huge financial and informational resources, rather jostle for position in what was by then a very crowded market. Eventually, all LVMH's champagne brands were indeed brought together under one roof. Job done.

At around the same time, I got together with three old friends to form what the respected trade magazine, *Off Licence News* heralded as a 'Consultancy to advise the UK trade'. Taking our cue from the leading advertising agencies of the day, we rather pretentiously called ourselves 'Howkins, Liddle, Novis and Spurrier' and set up shop in Adam and Eve Mews off Kensington – appropriately the same little street in which I had once shared a bachelor house. Richard Novis, of course, was the wine trade's leading headhunter, while Alan Liddle brought an immense amount of experience in corporate marketing strategy to the party. As for my old school friend Steven Spurrier, he had just been ousted from his job as wine buyer for Harrod's by the not-so-delightful Mr Fayed. As one trade wit put it, if we'd used our first names, it would have spelt BARS. What better name for an outfit serving the drinks trade? Quite possibly we might all have continued in this direction for longer, but in late 1992, an amazing opportunity presented itself. It is a rather extraordinary story.

CHAPTER NINE

To the Manor Born

'Lord Rothschild would like to meet you.' How could I forget those words? It was not exactly a royal command, but even in 1992 I was familiar enough with his lordship's reputation to know that 'even the Pope would get out of the bath to speak to him,' such was his worldwide influence and authority.

It had begun innocently enough, when a friend suggested that I should apply for the newly created role of 'drinks analyst' at Barings Bank – proof that the drinks industry was being taken increasingly seriously by the City. The people at Barings were very nice, but in the end decided not to make the appointment (indeed, three years later the bank went bust). However, they suggested that other private merchant banks might be interested in what I had to offer.

I duly wrote to Lord Rothschild on the assumption that he owned a bank, which he didn't. I also addressed the envelope to 'Mr' Rothschild, which of course he wasn't. Nevertheless, his secretary called me on each of three consecutive days at different branches of the Nicolas retail chain, where I was doing some consultancy work, to arrange a meeting. On each occasion I was greeted by a somewhat baffled French store manager, saying 'Monsieur le Baron Rothschild wants to speak to you.' They were clearly impressed. I was nervous, and couldn't even contemplate calling him back from the shop. Did I think I was being cool?

Eventually I made the appropriate arrangements and turned up, incorrectly, at his private entrance in St James's Place, where he was in the middle of another meeting. Things could only get better, as they say.

Five interviews later, I got the job – not as a drinks analyst, but as the wine advisor to Waddesdon Manor – sole survivor of the 50 or so residences that the remarkable Rothschild family had built in Europe in the late 19th century, and which was currently undergoing a spectacular redevelopment. I was duly installed in a nearby office in St James's Place – an address I was to occupy with great pleasure for the next dozen years.

Lord Rothschild loves projects, and the grander the better. At the time he had just assumed responsibility for running Waddesdon – a vast Loire château lookalike tucked away amid the hills of rural Buckinghamshire. His Lordship is also a serial collector, as all good Rothschilds are, and fine wine did not escape his notice. Being a shareholder in Château Lafite gave him a head start. When the renovation of the Manor was completed, which was scheduled to be in 1994, the plan was to turn Waddesdon into a mecca for the Rothschild family's wines. Among other things, the wine cellars would have to be filled, and a shop constructed to sell the wine.

That left us two years to plan. The first, and only, wine commissioned at that stage was a generic Pauillac from Château Lafite – in effect, its third-tier wine. On the label was to be a drawing of Waddesdon Manor, which made it look for all the world like wine made in Buckinghamshire rather than the Médoc. I implied that this was not the way to go. Shock, horror. Raised eyebrows. In classic Rothschild fashion – as I was to discover – my views were subsequently relayed to a senior corporate marketing executive outside the wine industry to get a second opinion. Fortunately, he concurred. I had passed this vital first test of loyalty.

We were essentially a team of four: Jacob Rothschild himself; Fabia Bromovsky, his delightful and incredibly bright right hand; an enticing marketeer, Martine d'Anglejan, and me. As luck would have it, the one large private wine cellar that I had got to know quite well was not far away. At Buckingham Palace, we made a close inspection of the wine racks and bins, the chestnut staves, the temperature and humidity levels. We looked at lighting and at spaces for tasting wines.

The Waddesdon architects, led by Peter Inskip, did a fantastic job of creating the Manor's new wine cellars and in due course I found myself in the enviable position of corralling more than 15,000 bottles of Château Lafite wines to fill them. These mostly came from Lord Rothschild's personal collection, which at the time was divided between Château Lafite itself, and his English homes at Eythrope, near Waddesdon, and in London. The oldest of the wines was dated 1870.

Lafite and Mouton Rothschild, the Rothschild family's two great First Growths, have long enjoyed a (mostly healthy) rivalry since the latter was elevated to Grand Cru status in 1973. Jacob and I therefore discussed whether we should invite Baroness Philippine, the mercurial ex-actress and owner of Mouton, to contribute to this unrivalled stash of Rothschild wine – a gesture that seemed both friendly and commercial. Having enquired what was the oldest vintage in our collection, Philippine lost no time in including a gratis bottle of Mouton 1868 among the wines we bought from her. Rothschilds, wherever they live, thrive on one-upmanship.

Every single one of these bottles was binned by yours truly and Duncan McEuen, a good friend at Christie's. I had never imagined that my binning apprenticeship, served all those years ago in Northampton, would come in so handy – or that it would be so satisfying.

* *

By the time Waddesdon Manor opened to the public, and again thanks to Jacob Rothschild, I had been presented with yet another quite remarkable opportunity that entailed dividing my time more or less equally between the Home Counties and the rolling hills of northeast Hungary. More on that in the following chapter, but for the moment let us remain in Buckinghamshire.

Naturally, the wine cellars at Waddesdon were an integral part of the overall visitor experience. In *Decanter* magazine, Steven Spurrier announced 'A Rothschild Goes Retail', while readers of *The Briefing*, the British Airways Concorde magazine, were greeted by the headline: 'The Grape and the Good'. In the *Financial Times,* Jancis Robinson wrote 'Lord Rothschild and his team have transformed Waddesdon's substantial below-stairs area into an example of a 'gentleman's working cellar.' Elsewhere in the *FT*, Edmund Penning-Rowsell wrote a piece entitled 'Pauillac rivals join hands in an English Château,' while Hugh Johnson in *The Daily Telegraph* echoed this theme by writing: 'The Rothschilds wine interests are united in a manner never seen before... Lafite and Mouton's wines...make a whole Rothschild wine list with which visitors, dazzled by the splendour all around, can console themselves.'

In due course we started 'Waddesdon Wine Days in the Cellars', at which I would explain the extraordinary history of the Rothschild family, and how Nathaniel bought Mouton in 1853 while his cousin James bought Lafite in 1868. Mouton at that time was still classed as Second Growth, whereas in 1855 Lafite had been proclaimed the first of the First Growths and could therefore command higher prices in the marketplace. So it was that the famous Rothschild rivalry, which had begun life deeply embedded in the terroir of Pauillac, was now being resolved in a quiet corner of the English countryside.

We tasted wines from both Lafite and Mouton, which was a unique experience and much enjoyed by our visitors. At one such session, I remember saying: 'Don't wait for that special occasion to open your bottle of Lafite, Duhart-Milon (a Fourth Growth), Mouton or d'Armhaillac (a Fifth Growth); that special occasion will never come. You have to make the occasion special by opening whatever particular bottle has been lurking in your cellar.' One gentleman who had attended a Waddesdon Wine Day returned a year later. 'I just want to thank you for that suggestion last year,' he said. 'I have never enjoyed myself so much. I have finished all those "special" bottles and now I want to buy some more.'

Among the many artefacts in the Waddesdon cellars were empty magnums of Lafite, whose back labels were signed by the Queen Mother, the Queen, Prince Charles and Princess Diana among others, and an exquisite set of prints depicting Château Mouton Rothschild's famous 'artist' front labels, first introduced in 1945. Perhaps the most fascinating artefact of all, though, was an empty bottle of what at the time was the most expensive wine in the world: a Château Lafite 1787, believed to have been owned by Thomas Jefferson, the second President of the United States. Michael Broadbent had famously auctioned a similar bottle at Christie's in 1985, which Malcolm Forbes, equally famously, had bought for £105,000 – then a world record. Michael kindly offered us the companion bottle, which had been opened for analysis and to verify its authenticity. He thought 'it would be a great coup for the Cellars' and duly handed it over to Jacob in a formal ceremony at which I was the witness. Little did I know that this seemingly innocent act would later lead to a gentle quizzing by my local police at the behest of the FBI.

Benjamin Wallace explains all in his 2008 book *The Billionaire's Vinegar*, which questions the authenticity of the 1787 Lafite bottle and delves into the 'mystery of the world's most expensive bottle of wine'. One day, Michael called me to ask whether he could take another look at the bottle. 'Of course,' I replied, momentarily forgetting that nothing can be removed from Waddesdon Manor without Jacob's expressed permission. I duly remembered to ask Lord R, as he is affectionately known by his team, just as Michael was wending his way up the drive to the Manor to take delivery. The timing could have been better. Lehmann Bothers had collapsed the same day, beginning the most serious economic downturn since the 1929 Wall Street Crash. In his wonderful, somewhat world-weary way, Jacob asked me: 'Ben, do I understand you right. On the day when the world is facing its biggest financial crisis ever, you want me to come downstairs and take an empty bottle off the wall?' I hastily explained that my question was a necessary formality, thanked him graciously, and fled the office.

Needless to say, Waddesdon provided a perfect backdrop for entertaining on a grand scale. The classic Revivalist French Renaissance architecture of the exterior and the sumptuous interior, the delightfully informal setting of the adjoining Dairy, the solemn ambience of the Wine Cellars and the immaculately maintained formal gardens all cried out to be appreciated. Among the first guests to experience a Summer Dinner in the Dairy were the members of Lord Montagu's Wine Guild, 100 of whom sat down to enjoy Château d'Armailhac 1989, Château Duhart-Milon 1986 and Château Lafite 1983 after a welcoming glass of champagne on the Parterre in front of the house. This proved to be an easy pattern to follow, although it still took a huge amount of organizational effort to make it happen. Fortunately, others did the work; I simply banged on about the wines – a task, I'm glad to say, that I never tire of.

One wine dinner at which I refrained from banging on, though, was among the most fascinating ever staged anywhere in the world – despite receiving almost no publicity. It revolved around the unique idea of inviting Charles Chevallier, head winemaker at Lafite, and his opposite number, Patrick Léon at Mouton, as guest speakers. Both represented Rothschild First Growths; both were commercial rivals: it had never been done before, nor has it since.

On the appointed day, July 3rd 2003, we all met up a few hours before kick-off. 'But what shall I say?' queried Charles; 'What do you want us to do?' pleaded Patrick. Both were clearly outside their comfort zone. 'Just talk about yourselves and each other. Talk about your experiences,' I replied rather feebly. In the end, as the Lafite 1983 and the Mouton 1986 flowed freely, they both relaxed and were hilarious about each other's exploits in the vineyards: 'Ah ha… that was the year when you stole a few of my grapes. No wonder your vintage was so good.' Later, Patrick wrote on my copy of the menu 'What a great idea,'while Charles added 'So exceptional.' Yet again, the behind-the-scenes the organization was a feat to behold – not least, the negotiations about which vintages to serve.

Also in 2003, Jacob was keen that we should honour and celebrate the 150th anniversary of Château Mouton Rothschild at Waddesdon, thereby sending an important message that all Rothschild wines were equally welcome there. It was to be a private party, hosted by Lord and Lady Rothschild themselves and limited to 50 guests. Michel Roux Sr was engaged to present the dinner, in recognition of his long association with the Rothschild family, while Baroness Philippine was naturally the guest of honour. Baron Eric was also there, together with Sir Evelyn and Lady de Rothschild. Charles Chevallier and Patrick Léon were at their respective vineyard owner's sides. The guest list also included many other leading personalities from the wine world, including Michael Broadbent, Hugh Johnson, Jancis Robinson, Steven Spurrier and Michel Bettane from Paris. Robert Parker, sadly, was on holiday.

The seating plan was a nightmare and was completed only minutes before we all sauntered, champagne in hand, onto the Parterre, which had been specially planted with a carpet bedding depicting the original 1924 Mouton label, designed by Jean Carlu. Everyone and everything was being filmed. The thought occurred to me that after our nervous start, things were going rather well.

Then my heart stopped as I suddenly realized that I had not asked anyone to talk about the wines. Utterly aghast, I quickly put myself in step with Jacob and enquired, as casually as I could: 'Would you like someone to talk about the wines?' Jacob looked up and gave me a barely discernible nod. I stepped away. There was less than five minutes before we filed into dinner, by which time it would be too late. But who should I ask to talk about which wines? It was a minefield: just as there was a prescribed order in which the wines should be served, so there was an unspoken pecking order of speakers that needed to be observed.

Jancis Robinson was closest to me and cleverly agreed to take the first wine, Mouton's white Aile d'Argent. Hugh Johnson then kindly volunteered to take the somewhat wider brief of the Rothschild family's winemaking history. I duly sidled up to Michael Broadbent and his opposite number at Sotheby's, Serena Sutcliffe, knowing full well that Serena was close to Mouton and that Michael revered Lafite. I allocated the speaking duties accordingly. Almost at once Steven Spurrier bore down on me. 'I gather you have allocated Serena to Mouton. This is wrong. Michael is the most senior. He must talk about Mouton.' Steven was as stern as I had ever seen him. As we all filed in, I reallocated the speaking duties according to Steven's wishes – whether to the annoyance or the delight of the respective speakers, I know not – before slumping into my seat exhausted. Luckily, I was soon revived by draughts of Château Clerc Milon 1982, followed by double magnums of Château Lafite Rothschild 1975 and jeroboams of Château Mouton Rothschild 1955.

A few years later, Christopher Campbell, the enterprising head of wine at Waddesdon, had the great idea of celebrating the 30th anniversary of Steven Spurrier's legendary Judgement of Paris tasting in conjunction with Copia, the newly created not-for-profit wine education centre in Napa, in an event that would take place simultaneously in real time. Going through my old files recently, I was amazed at the amount of correspondence and decision-making that such a seemingly innocent-sounding project entailed. Steven quickly came on board, as did Copia, but then the trouble started: should the choice of wines reflect those of the original tasting, or should we serve their modern-day equivalents? Who would serve on the panel of judges, of which, of course, we needed two – one in England, one in California. Would Aubert de Villaine, owner of the fabled Domaine de la Romanée-Conti, chair the Waddesdon panel? Would Robert Parker do the honours at Copia? A month before the event, on April 28th 2006, while finishing up the Decanter World Wine Awards in Australia, Steven took it upon himself to change the methodology of the tasting. The same week, Baroness Philippine decided to withdraw Mouton 1970 from the competition in a somewhat hysterical letter to Jacob. (I suggested to him that it must have been dictated while she was out jogging.) Without the Baroness's conditional support, Waddesdon felt that it could no longer host the event – which left us less than a month to find another venue. I drew up a list of possible options and got on the phone. The day was eventually saved by Simon Berry, then Chairman of Berry Bros, who put his company's wonderful premises in St James's Street at our disposal.

We started with an expert panel to taste the original wines, followed by a panel of invited guests to taste the current crop. When it was all over, we enjoyed a few more glasses for relaxation purposes before repairing to the Royal Automobile Club around the corner to hook up for a live video link with Copia. It was noon in Napa, which was somewhat at odds with the rowdyish atmosphere of an early evening in Pall Mall. It is fair to say that the communication links between these two venerable establishments could also have been better. Even so, it was fun.

* *

My frequent visits to the West Coast at this time, especially San Francisco, enabled me to maintain a wonderful relationship with the late Dennis Foley, then one of the world's leading exponents of fine and rare wines. Gordon Getty, head of his family's eponymous oil company as well as a composer of music and the owner of the Plumpjack Winery in Napa Valley, had asked Dennis to organize bespoke trips in the Gettys' private 727 jet to London and elsewhere to enjoy the very best that the wine world had to offer.

Most of these trips were under the auspices of the Friends of the Russian National Orchestra (RNO), a charity possibly supported by Gordon Getty on the basis that the orchestra played his compositions in return.

The high spot was a tasting followed by a dinner at Waddesdon in December 2000, where the theme was 'Extraordinary California Wines: a tasting of vertical vintages 1990–97'. This featured, in alphabetical order, an Araujo Eisele Cabernet, a Caymus Special Select Cabernet, a Dalle Valle Maya Cabernet, a Harlan Estate Cabernet, a Ridge Vineyards Monte Bello, a Screaming Eagle Cabernet and a Stag's Leap Wine Cellars Cask 23 – an astounding selection of wines.

Jacob was busy elsewhere, so I was the host for this extraordinary event, which had taken weeks of planning even though there were only 30-odd guests, including Michael Broadbent, Hugh Johnson and Jancis Robinson. The tasting started at 12 noon and ended at 4.00pm. Gordon Getty sat on my left, Hardy Rodenstock was opposite. I had already gleaned that Mr Getty was a man of few words, but we had friends in common at the US importer Wilson Daniels, so I decided that this would provide me with a suitable entrée; four hours sitting next to someone without speaking to them is a painful experience. After about an hour of silence from my left, I decided to open the batting. 'I believe you know my friends from Wilson Daniels,' I began cheerfully. 'Nope,' came the reply. An hour or so later, I tried again, this time mentioning my friends by name. 'Win and Jack…' I ventured, only to be told: 'I don't know who I know. My wife knows who I know.' And that was that. I suppose that if, as was rumoured, you openly run two families, one with your wife in San Francisco, the other with your mistress in Los Angeles, it's perfectly possible to get confused on occasions. Hardy Rodenstock, the infamous wine collector behind the 1787 'mystery' Lafite, sat immobile throughout. We caught each other's eye, at which point the thought struck me that Hardy was more of a taker than a giver. He probably wondered who on earth I was.

At dinner, we took refuge in Château Lafite Rothschild 1952 en magnum followed by Taylor's 1935 and in recognition of my Hungarian benefactors I even managed to slip in a Royal Tokaji 5 *putts* to pair with the pear tart. It was then I realized that trying to compare Old World wines with those from the New World is a little like comparing Savile Row with Armani. Both are wonderful, and both rightfully occupy their places among the best – but they are very different.

Dennis Foley was a brilliant, if exacting, organizer. A few years later, we put on a dinner at Spencer House in St James's for Gordon Getty's beloved RNO. Among a spectacular array of wines flown over specially for the occasion in the Getty jet were Salon and Roederer Cristal 1979, a pair of Montrachet 1982 Grand Crus from Domaines Ramonet and de la Romanée Conti; and Cheval Blancs 1971, 1970, 1964, 1961, 1959 and 1947, plus a Château d'Yquem 1959 and a Croft 1945. To paraphrase Oscar Wilde, to taste one Cheval Blanc at dinner may be regarded as fortunate; to taste six looks like extravagance.

Whether at Waddesdon or at Spencer House, there was always some request, idea, or event that involved weeks of painstaking organization and a veritable army of people. We hosted Christie's masterclasses with Michael Broadbent and Steven Spurrier, a Sunday Times Wine Club dinner, a Riedel tasting and dinner with Georg Riedel, a Bibendum portfolio tasting, a new season preview dinner with Michel Roux and a Wine at Waddesdon dinner featuring 21 different wines, not to mention endless Champagne evenings on the Parterre and an historic dinner based on the menu and wines enjoyed at Waddesdon on December 7th 1937.

Incidentally, talking of history, we once excitedly opened a bottle of the Heidsieck 1907 champagne that had been famously lost in the Baltic Sea in 1916, when the cargo ship *Jonkoping* was sunk by a U-boat en route to Tsarist Russia. After a lot of fumbling around, I managed to extract the ancient cork – and yes, after 80 years in the sea, the aromas and tastes were a tad salty, but still recognizably champagne. Most champagne was well *dosaged* then, the sugar levels contributing to the wine's survival. A single bottle is currently on sale at the Ritz Carlton in Moscow for more than a $250,000. I must say, ours was very good.

Perhaps the most extravagant evening I ever witnessed at Waddesdon took place on June 11th 2001. 'It's Fashion' was a celebration of style in the presence of the Prince of Wales, in aid of Macmillan Cancer Support. Sponsored jointly by Vogue and Jaguar, the ticket price was £10,000 (plus VAT) for a 'Patron' table seating 10 guests. The entrance was pure red carpet. As Clarissa and I made our way through an army of photographers, they began by ignoring us and then suddenly took an interest and started flashing excitedly. We smiled graciously in acknowledgement, little realizing that right behind us was Naomi Campbell.

The champagne was provided by Laurent-Perrier, the wines at dinner were of course furnished by Lafite and Mouton Rothschild and my friends in Hungary supplied a Royal Tokaji 5 *putt* Aszú 1996 to accompany the delicious vanilla-pod pannacotta with crushed raspberries. We duly sat down at our tables. Everywhere you looked, there was a celebrity or a famous face. Ben Elliot, the then Duchess of Cornwall's nephew, was on my table and we had a long chat about his new luxury lifestyle management company Quintessentially. Joan Collins sat opposite. Amid the general hubbub I managed to yell across the table 'I so much enjoy your Diary column in *The Spectator*.' 'What did you think of this week's?' she replied. Needless to say I hadn't read it; immediate collapse of stout party.

Clarissa was on the same table as Ruby Wax, who kept crawling under it looking for her handbag. 'She's always doing that,' sighed her exasperated husband. Later, while on the dance floor with Beth Rothschild, I inadvertently trod on someone's stunning full-length dress. I turned round to apologise and came face to face with – The Body. Elle Macpherson could not have been more charming as I spluttered my apologies. Towards the end of what had been a truly amazing, star-studded evening, another young blade rushed past me shouting: 'Where's the coke, I need some coke.' Being naive at the best of times, I duly pointed him in the direction of the bar...

CHAPTER TEN

Mád World

Two years before the opening of Waddesdon Manor to the public in 1994, I was dispatched by Jacob Rothschild on a vineyard-buying mission to Hungary. I was hardly the ideal person for the job: I had never been to Hungary, I had certainly never bought a vineyard and the only time I had ever tasted Hungary's famed Tokaji wines was while Clarissa and I were staying with Michael and Daphne Broadbent at their home in Wiltshire. Michael was in the middle of writing *The Great Vintage Wine Book* at the time. Having reached the letter 'T', he asked me if I wouldn't mind tasting some of his Tokaji samples before we moved on to something more interesting. I remember that neither of us were particularly wowed by what we knew had once been one of the great wines of the world before it was virtually snuffed out during the post-war Communist era. 'Interesting,' I thought, though it wouldn't have troubled me if I'd never tasted Tokaji again. Little did I suspect that less than six months later, I would become deeply involved in what proved to be the renaissance of these amazing wines.

Jacob, it transpired, had been approached to see if he might be interested in acquiring an important estate in the legendary Tokaj[1] wine region of northeast

---

[1] In Hungarian, 'Tokaj' is the name of the wine region, 'Tokaji' the name of wines that come from it. 'Tokay' is the acceptable English translation.

Hungary. Prized for centuries by Europe's aristocracy, the area's once-famous wines had fallen into sad neglect after 40 years of Communist rule, which favoured bulk production and collectivization over the skills of small independent producers. Now, though, the Soviet bloc had collapsed and the wine world was once again taking an interest.

Jacob, who also had a Hungarian aunt – Rozsika von Wertheimstein – was more interested than most. Would there be an opportunity for the Rothschilds to invest? wrote Jacob to his cousin, Baron Eric, at Château Lafite. Ever persuasive, always hassling, Jacob was keen to take an option on one of the former Tokaj estates before others stepped in. So it was that in March 1992, I undertook a recce of the Chateau Megyer estate near Saraspatak in the company of Charles Chevallier, then head winemaker at Château Rieussec in Sauternes before his move to Lafite.

In my report, I described the trip as being like 'Going up the Douro,' since Tokaj was three hours' drive from Budapest – roughly the same distance as my beloved *quintas* were from Oporto. I likened my arrival to: 'Arriving in the Côte d'Or without any signposts. Undulating vineyards with aprons of different vineyards and terroirs.' It was indeed a magical, if derelict, region. Charles and I tasted over 40 wines in a damp underground cellar that measured nearly a kilometre in length. Among them were dry furmints, dry and sweet szamarodni, and 3-, 4- , 5- and 6-*puttonyos* Aszú dessert wines[2] including the much-prized Aszú Essencia and the almost impossibly exotic Essencia – the essence of wine. Suddenly, I was confronted not only by a whole new wine vocabulary, but by a wave of new taste sensations that ricocheted through my nose and around my mouth; my imagination was on fire.

I returned to London, Charles returned to Paris. In his opinion, one sweet

---

[2] The sweetness of Tokaji wines is measured by the *puttony* ('picker basket') of Aszú grapes, with 6 *puttonyos* (commonly shorted to '*putt*' or '*putts*') being the sweetest. Ever keen to promote higher quality, the Hungarian authorities now prefer only to recognize the 5 and 6 *puttonyos* levels of sweetness, at minimum levels of 120 and 150 g of sugar respectively.

dessert wine (ie, Château Rieussec) in the Lafite Rothschild portfolio was enough. His boss agreed. Meanwhile I reported back to Jacob and to Tony Bromovsky, Fabia's husband, who also worked with Jacob on some of his projects. I did so with huge enthusiasm, as I could see a unique marketing opportunity in the offing.

Jacob, however, would not go ahead without Eric, which after months of negotiations and meetings left us at something of a stalemate. I happened to relay this to my old friend David Orr, who by now was President of Château Latour, where Hugh Johnson was also a director. Did I not know that Hugh and another friend of his, the pioneering Danish winemaker Peter Vinding-Diers, had recently invested in a vineyard in Tokaj, but had subsequently run out of money due to the current recession? No, I did not. I had met Hugh several times and I knew Peter, a much-respected oenologist, from my Loudenne days. A quick phone call to Peter at his new home, Château Landiras in the Graves, and I soon learned all about the Royal Tokaji Wine Company. Peter also told me that the Megyer estate was in the wrong part of Tokaj.

Tony Bromovsky and I felt a fresh surge of enthusiasm and that June, while on a Waddesdon fact-finding visit to Lafite, Martine d'Anglejan and I dropped in on Peter at Landiras. Yes, there did indeed seem to be scope for cooperation. And so began my 'double life' for the next 20 years or so. Synergy in spades – the noble and the Royal.

Tony, Peter and I subsequently got together with Nigel Wilson, an old City friend who had been asking for some time how he could best invest in a wine business, and together we raised enough money through our various contacts to buy out the local Hungarian farmers who had been equal shareholders in the fledgling Royal Tokaji Wine Company. Lord Rothschild was also good enough to invest, which lent all-important gravitas to the project. On listening to what had been achieved so far by Hugh and Peter and to our proposed plans, he observed ruefully as he signed the cheque and wished us luck: 'Well, it seems you are half pregnant. You cannot go forwards and you cannot go backwards.'

By 1993, my working life was essentially split between Waddesdon Manor and our Royal Tokaji offices in the splendidly named town of Mád, whose fine bishop's palace had relatively recently been converted into a supermarket.

In those early days, nothing was simple in post-Communist Hungary. There were no hotels, so we lurched between a succession of B&Bs. The local pub, which turned into a strip club after dark, only served soup and bread at lunchtime. In an early instance of recycling, wine was served out of used plastic Coca Cola bottles, since no glass bottles were available. Yet on a more serious note, the Hungarians we were to come across and work with were charming and friendly. Yes, there was the odd one who 'entered the revolving door last and came out first,' but for the most part they were tired of four decades of Soviet domination and were only too delighted to look West as a prelude to joining the EU.

We were advised early on to seek out someone to guide us through the various political and bureaucratic minefields that awaited us, and in due course Peter and I called upon Dr George Rasko, the Minister of Agriculture, in his Budapest office, to sound him out. 'I will help you,' he said, and that was that – no hint of a conflict of interest and no complicated arrangements to be made. The indefatigable George subsequently negotiated on our behalf to buy the 14th-century underground cellars behind our offices in Mád from the Hungarian State Winery. He dealt with the tricky subject of labelling after it was decreed that our front labels had to show the region, Tokaj, in larger letters than our brand name of Royal Tokaji. And he smoothed the way with the OBI, the government's so-called quality-control department, which at one point questioned our definition of what an Aszú wine actually was. Softly spoken, but always delightfully articulate, George has been our chairman in Hungary ever since.

All the while, we spent time chatting up the local press, one of whom was an American editor based in Vienna. One day I was innocently bathing in the famous Gelhert steam baths in Buda, wearing nothing but a glorified handkerchief around my waist, when I received a holler from across the water. The aforementioned newshound then unashamedly waded up to me to be updated on the latest developments at Royal Tokaji – both of us naked except for our floating hankies.

While Nigel and Tony focused on the financials – which were a story of their own – I attempted to devise a five-year marketing plan for what had once been one of the world's greatest wines, albeit one that did not produce a vintage every year. Among the many problems I faced was that the most highly prized Aszú wines relied on the grapes being infested by the wholly natural but notoriously fickle *Botrytis cinerea* fungus (aka 'Noble Rot') to shrivel their skins and concentrate their juices. This in turn made it very difficult to estimate production volumes. Equally, there was no international price structure that I could use to determine the selling price of the wines. Where to start? Berry Bros had effectively been the exclusive UK importer of Tokaji Aszú during the wines' 1930s heyday and still stocked a 5 *puttonyos* Aszú produced by the former Hungarian state winery, the Borkominat. The style was a touch rancid, and the colour more brown than the golden hue of days gone by, but the retail price in St James's was £16.50 for a half-litre (50cl) bottle. We therefore built our entire commercial plan on the basis that we would sell our flagship 5 *puttonyos* Aszú for £16.50, or its dollar equivalent in the US. Today, some 30 years later, Royal Tokaji 5 putts Aszú sells for less than £30 retail.

Meanwhile, Peter was hard at work using the 1990 and 1991 vintages that Royal Tokaji had procured and blended to determine how 'real' Aszú wines should taste. All of us were firmly of the opinion that the Aszús of old had been gloriously rich and fruity, but with a fresh acidity that prevented them from ever being cloying. The Communist-produced wines of the last 40 years, which included the ones Michael Broadbent and I had sampled, were not only dull in colour but in aroma and taste. The new French owners of the other previously state-owned wineries in Tokaj wanted to produce one-dimensional, dry or Sauternes-style wines at competitive, rather than premium, prices[3]. Peter and Hugh were adamant that Royal Tokaji must produce the style of Aszús that for centuries had so entranced kings, popes, emperors and tsars in equal measure – 'Wines that pulled nails from coffins,' as one customer of Berry Bros wrote in admiration.

We tracked eventually down Miklos Nemeth, who had served as first President of the newly democratic Hungary, and gave him a sample of our 5 *puttonyos* Azsú 1990. He was immediately in raptures. 'This is the wine that I remember while sitting on my grandfather's knee,' he told us. Shortly afterwards I flew to the States to give an unlabelled sample to my old friend Peter Morrell, the trend-setting New York wine merchant who had recently bought a sizeable stash of pre-communist Tokaji from the then leading wine auctioneers Heublein. He, too, was ecstatic. He rushed out of his shop and down the road to the nearby celebrity restaurant, the Four Seasons, where Paul Kovi, an expat Hungarian, held court. Having tasted my sample, Paul later wrote to Hugh Johnson: 'This is the fiery style of Aszú that we Hungarians thought we would never see again.' I was assured that 'fiery' in this context was highly complimentary. We were ready to launch Royal Tokaji on an unsuspecting world.

The big question, though, was to whom? In spite of the positive noises that had been made, we still needed a customer or two. During my Morgan Furze days, I had been happily courted by Laurent-Perrier, which was keen to increase its London distribution among top restaurants. I also very much appreciated holding a glass of its excellent champagne in my hand as we all watched polo together at Smith's Lawn in Windsor Great Park. Their UK MD, Dickie Nicholson, was a friend, so we duly asked Laurent-Perrier to be our UK agents. Our first retail customer was Lea & Sandeman, now deservedly Royal Warrant Holders. Le Gavroche was the first restaurant in London,

---

[3] Somewhat surprisingly, in his autobiography *From Bordeaux to the Stars* (Académie du Vin Library, 2023) the late, great Jean-Michel Cazes, the owner of Château Lynch-Bages and probably the most influential investor during Hungary's new wave of foreign ownership, states that from the beginning, his plan was to produce and sell mainly dry white wines rather than focus on the sweet, rich Aszú wines – the opposite of the way we were thinking at Royal Tokaji.

in fact the first in the world, to stock and promote Royal Tokaji 5 *putts* Aszú. Again, those Morgan Furze lunches had paid off: Silvano Giraudin, Le Gavroche's outstanding *maitre d'*, was instrumental in getting Royal Tokaji noticed on London's restaurant scene, ably aided and abetted by Stephen Clark, Laurent-Perrier's genial tousled-haired sales manager.

Cracking the States took a similar route of friendship. As previously mentioned, during my Croft days, IDV had created a worthy Gilbey Vintners' Wine Education School at which I sometimes used to lecture about port. In the audience one day was a tall, blond American from the West Coast called Win Wilson. We had a chat and subsequently kept in touch. Win later joined forces with Jack Daniels (no relation), who hailed from Wisconsin, to form what today is arguably America's leading wine importer, Wilson Daniels.

In the meantime, after leaving Peter Morrell, who wanted exclusivity for the USA – good to hear, but impractical given the US's three-tier distribution system – I stepped around the corner on Fifth Avenue to darken the door of New York's longest established wine retailer, Sherry Lehmann. My erstwhile friend and the current owner, Michael Aaron, was out; his second in command, Michael Yorch was in, but on the phone. I was ushered into his office just as he put the phone down. 'Goddam,' I heard him exclaim (or something to that effect): 'They are so tight with their DRC allocations.' Michael had just been talking to Win (or maybe it was Jack?), who held the immensely valuable Domaine de la Romanée-Conti agency for the US. I nodded in sympathy while quietly thinking to myself what a great place 'allocation land' was to be. 'That's who you want in the US,' Michael concluded.

My next call was a little further downtown to Kobrand, the agents for Taylor's port agents, with whom I had a strong relationship and who I really wanted to take on Royal Tokaji. Their urbane CEO, Gérard Yvernault, listened attentively, but in the end shook his head. 'Too small for us. I'm afraid.' The irony is that many years later, when our paths crossed again at a New York *Wine Spectator* event, Gerard ruefully admitted to me that he greatly regretted not taking on Royal Tokaji.

Undaunted, I raced back to the Knickerbocker Club where I was staying and put a call through to Wilson Daniels in Napa Valley. Jack was in, so we chatted away. He kept mentioning 'Hungarian wine' in a way that did not sound over-complimentary, but when the talk turned to the rarity of Aszú wines and the Essencias that were once the exclusive preserve of European royalty, he immediately got it. Three weeks later I flew out to San Francisco, met with Jack and Win, and we did the deal. That was 30 years ago and it is still going strong.

For Jack and Win, wine was all about authenticity, provenance, style and presentation. When Royal Tokaji first took a stand at Vinexpo, the annual wine fair in Bordeaux, they clearly approved of how the brand was being presented. Later, when they brought their first customers out to the winery in Mád, they proposed that we include Waddesdon Manor in the itinerary to give the brand yet more gravitas. We duly had lunch with Jacob Rothschild, which went down particularly well.

In those early days during the early 1990s, our international network was largely built around Hugh Johnson's and my contacts. We also made a point of writing to the Hungarian Ambassador in each of our major markets, which resulted in some wonderful launch parties, such as one given at the Hungarian Embassy in Washington DC. It was touching to hear more than one grateful ambassador say: 'Thank you for what you are doing. Hungary does not produce many world class products, but Tokaji is one of them. I can now raise a glass of Tokaji and look my opposite number from Paris, London or Washington straight in the eye.' This was reward in itself.

Meanwhile. back in Hungary, a representative from the highly influential *Wine Spectator* in the form of Per-Henrik Mansson visited our centuries-old underground cellars. Per must have been the first person ever to bring a laptop to an Aszú cellar. He tasted from the barrel while we held our collective breath, then waved his arms in jubilation: 'I don't know what you guys do to these wines, but they are certainly world class.' This simple utterance changed our lives. We knew we were on the right track.

All this positive feedback spurred us on to position Royal Tokaji in the best possible light. Other world class European wine regions – Bordeaux, Burgundy, Champagne, Sherry, Port and so on – had been in continuous existence long enough to evolve their own clear personas. Tokaji, once the most famous of them all, had been ignominiously ignored for the best part of half a century. We badly needed to establish its working identity. Perhaps a figurehead was what was needed?

Jack and his delightful wife Gayle had kindly invited Clarissa and me to spend a few days together in Hawaii, on the pretext of attending a Food & Wine festival. On our first day, I explained our thinking to Jack. That same afternoon I conducted a masterclass on Royal Tokaji to Shep Gordon – not only one of the original hippies, but a keen wine collector and, I was soon to discover, agent to leading Hollywood stars: Shep's clients included Frank Sinatra, Michael Douglas and Sharon Stone. I thought Sharon Stone might be ideal, but trod gingerly and started with Michael Douglas. 'No. You don't want Michael. Too erratic,' replied Shep. 'You want Sharon.' I could not have put it better myself, I thought, as we joined the others by the pool.

After dinner, no less a personage than Burt Baccarach himself was there to entertain us with 'Magic Moments' and other memorable hits as the night wore happily on. As we bid farewell, Shep and I agreed to keep in touch about Sharon. Royal Tokaji had neither the budget nor the money, but we didn't let that deter us. Later, Sharon and I faxed each other (does that sound quite right?) and agreed to meet up in LA, but her filming schedules kept changing and in the end we never made it. She did, however, gratefully acknowledge the gift of Essencia that we sent her as a wedding present. She said it made her feel 'imperial'.

Some years later, I bumped into Shep strolling down St James's Street. 'I just wanted to thank you so much for helping with Sharon,' I reminded him. 'On the contrary' he laughed, 'I wanted to thank you for the idea. You wine and spirit guys were searching for a star to front your brand, so I simply turned the idea around; why shouldn't celebrities endorse drink brands?' He then went on to inform me that another of his stars, the American singer-songwriter

Sammy Hagar, endorsed the Cabo Wabo tequila brand in 1996 which he then sold for $11 million 15 years later. Whose idea was it anyway?

* *

The richness of our Aszú wines inevitably raised comparisons with Sauternes. We thought ours were more complex and, in any case, wines from Tokaj had existed long before their French counterparts. In addition, we could boast double the acidity and 2 or 3 degrees less alcohol, both of which became selling points. Nevertheless, Sauternes was the unquestioned market leader in the sweet dessert wine market and at the top of the tree was the First Growth Château d'Yquem. At one of the earliest New York Wine Experience weekends, I was manning the Royal Tokaji stand where we were debuting our first vintage of Aszú Essencia – 1993. The crowd was four or five deep when, out of the corner of my eye, I spotted d'Yquem's illustrious owner, the Marquis Alexandre de Lur Saluces. There he was with his arm outstretched, glass in hand, waiting in line to taste our wine. 'Yes,' I thought with a deep feeling of inner triumph: 'We have made it.'

Royal Tokaji's most successful restaurant account was the wondrous but ill-fated Windows on the World on the 107th floor of the World Trade Centre. Presided over by Kevin Zraly and Andrea Immer, it was the highest-grossing restaurant in the US of the day. I did staff training courses there on several occasions and lunched there more than once.

During my first visit, they were keen to show me the fitness centre adjacent to the dining room. The light switch could not be found, and I swept in grandly – only to step straight into the swimming pool. My left leg was sodden, and as I walked back to the dining room I left a trail of water behind me. They closed the fitness area soon afterwards.

Among my most treasured possessions was a Windows on the World wine list featuring Royal Tokaji 5 putts. Some years later, at a ceremony to celebrate the opening of Wilson Daniels' wholesale company in New York, I gave it to the company president, Rocco Lombardo. Rocco, a charming, highly moti-vated but full-on businessman, graciously accepted it with tears in his eyes.

I subsequently flew to New York just a few weeks after 9/11 for the biannual New York Wine Experience. On the way over, it was confirmed on the news that nearly 3,000 people had died that day. My mind turned to the Troubles in Northern Ireland, where the death toll had been roughly the same, albeit over some 30 years. When the subject of Noraid came up, as it inevitably did, I pointed this out to my American friends. Most saw my point.

In fact, I had been in Northern Ireland both at the beginning of the Trou-bles, with Charles Piat, and at the end, with Taylor's port. On the latter occa-sion, we were dining in a restaurant after a tasting at Queen's University in Belfast when the chef rushed in from the kitchen shouting 'Vacate the premises immediately. We have a bomb scare'. Hear those words said in a thick North-ern Irish accent and you run instinctively – and indeed, we did. I recall that I was still holding my napkin as we repaired to the Hotel Europa, where we filled up on sandwiches.

Another good New York account for Royal Tokaji was the 21 Club on West 52nd Street, which had been a famous speakeasy during the era of Pro-hibition. In the restaurant, I once spotted Jackie Onassis. Another time I was in the downstairs gents' urinals where there was only one other person. I stood nearby. I looked to the left. It couldn't be. It was. Salvador Dalí eased his unmistakable features slowly towards me. Our eyes met. I wished we had exchanged words, but what words?

Words also failed me when Jack and Win, knowing that I was serving on the Royal Household Wine Committee, arranged for the three of us to visit the White House – ostensibly to see the wine cellars. The delightful Daniel Shanks was to be our guide. After a personal tour of the main building, which included seeing Hilary Clinton through a window going through her fitness routine, earphones and sunglasses in place, we arrived at the wine cellar. 'Ahem,' coughed Daniel nervously. 'I'm afraid I can't show you the cellars; it's too

The author with Jack Daniels (left) and Win Wilson, who together created the leading US fine wine importer Wilson Daniels, during their visit to the White House in 2001. Right: A letter from their guide for the occasion, Daniel Shanks, confessing that the cellars weren't quite up to Buckingham Palace standards.

行程亮点 | 世界葡萄酒行业泰斗
英女王葡萄酒顾问·全程随行

本·霍金斯 先生

- 世界葡萄酒行业泰斗级人物
- 英国女王伊丽莎白二世御用葡萄酒顾问
- 英国皇室家庭葡萄酒委员会重要成员
- 罗斯柴尔德家族葡萄酒首席顾问
- 罗斯柴尔德沃德登斯庄园酒窖设计者
- 国际葡萄酒比赛评委
- 葡萄酒与烈酒教育基金会(WSET)理事
- 世界著名葡萄酒著作家

Above: the author pictured in the wine shop at Waddesdon Manor as part of a presentation to wealthy Chinese individuals arranged by his friends Lily Zhu and Emma Feng.

Left: Jacob Rothschild, 4th Baron Rothschild OM, GBE, CVO, financier and philanthropist, who has been responsible for the outstanding restoration of Waddesdon Manor (below), the magnificent house built by Baron Ferdinand de Rothschild in the late 1880s and affectionally known as 'the French château astride a Buckinghamshire hillside'.

舍
THE COUNTRY MANOR HOUSE
英人庄主俱乐部

GALA DINNER
5TH OCTOBER 2017

原味和黑麦迷你法国面包
鲜黄油
Mini baguettes, plain & rye
Fresh butter

挪威鳟鱼，顶级鱼子酱
橘子沙拉，细葱，细叶香芹，桔子汁
Confit of Norwegian trout, Beluga caviar
Citrus segment, chives, chervils, yuzu dressing

温莎城堡式羊肉根茎蔬菜汤
Brown Windsor lamb soup

香煎鹅肝，天然盐片
嫩炒抱子甘蓝叶，无籽露
Pan fried foie gras, Maldon salt flakes
Wilted Brussels sprout petals, seedless grapes

香草烩鹌鹑蔬菜墩，黑蒜汁
Timbale of quail and root vegetable ragout, black garlic nage

香烤巧克力和牛柳，鲜松露汁
黄土豆西红柿墩，香槟细葱汁
Grilled chocolate wagyu beef tenderloin, fresh truffle jus
Timbale of yellow potato and tomato, champagne chive nage

现烤开心果蛋奶酥，焦糖香草奶油，鲜树莓
Fresh baked pistachio souffle, toffee, vanilla cream, fresh raspberries

BARONS DE ROTHSCHILD BLANC DE BLANCS NV
AILE D'ARGENT BLANC DU CHÂTEAU MOUTON ROTHSCHILD 2014
CHÂTEAU LAFITE ROTHSCHILD 1988
CHÂTEAU LAFITE ROTHSCHILD 1982
ROYAL TOKAJI ASZU 6 PUTTONYOS LIMITED EDITION 2011
CHURCHILL'S VINTAGE PORT 1997

Inspired by the menus served when the Rothschild Family hosted the Queen

Above: a typical menu for our
private dinners in China.
Above right: the author signing
a copy of his 2019 book Sherry,
Maligned, Misunderstood and
Magnificent! at a launch party.

Centre right: A presentation of
Graham's Tappit Hen Vintage
Port 1997 to a group of wealthy
Chinese wine lovers.
Right: The author with a
bespoke luxury case of Château
Lafite Rothschild in the wine
cellars at Waddesdon.

Above: Jacky Zhang, our friend in China, evaluating two separate glasses of Chateau Lafite Rothschild 1982, one from a magnum, the other from a bottle, at a private banquet just south of the Great Wall.

Below: toasting a sample of the stunning 1870 colheita port for the Last Drop Centenario duo collection, consisting of a bottle each of 1870 and 1970 (l-r) the author, Francisca van Zeller, Manuel Aranha Furtado de Mendonça, Production/Wine director and Cristiano van Zeller.

Above: Royal Tokaji's offices and cellars in Mád.
Right: The beguiling entrance to the cellars,
which stretch for nearly 2 km undergound.

Below: Hugh Johnson, founder of Royal Tokaji,
in front of his bust outside the company's offices.
Below right: The author in Royal Tokaji's
'sacristia' in the cellars, where old and rare
vintages are kept under lock and key.

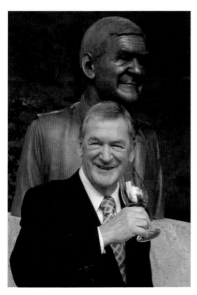

Above: the author with Charlie Mount, MD of Royal Tokaji, viewing the company's First Growth vineyards at St Tamas, Nyulaszo and Betsek.

Above right: different vintages of Royal Tokaji Essencia maturing in demijohns in the 14th century underground cellars.

Right: the magnificent and rare magnum of Essencia, of which only a handful exist, and (inset) the fabled crystal sipping spoon.

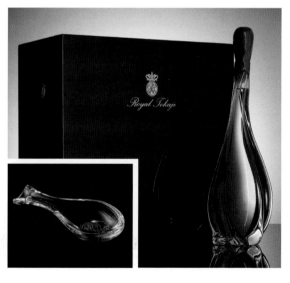

Above: son Jamie and daughter Lucy graduate from Edinburgh University.
Left: three generations of the Howkins family – with Jamie and Oliver, our first grandson.

Below left: feeling on top of the world.
Below: the husband and wife team Howkins – still skiing, still winning.

Above: The author's family celebrating his 80th birthday in the garden at Staverton, Northamptonshire.

Right: standing in a wine press in Georgia's oldest cave town, Uplistsikhe, which dates back to the Iron Age. Far right: Clarissa reposing in the author's brother's set in Albany, London.

embarrassing. You see, the President cannot sit still for more than 45 minutes, so dinners are always rushed and there are barely any fine wines there – only six bottles of Château Latour 1945.' We gently pleaded our case, but Daniel was adamant: he simply couldn't let someone who was familiar with the cellars at Buckingham Palace draw comparisons with the White House's current feeble offering. In fact, the oldest clarets in the Palace at the time were six bottles of Lafite 1945 – reminders, perhaps, of a successful Allied war effort?

As previously mentioned, the ultimate Royal Tokaji wine is Essencia, which is as rare as it is unique. It was once the nectar of Emperors and Popes, if not the gods. It can only be produced in outstanding vintage years and it takes years to ferment. It is rich beyond all reason. And it is expensive.

We launched with the 1993 vintage, whose viscosity was such that it was almost impossible to drain the last few precious drops in the bottom of the glass. What was needed was a smaller implement to transport these last drops to their rightful home. Years ago, in Hong Kong, I had bought some small Chinese snuff bottles with tiny ivory spoons inside them. That gave me an idea. We subsequently did our research and sure enough – spoons of pure crystal had indeed once been used to sample Europe's most precious wine. Essencia by the spoon duly became the must-try tipple in up-market restaurants across the world. My good friend Daniel Mahdavian even featured a 1oz-pour of Essencia on a crystal spoon at the October 2016 opening of the jaw-droppingly glitzy Trump Hotel in Washington DC[4]. And the price? A mere $150.

In our efforts to restore Essencia's reputation of old, we furnished Pope John Paul II with bottles of Essencia 1993 and presented the current Pope, Pope Francis, with bottles of Essencia 2009 during his visit to Budapest in May 2023. Less proudly, given the way things have turned out, we also acted on a request from President Putin to send some Betsek 1992 6 *puttonyos* first growth for a dinner in St Petersburg.

---

[3] The hotel has since been sold to the Miami-based CGI Merchant Group and is now called the Waldorf Astoria.

Rather cheekily, we even tried to bestow a glass of Aszú upon the Queen Mother, when we spied her car parked outside the West End club where she was dining (we happened to be dining nearby). Quite correctly, her chauffeur refused our kind offer, although I know for a fact that Royal Tokaji is now a fixture in the cellars at Buckingham Palace.

CHAPTER ELEVEN

Spreading the Word

When I am asked, which I often am, how to get into the wine trade, I point out that some of the best jobs in wine are created, not filled. Neither my Waddesdon nor my Royal Tokaji roles existed before I took them on; I was simply fortunate to be in the right place at the right time. It was the same with my next adventure, which involved not wine people but two titans of the spirits industry – both of whom had been senior colleagues at IDV and were now personal friends.

It so happened that the ever-inventive Tom Jago and the dynamic James Espey had just created a spirits business, Last Drop Distillers. Their idea was to seek out ancient or rare casks of forgotten whiskies, present them beautifully and in due course lead the luxury end of the market. James and Tom had already changed the face of international branding by creating Baileys Irish Cream, Malibu and countless other successful brands. James had also started the Keepers of the Quaich to promote Scotch whisky in much the same way as the centuries-old Confrérie des Chevaliers du Tastevin did for burgundy.

Tom and James were A-listers to their fingertips – drinks business insiders who above all knew how to tell a story. Whisky, they realized, had been too long in the doldrums: it needed a route to the luxury market, with a price tag to match. This time, though, it was their own necks on the line and they needed help to reach what was a small, but potentially hugely profitable, target market. We duly chatted, after which I made some calls to contacts on both sides of the Atlantic. As luck would have it the Underwood family, who had recently bought Wilson Daniels, expressed an interest. Jack and Win, who were still personally involved in WD, were equally supportive. The first release was the incredible, mouth-tingling Last Drop 1960 blended Scotch whisky, produced in a limited run of 1,347 bottles that retailed for $2,000 each. We had aimed for the US to take around 25% of this total, but they quickly became hyper-excited and wanted more. We, in turn, played hard to get. We eventually settled for 330 bottles – our first big deal. Timing, as they say, is everything. Just one month later, in September 2008, the storm of the Financial Crisis hit full force: we had signed the deal just in time. As things progressed, Tom and James kindly asked me to become both a director and a shareholder in Last Drop. Another journey had begun, this time blending the worlds of high-end wines and high-end spirits.

From the beginning, it was fascinating to see how much high-end consumers of wines and spirits had in common. Both had money; both had a taste for luxury; both collected and/or invested, and both thoroughly enjoyed being entertained. We duly resolved that Last Drop must be driven not by gimmicks, but by provenance and authenticity. No trendy shapes or 'bling' for us: our bottle design was classic and elegant, reflecting, we hoped, the profile of our customers.

Incidentally, while we're on the subject of brands, it occurs to me that in general, the shorter the name, the better. I recall that in my Croft days, two of the leading cartoonists of the time – Wally Fawkes, who created Flook in the *Daily Mail*, and JAK of the *Evening Standard* – regularly used the name 'Croft' on the label whenever their cartoons depicted port. I thought it might be fun to obtain an original, so one day I found my way to JAK's office in Fleet Street to ask him about his cartoon featuring a group of bishops in their club enjoying a decanter of Croft port. I assumed JAK preferred Croft to other brands. 'Oh no,' he replied cheerfully:' 'It's just that "Croft" fits neatly in the space.' Nevertheless, I slipped a bottle onto his desk and took the (giant) original home, where it still hangs to this day in my study.

* *

Somehow, without consciously ever seeking it out, I realized by this time that my former bosses had all been rather exceptional people. Lord Rothschild is without doubt one of the most remarkable personalities of his generation. His friends are the people who influence our lives, and he cares as much about the details as about the many wider issues in which he has an interest. A visionary like no other, but with a gravelly sense of humour, he inspires great loyalty. In the early days of email, his secretaries were concerned that 'Lord R' should not fall prey to 'phishing' emails or scams. 'Even a very rich man can press the delete button,' he told them. I learned so much from him, and from his equally delightful right-hand, Fabia Bromovsky.

Another inspirational person was Viscount Astor, who became chairman of Royal Tokaji, having taken over from Dickie Nicholson of Laurent-Perrier, who in his turn had taken over from Sir Hugh Bidwell, a former Lord Mayor of London. William Astor's step son-in-law was David Cameron. Later, when the latter became prime minister, William was good enough to stick a copy of my second book, *Real Men Drink Port... and Ladies do too!* (2010), in his Christmas stocking.

In addition to our day-to-day business chats, William and I used to have fascinating political discussions. Again, I learned much from him. Once, on a fact-finding trip to Mád, he brought along his friend Lord Lamont, the former Tory Chancellor who had presided over the infamous 'Black Wednesday' financial crisis. William warned me that Norman Lamont was seldom on time and was apt to get 'diverted' at the drop of a hat. Sure enough, on our way home after dinner in Tokaj, we did indeed lose him – only to find him again, happily chatting away to some largely uncomprehending locals in a very rustic pub.

Families such as the Rothschilds and the Astors have, of course, effectively become international brands in their own right. Without such a kick-start, you need to invent your own. 'Royal Tokaji' was the brainchild of Hugh Johnson. His original suggestion had been 'Imperial' Tokaji, inspired by the Austro-Hungarian Empire of which Hungary had once been a part. Unfortunately, this was greeted with dismay by the region's farmers: 'We are no longer an empire, we are back to being a kingdom,' said one. So 'Royal' Tokaji it was.

Whenever Hugh and I travelled on promotional tours, whether in California or China, I thought I pretty much knew what he was going to say when relating the background to our wonderfully aristocratic wines. Somehow, though, he always surprised me with an evocative word or description that cut straight to the heart of the matter.

Hugh is a veritable giant among wordsmiths who, perhaps more than any other person alive, has defined the ways in which the fruits of the vine are best enjoyed. With an inimitable twinkle in his eye, and in spite of his worldwide fame, he is also wonderfully approachable. Although the two of us had met previously on several occasions while 'on the circuit', it was through Royal Tokaji that I really got to know this remarkable man. Today, Hugh's vision and thirst for knowledge run as deep as ever; in the intervening years, he and his delightful wife, Judy, have become firm friends.

* *

But let me return to Last Drop. The brand was created when a friend of James Espey's, who had founded a luxury hotel chain in South Africa called The Last Word, asked James to find him some own-label whisky. Quick as a flash, James suggested that the drink could be called The Last Drop, and so Last Drop Distillers was created. James has since deservedly been awarded the OBE for his contribution to the whisky industry and remains a dynamic force behind the scenes.

Wearing our Last Drop hats, James, Tom and I soon found ourselves criss-crossing the globe in pursuit of new business. At dinner, we strove to pair our whiskies with each course. One such, at Crustacean in Beverly Hills, involved no less than six courses, which we paired with Last Drop's 1971 blended, a 1977 Dumbarton single grain, a 1969 Glenrothes single malt, a 56-year-old blended whisky and an 1870 Colheita port.

In Beverly Hills we also teamed up with one of LA's more intriguing residents, Karen Setian, who knew absolutely everyone and in due course became Last Drop's de facto ambassador to the rich and the famous.

I first got to know Karen through the legendary Beverly Hills wine merchant, Dennis Overstreet – the man credited with introducing fine wine to the Hollywood stars through his friend, Dick Martin, one half of the long-running TV comedy series *Rowan & Martin's Laugh-In*. Dennis was far-sighted enough to realise that in order to sell fine wines to such people, it was not only necessary to guarantee their provenance but also to provide facilities for their proper long-term storage at the correct temperature and humidity. So it was that in the mid 1970s, he pioneered the concept of refrigerated wine storage by opening a 20,000 square foot facility in west Los Angeles called, unsurprisingly, The Wine Cellar[1].

I was delighted when Dennis invited me and Joe Bogorad from Wilson Daniels to host a Royal Tokaji tasting and dinner there. From the outside it looked much like any other warehouse, but as we stepped inside I was flabbergasted: it was as if we'd just entered the hall of a Scottish country house, complete with antlers on the wall and blazing log fire. (In fact, Dennis was well known for his slightly eccentric sense of humour; when excited he frequently used to jump up and down on both legs.) Charged with glasses of champagne, Joe and I and the invited guests, mostly American and Chinese, were led back stage to the labyrinthine wine cellars, of which there was one per customer. There was not a straight line in sight, and famous labels with mouth-watering vintages beamed back at us around every corner. At this point, Dennis disappeared back to his office, leaving us to find our own way out of the maze.

---

[1] This was a hugely important innovation in the history of the wine industry, since it paved the way for fine wine to become the globally recognized investment asset that it is today.

The charming Chinese, not quite in on the joke, started to panic, whereupon Dennis reappeared and led us to the dining room. True to form, flushed with the success of what had evidently been his party trick, he did indeed jump up and down on both legs with undisguised joy.

At dinner, the Royal Tokaji flowed liberally while I banged on relentlessly about our amazing wines. Among those listening was Karen Setian. He asked me if I would join him for breakfast the following morning in the Polo Bar at the Beverley Hills Hotel – at the time, the go-to meeting place for the great and the good of Hollywood. 'If Karen has asked you, then you go,' was Dennis's advice, and so I began a friendship with a most unique and engaging man.

Karen's story was a Hollywood classic. Born in Armenia, virtually penniless, he moved this family to the US to make his fortune and became a leading light in the Beverley Hills community. Tragedy struck when his 17- year old son was killed in a drink-driving accident, after which he worked tirelessly to raise money for good causes. Having enjoyed my Royal Tokaji stories, Karen became a much loved and respected honorary ambassador for Last Drop whiskies – and yes, he did indeed know everyone...

Karen and I happily shared both dinners and cigars together in Los Angeles, Las Vegas and Monte Carlo. He once took me up to enjoy the view from The Vineyard – at the time the largest and most expensive undeveloped property in Beverly Hills, in which he had a financial interest. Another time in Las Vegas, I noticed some filming taking place in my favourite casino, the Bellagio. When I enquired what the film was, someone mentioned something about 'oceans'. A film about the sea? I thought. In Las Vegas? It was only later, when the film *Ocean's Eleven* was released, starring Julia Roberts and George Clooney, that I realized what I had missed that day.

While Last Drop was predominantly spirits-driven, we all agreed that very old ports, containing up to 20 percent grape spirit, could also qualify. Cristiano van Zeller, scion of the previous owners of Quinta do Noval, duly rose to the occasion. On a visit to the Douro, he showed me no less than three different blends from the 1870 vintage that had been locked away in their oak barrels for nearly 150 years. One was absolutely delicious, but sadly not for sale: the owner, a cousin of Cristiano's, had reserved it for HM the Queen Mother, who had been a regular visitor. He would not part with it.

There is something quite humbling about standing in an ancient small family wine cellar on the banks of the majestic River Douro and tasting from an oak wooden barrel that has sat there in the darkness for maybe six generations. What has it been doing since the reign of Queen Victoria I wonder? Is it still alive?

In Cristiano's tasting room we joyfully pulled several vintages from their reverie. All were different, yet all shared the most wondrous flights of colours and aromas, and all were marked by their exquisite length – the hallmark of greatness. After much healthy debate, we selected another 1870 and then, to create historical interest, a 1970 harvested from the same vineyards in the Baixo Corgo exactly 100 years later. The vineyards were in sight of our tasting session, which lent the occasion added poignancy.

One trick of the trade that I learned along the way is that such wines, so well rested for so many years, invariably benefit from a little freshening up before they make their appearance in polite society. In this case, a shot of grape spirit to restore a marginal loss of alcohol did wonders for their physique and wellbeing. Thus restored, they were ready to join the party.

Two classic outlets for our wares were Club 33 at the Disneyland Park in Anaheim, California, and the former Trump Hotel in Washington DC. Club 33 was arguably the least known but most exclusive club on the West Coast, having once been where Walt Disney persuaded his friends to bankroll his new theme park venture. The security there is tighter than at Buckingham Palace, although once you are in you are greeted by characters from Disney cartoons and Star Wars rather than guardsmen in bearskins. Matt Ellingson was the delightful manager in charge of food and beverages. In a highly convenient partnership with Royal Tokaji, we held the club's first ever wine tasting dinner there.

As mentioned earlier, the former Trump Hotel, now the Waldorf Astoria, was fortunate to have the enterprising Daniel Mahdavian overseeing both the kitchens and the bar. A good friend, Daniel made a point of highlighting Last Drop's wares in his amazing private cellar. The hotel itself was formerly the Old Post Office on Pennsylvania Avenue and boasts a vast atrium. During one visit, I was scheduled to meet several journalists there for dinner, but they refused to enter any establishment owned by Mr Trump. Instead, Daniel and I enjoyed an excellent, if quiet, dinner by ourselves.

And so we come to China: a land of opportunities, and of challenges almost equally great. In vinous terms, China in 2000 was where the US had been in 1970 – that is, roughly two generations behind Europe. In the America of the early 1970s domestic wines, led by Gallo, still took precedence over imports. It was the same in China in the early 2000s: wine, which included some imports labelled 'domestic', was just beginning to make inroads into the more traditional market for beer and (very strong) spirits.

Just as the 1970 vintage began Bordeaux's acceptance in the States, so the 1982 vintage – especially Château Lafite – sparked off what turned out to be a ballistic demand for claret in China. In both nations, fine wine lovers initially expressed their enthusiasm by insisting on drinking the very best before venturing further down the quality ladder. In the more established wine-producing regions, where wine drinking has always gone hand in hand with eating, the reverse tends to be the case.

Both Royal Tokaji and Last Drop were determined to crack China. It helped that I was associated with the Rothschilds and thus, by implication, Château Lafite. But where to start? The traditional Hong Kong traders weren't really interested – China was still a foreign country so far as they were concerned – but in China itself, bona fide licensed importers were just starting to appear. Until the 1990s, the wine business had been largely dominated by old-established domestic producers such as Changyu and Great Wall. But now, again thanks to the major political and cultural changes that accompanied China's entry into the 21st century, a significant number of very wealthy Chinese were beginning to take a keen interest in luxury Western goods and lifestyles, and naturally they wanted the best of everything.

Among the first licensed wine importers was a charming father and son team, Don St Pierre Sr and Don St Pierre Jr, who had built up a very successful tractor business in China that they later sold to the government. Casting around for their next venture, they married their knowledge of distribution in China with their personal love of wine and concluded that there was no better way to cash in on the burgeoning luxury market. I first met Don St Pierre Jr when we appeared on stage together during a wine trade show in Paris. Don was there to let the world know about his new company, ASC, while I was giving a somewhat more prosaic talk on cross-Channel trading. I knew at once that Don would be the ideal importer and distributor for Royal Tokaji in China, but although he liked the idea, he felt that ASC wasn't yet well-established enough to take on such a niche product. Unfazed, I decided to bide my time. I also introduced the WSET programme to ASC, which proved to be hugely beneficial to both organizations.

Three years on, during which time I kept in touch with Don and gave him the occasional gentle prod, ASC had grown from a few dozen employees to over a thousand. The foundations of a healthy, import-led wine and spirit industry had been well and truly laid; the time had come to introduce Royal Tokaji to China. At the time, the imported sweet wine market in China, small though it was, was dominated by Château d'Yquem – then being run by Pierre Lurton. We were determined to overtake it. At one Gala Reception (I think it was in Chengdu), which the Chinese do very well, we ran a competition that was won by a lady Chinese banker. Offering my congratulations, I asked her which bank she worked for. 'My own' she smiled sweetly.

I asked Don why d'Yquem was so successful. In his opinion it was not so much to do with the wine itself, but with the fact that Pierre Lurton had taken the trouble to visit China on numerous occasions and made sure that he was introduced to the right people.

A few years later, by which time Don had also taken over the Château Lafite Rothschild agency in China, I asked him the same question – this time with Lafite's dominance of the Chinese red wine market in mind. Again, Don ascribed its success not just to the wine itself but to the person selling it – in this case Christophe Salin, Rothschild's charming and enigmatic CEO, who had spent years in both tier one and tier two cities making sure that Lafite was enjoyed by the 'right people'.

It was on one such visit for Royal Tokaji, which took in Beijing, Shanghai, Chengdu, Shenzhen and Guangzhou – all cities of more than 10 million people and thus all larger than London – that I strode into the renowned Long Bar in the Waldorf Astoria, opposite the Bund in Shanghai. I was there to meet one Jacky Zhang – a friend of James Espey who was in line to be our Last Drop importer in China. It was 5.00pm and the bar was almost empty. To my left, I spied a young, well-dressed man drinking whisky and smoking a serious cigar. My heart immediately warmed to him whoever he was. 'Yes', I replied when he offered me a whisky, and 'Yes' I replied again when he followed up with a cigar. Years later, Jacky and I recalled this moment. He confessed that at the time he did not know how I would react, but he took a chance, and our friendship was sealed.

Jacky and his lovely girlfriend Jennifer were to become our eyes and ears in China. Jacky was a well-connected 40-something businessman who had built up a formidable list of private clients. Through his company Golden Glen, he masterminded Last Drop's luxury positioning among what turned out to be a group of exceptionally 'High Net-Worth Individuals'. In the meantime, ASC had gradually fallen under the control of the Japanese conglomerate, Suntory, and were no longer giving us quite the attention we felt we deserved. In due course, this time with my Royal Tokaji hat on, we took the decision to move the company's top-end Aszú wines over to Jacky, too.

By the mid-2010s, Damon de Laszlo, a true renaissance man whose Anglo-Hungarian grandfather was the acclaimed early 20th century portrait painter Philip de Laszlo, had taken a major financial interest in Royal Tokaji. Up to this point the company had never enjoyed the best of financial health, but Damon's desire to honour his grandfather's reputation in Budapest coupled with his visionary belief in the wines themselves gave Royal Tokaji the financial stability that would see it go from strength to strength. Around the same time, Charlie Mount, a delightful and innovative marketer who had achieved great heights at Krug, took over as MD of Royal Tokaji, while Rebecca Jago and Beanie Espey succeeded their respective fathers as joint MDs of Last Drop. The latter was eventually sold to Sazerac in the USA in 2016, but our joint forays into China were always memorable.

During one of these visits, Jacky and I dined with a very wealthy lady who had recently secured a generous consignment of Burgundy's most desirable wine, Domaine de la Romanée-Conti, but had nowhere to store it under the right conditions. It just so happened that a good friend of mine, Nik Boulting, whose father and uncle were the pioneering UK film producers – the Boulting Brothers – had recently asked me to join him in a new venture called Wine Cellar Consultants to build bespoke wine cellars for people in London. (The irony was that both Nik and I were too busy with our day jobs to really give it our full attention, although our promotional video clearly inspired others to fill what proved to be a highly profitable gap in the market.) Jacky, forever on the lookout for new opportunities, thought that we might do the same in China and to this end created a promotional booklet he called *The Cellar*. It was written in Mandarin, so I have no idea what it said, but it seemed to have the desired effect and before long we had our first customer. This was a well-connected lady I shall call Annie, who had founded the 'House of I Heritage Chateau' north of Beijing – the first in a network of eco-village projects that would eventually extend across the whole country. In due course we built and filled a cellar for her, and to my surprise she asked me to become her 'spiritual advisor' – a great honour in China, since it confers a position of deep trust. For my part I was more than happy to oblige: not only was Annie a great supporter of both Royal Tokaji and Last Drop, but her exclusive dinners, set overlooking a spectacularly beautiful lake, were something to behold.

For one of these dinners, Jacky persuaded Clarissa and me to bring over in our luggage a bottle and a magnum of Château Lafite 1982 – unquestionably the most sought-after wine in China. We met up with Chris Campbell, CEO of Waddesdon Wine, and a brand-new Bentley duly whisked us to our desti-nation, where the surroundings were a curious blend of the Scottish High-lands, Vail, Colorado and Milton Keynes. The fact that our Lafite had come directly from the Château, via Waddesdon, and was therefore emphatically not fake was widely applauded by our fellow guests, who were ever-wary in a land awash with counterfeit luxury goods. I even managed to convey, as night fell over the lake, that there really was a taste difference between a bottle and a magnum of the same vintage.

At another dinner, the main course was Peking Duck – a much-revered dish in China, and one with (if you'll forgive the pun) a very clear pecking order as to which bits are consumed by whom. The most highly prized deli-cacies, it so happens, are the eyes. The attention of several diners around the table turned to me for some reason, and I, in turn, sensed what lay ahead: there was absolutely no way that I was going to scoff the eyes. Next in line were the feet – only marginally less off-putting. With a wan smile I picked one up and dropped it into my mouth, where I crunched it to smithereens and washed it down hurriedly with a dram of whisky. Never has a drop of Last Drop tasted so good.

The following year, I presented a magnum of Royal Tokaji Essencia 2008 to Annie and her guests. This hand-crafted beauty, the brainchild of Charlie Mount, was the only one of its kind at the time, having been commissioned as a prototype. We put a price of €30,000 on it, which made it the most expen-sive bottle of white wine ever sold. As is customary, the chief guest and the producer signed the label in gold. In this case the chief guest happened to be Princess Beatrice Marie Caroline Louise Françoise of Bourbon-Two Sicilies, who signed first – not without difficulty. As I signed as the producer, the Prin-cess was heard to sigh: 'How wonderful to have a short name.'

Annie insisted on buying the signed magnum – and as her 'spiritual advi-sor', what could I say? It subsequently transpired that the hand-made cork didn't fit properly, so we took the bottle home with us, had it re-corked, and sent it back to her.

Around this time, President Xi himself had expressed an interest in 'artisan work', and we were delighted to hear from one of his colleagues that Last Drop fitted into this category. The President was also keen that his fellow country-men should learn more about Western culture and etiquette, and to this end he was offering selected Westerners with the requisite knowledge a chance to spend a year in China for the not inconsiderable fee of $1 million. Jacky asked me if I would be interested. Over a cup of Chinese tea, Clarissa and I looked at each other very much as we had done all those years ago when a move to Manhattan had been on the cards. 'It might be fun,' we concluded. Jacky duly made a call to the relevant person, only to return looking crestfallen: 'I'm afraid you're too old,' he grinned.

Not long afterwards, Clarissa and I found ourselves at another tea cere-mony, this time with Annie, her MD, and Jacky. Normally Jacky did all the translating, but on this occasion Annie and her MD had an interpreter of their own in attendance. It soon became clear that something was wrong: Annie was evidently under the impression that I would be staying in China for three months, which I had no intention of doing. Later, out of earshot, Jacky explained to me that Annie's interpreter had been lying to her, apparently on the instruction of her MD, who was desperate to hold on to his job by securing my services. We spent half the night working out how to save face.

Once, when Jacky and his girlfriend Jennifer were in London, we treated them and their clients to cigars at Davidoff, then crossed St James's Street to dine at my club, Brooks's. Seeing a group of English people crossing the road sporting red smoking caps and puffing on cigars would have been funny enough; the sight of a group of Chinese people doing so was nothing short of hilarious.

The next day, we all paid a visit to the highly innovative Last Drop pop-up in Piccadilly Arcade, which runs between Piccadilly and Jermyn Street. The star attraction there was 'Penelope' – an ingenious but elegant decanter-pourer of Last Drop whisky that had been the brainchild of Rebecca and Beanie and was named after Tom Jago's wife. 'Penelope' intrigued everyone. Everyone wanted her, but she was not for sale.

Just as intriguing in its way was the time when Jacob Rothschild asked Hugh Johnson and me to have a look at Château Thénac in Bergerac, which had just been acquired by Eugene Schvidler, a youthful Russian oligarch who was the president of the energy company Sibneft. We duly arrived at Farnborough and boarded Eugene's expensive private jet at 8.30am precisely. Having settled our choice of breakfast, the three of us then sat back in our armchairs for the short trip to the Dordogne. Hugh and I both knew that Eugene was in partnership with Roman Abramovich, but we were slightly unnerved when we thought we heard, via the plane's telecom system, that 'Roman' would be at the château to greet us. It turned out that Eugene's general factotum shared the same first name.

We did learn from Eugene that Roman A had imagined that buying Chelsea FC might be a three-day wonder for the press, while Eugene himself thought the furore could last a week. He also admitted how ingenuous they had all been back then. We were most impressed, though, by the way Eugene went straight to man his stall at the local fair – and also by the wines themselves. He later confided that although he could have afforded to buy any First Growth château, unlike his more extrovert friends he wanted to own somewhere with a lower profile place for the sake of his family.

Hugh stayed on in Bordeaux, while Eugene and I flew back together. I was somewhat taken aback that the plane did not seem to have a bar on board. This was in stark contrast to the old Pan Am, which had once had the extraordinary idea of asking wine merchants to conduct mid-air wine tastings in its First Class cabins. There was certainly plenty of time between London and New York to get stuck in. I remember giving a copy of *Rich, Rare & Red* (my book published in 1982) to Cyrus Vance, Secretary of State under President Jimmy Carter, and I seem to recall we also toasted the crew with Croft 20-year-old tawny.

An even more relaxing form of travel was lecturing aboard cruise ships. Chris Campbell first got me going on Saga's *Spirit of Adventure* with a Waddesdon/National Trust cruise to France, Portugal and Spain. First Growths were eagerly dispatched, much to the envy of those who could not afford the ticket price.

The International Wine & Food Society also invited me to be the wine host for their Danube River Cruise from Budapest to Passau in 2016, possibly mindful of my Royal Tokaji connections. This outstanding eight-day bonanza was superbly organized by Andrew Jones and Steve Hipple of the International Food & Wine Society Americas Inc, and the discussions on pairing menus and wines occupied many happy transatlantic hours. Our party of 80 started in Budapest with a reception aboard the *River Beatrice*, at which we drank Taittinger 2006, Pol Roger Winston Churchill 2002, Billecart-Salmon 2004, Bollinger 2005, Krug Grande Cuvée, Ruinart 2005 and Dom Pérignon 2004. The dinners comprised six courses, each paired with local wines that included Furmint 2013 and Mézes Mály 2009 from Royal Tokaji, along with other gems of the Danube including Somlói Cuvée, Spiegelberg 2011, Sauska Cabernet Franc 2011 and St Andrea Merengö 2011. What a trip!

* *

All the while, I had been putting pen to paper in various forms. My first published article appeared in *Ashfold*, my old prep school magazine, when I was 10, and by the ripe old age of 12 I was the magazine's editor. Later, I wrote articles on wine for our local Northampton paper, for which I was paid £1 per column.

At various times during my career, I resolved to maintain the scribbling habit. Some of these efforts were educational, but most had a more commercial purpose in mind. They were nearly always about wine, except for one occasion when I recall I branched out into hot pants.

During my brand manager/Croft/Morgan Furze days, I was often asked to contribute to what turned out to be an impressive list of publications including the *The Wine & Spirit Trade Record*, Egon Ronay's *Good Food Guide*, Boardroom, Grand Met's *Bienvenue*, *Sheraton* magazine, *Decanter*, *Drinks International*, *Harp-*

ers Wine & Spirit Gazette, Wine & Spirit magazine, *The Drinks Business, Wine Mine, Which? Wine Guide, International Wine & Food Society* and *Thoroughbred Express.* Neither were my efforts confined to the UK; I also wrote for *La Revue du vin de France* and the *International Herald Tribune.* At one point my name appeared even in the *Financial Times,* in addition to which I compiled crosswords in French for *Harpers* and quizzes for *The Wine & Spirit Trade Record.*

Sometimes I offered to write an article instead of taking advertising space – a time-consuming but thoroughly enjoyable way of getting free publicity. Similar conversations took place with the organizers of various seminars when I would decline to buy advertizing but offer my services as a guest speaker. After a particularly good lunch at Morgan Furze one day, I was invited to address an Institute of Marketing seminar, sponsored by American Express and *Business Travel Weekly,* on 'What Motivates People to Buy'. James Espey also lured me into joining the editorial board of the Australian publisher of *International Wine Marketing.*

It was my ad hoc scribblings that led me to write my first book on port, which was eventually published in 1982. This was originally commissioned by Pitman as part of a series on wine styles under the editorship of the unforgettable Pamela Vandyke Price, but then the series was axed and I was left high and dry. Fortunately, the book was subsequently picked up by the International Wine & Food Society, who ran with it as *Rich, Rare & Red* – a title I had thought up one day in Chelsea while crossing the road to have lunch with Pamela. Although I have almost completely rewritten it in the years since, it is now in its fourth edition.

Some 30 years later, I became intrigued by the idea of a 'port person' – someone who looked you in the eye, said what they believed in, and naturally enjoyed a glass or two of port. Margaret Thatcher would have been one such person; Tony Blair, perhaps, would not. Encouraged by Hugh Johnson and by Andrew Johnson, the publisher at Quiller, the idea gradually took shape and became my second book, the somewhat tongue-in-cheek *Real Men drink Port... and Ladies do too!* A friend of Andrew's, the brilliant Oliver Preston, kindly drew cartoons to accompany the text. Hatchards in Piccadilly took the book and it became one of its best sellers, much to the chagrin of my lovely brother John, who has an apartment opposite Hatchards in the Albany. As a world-leading academic, John has written many serious books, from *Understanding Television* (1976) with David Frost, through to the ground-breaking *Mass Communications in China* (1982) and perhaps his best-known work, *The Creative Economy: How People Make Money from Ideas* (2001). In the nicest possible way, it rather irked him that his upstart older brother had joined him on the best-seller list. We commiserated over a glass of port.

In between my books on port, I was asked by the International Wine & Food Society's to write a booklet entitled *Tokaji – A Classic Lost and Found*, in which I set out to explain the story behind this remarkable wine. By the mid-2010s, I felt compelled to do the same for sherry, which during my lifetime had sadly become something of a Cinderella among fine wines. This led to Clarissa and me paying several sun-drenched and sherry-soaked visits to Andalusia, where we were equally warmly welcomed Peter Dauthieu Jr, a family friend. In due course I submitted a manuscript to Quiller, only to have them pull out at the last minute – something of a recurring theme in my book publishing life. Fortunately, help was once again at hand.

A few weeks later during a long, lingering lunch at Brooks's with Hugh Johnson and Steven Spurrier, Steven announced his intention to found a new publishing house devoted entirely to books on wine. He told us that it would be called The Académie du Vin Library, echoing the Académie du Vin wine courses he had run in Paris in the 1970s. He also said that he was on the look-out for new books…

Balancing Steven's enthusiasm across the Atlantic in Toronto was Marc Nadeau, who was in the process of reviving Steven's original Académie du Vin wine courses in Canada and was still the financially savvy custodian of the brand. Marc's passion for wine is as infectious as his vision for new ventures, and he would go on to become a good friend. In the meantime, leadership of the Académie du Vin Library was entrusted to the dynamic but sure-footed

Simon McMurtrie, who had known Hugh Johnson since he was Hugh's publisher at Mitchell Beazley. A year later, Académie du Vin Library published my third magnum opus under the very apt title *Sherry – Maligned, Misunderstood, Magnificent!* (2021). I'm delighted to report that the book is now in its second printing and is playing its part in re-establishing the reputation of what for me has always been one of the world's great wines.

I am equally delighted that Simon's successor, the delightfully driven Hermione Ireland, has seen fit to make me Académie du Vin Library's global trade advisor, with a brief to further strengthen the links between the worlds of wine and publishing. It is a job that I relish, the wonders of Zoom giving me both the excuse and the means to contact old friends while quietly sipping a glass of sherry in the comfort of my study in rural Northamptonshire. There are so many people across the world now, particularly in China, who have grown to appreciate the wonders of fine wine yet are forever hungry to learn more about Western wine culture. It almost goes without saying that I am happy to oblige them wherever or whenever I can.

CHAPTER TWELVE

Old Friends

One of the most fascinating aspects of our trade, much envied, is that it involves largely subjective values that by definition invoke great passion. Relationships therefore have a huge part to play – not only in the structure of our business, but in evaluating the worth of the product itself. As my American friends are constantly fond of reminding me, the wine trade is, above all, a 'relationship business' – a quality that is apparent at many different levels. Loyalty to a particular wine can be inspired, for example, by a visit to a vineyard in the distant past, or by something as simple as sharing a bottle with old friends or colleagues.

I was once asked why it is that members of the medical and legal professions on both sides of the Atlantic have, over the past few hundred years, developed such a deep affinity with wine. Yes, they have always been able to afford it – but equally, both professions have a tradition of meeting to seek the opinions of their peers. It has always been natural for wine to be served at such gatherings, and for those wines to be mutually enjoyed, compared and commented upon. The same is true of clubs of one sort or another, whether they are specifically devoted to wine or not. The passion for appreciation is by no means exclusive to the trade; it is shared by discerning wine drinkers worldwide.

Wine and conversation are the *lingua franca* of our business. Friendship and rivalry go hand in hand, invitations ebb and flow, and menus are constantly perused to arrive at the most successful pairings. Attending tastings, luncheons, dinners can easily become a full-time occupation.

Equally, you never know who you might meet on such occasions. Restaura-teur Kevin Kennedy once asked Clarissa and me to one of his famous parties at Le Boulestin in Covent Garden, where we shared a table with the then business editor of the *Daily Express*, the redoubtable Kenneth Fleet, and his wife. Only a few weeks before, Dickie Nicholson had asked me on behalf of his brother-in-law, Anthony Tennant, who had just taken over the helm at Grand Met, how Anthony might get to know the business editors of the major news-papers. I duly asked Kenneth Fleet. 'No problem,' he said. 'I'll give you the names and then write to them'. Anthony, later Sir Anthony, was most grateful.

At my own club, Brook's in St James's Street, I am chairman of the Wine Committee, and for many years I have led annual trips to wine regions as far afield as South Africa and South America. The members, many of whom love their wines and have fine stocks at home, are only too keen to sign up for these jaunts in order to meet the producers of their precious vintages. The producers, in their turn, are more than happy to entertain such good customers. During these excursions, since we are generally a mixed party of 30 or more, we hire a coach to transport us around the countryside. On one occasion, Clarissa and a couple of girlfriends were waiting patiently for us to arrive back at Pisa airport when one of them asked: 'How will we know which is the Brooks's coach?' 'Oh, don't worry,' said Clarissa. 'Spot the one that unloads a bevy of jolly, Panama-hatted, blazer-wearing Englishmen.' And there we were.

* *

The wine trade, of course, will find almost any excuse to club together to share the odd bottle or three. Some of these clubs last only for a couple of outings; others exist for as long as their members are alive and willing, and few survive through the generations. Some of them are exclusively trade-led, others are enthusiast-led, but all have one thread in common: the enjoyment of wine in the company of like-minded human beings.

The first trade club that I belonged to was the Under Forty Club – unsurprisingly, for those us under the age of 40. One of the founders was Michael Grylls who went on to become an MP and was the father of Bear Grylls. Back in March 1975, we entertained members of the Scotch whisky industry at Innholders Hall – a big step in those days, since wine and spirits were regarded as two separate entities and the twain seldom met. Two other trade-only clubs are the long-established Old Codgers and Mr Pickwick. Each meets twice a year in London. The former has a club tie, the latter does not. The wine and conversation, though, flow in equal measure, with rivals in the field becoming friends over lunch to exchange banter and trade gossip. A more recent innovation is 'The Shortest Day, Longest Lunch', which is held at the Garrick on or around December 21st. There being at least 12 of us on such occasions, the rule is that we all bring a magnum.

Patrick Gwynn-Jones, the owner of Clarissa's and my favourite restaurant, Pomegranates, near Dolphin Square in Pimlico, was another great club man, and invitations to his splendidly boisterous 'Australian Beefsteak and Burgundy' and 'Tabasco Club' luncheons were always much in demand. A while ago, four of us, including the dedicated Christie's man Duncan McEuen, Giles Townsend, latterly of the Savoy, and Richard Parsons of Green's Wine Merchants, decided to celebrate the fact that we had all been born in the same year by holding an annual lunch there. On December 16th 1992, our 50th, we shared the best of what the notoriously poor 1942 vintage had to offer – Veuve Clicquot, Castillo Ygay Murietta, Château Coutet and Croft port, suitably supplemented by some younger wines. Incidentally, it was also Patrick Gwynne Jones who introduced gravadlax to London. He kindly used to give Clarissa and I a side of this Nordic delicacy each Christmas, and to this day we cannot contemplate Christmas Day breakfast without it.

The Cellarman Club, which I first attended in 1987 with menus going through until 2005, was one for the high rollers. Expertly run by genial Harley Street surgeon Dr Louis Hughes, a past president of the International Wine & Food Society, it numbered among its members the dedicated MWs John Clevely and John Boyes, extrovert winos Bill Baker, Tim Stanley Clarke and

John Avery, wordsmiths Hugh Johnson and Steven Spurrier and the chairman of Royal Opera House, Sir Colin Southgate. We always met in the same private room high up in the Savile Club in Brook Street, where the menu of sea trout and lamb or beef followed by cheese never varied. The wines we brought to each dinner usually followed a theme, for example: '1959, 1961 and 1979 clarets' or 'Northern Rhône,' which in turn obliged us to delve deep into our own cellars. The depth and range of the wines enjoyed at these dinners was both superb and very spoiling. The beauty is that no one felt honour-bound to defend what they had brought: if it was spot-on, the bearer would simply smile happily; if it was deficient in any way, this was accepted as proof that each and every bottle of wine has a life of its own.

The Aquitaine Society of Northampton was founded in 1956 and is still going strong, its membership drawn mainly from the medical and legal fraternities. Each member takes it in turn to host a dinner at their own home with four guests. My old friend Michael Orton Jones is currently the sixth Honorary President, and I have been fortunate enough to attend several of these splendid occasions, including the Society's 500th dinner on April 19th 2007.

At all these dinners, the wines were religiously tasted 'blind' – the forensic work in gauging the producer and vintage being all part of the fun. A fellow guest from the trade and I were asked not to give the game away, so instead we nodded sagely, hiding our ignorance in bliss. Imagine our faces when we opened the menu only to realize that we had just skimmed our way through a Château Latour 1990, a Château Mouton Rothschild 1989, a Château Pichon Longueville Comtesse de Lalande 1982, a Fonseca 1966 and a Noval 1955.

More recently, a few of us have taken part in similar 'Call my Bluff' events for charity. The first was to support the Arnold Foundation at Rugby School, where a vinous trio of Old Rugbeians, Hugh Johnson, Steven Spurrier and yours truly, entertained our old school mates in Salter's Hall under the watchful eye of organizational maestro, Peter Berners Price. Since the four of us knew each so well, the evening was hilarious – near misses in our descriptions of the various wines being very much par for the course. Another event, in support of Cure Parkinson's, took place in the 16th-century barn at our home in Staverton. Our gallant Lord Lieutenant volunteered to be MC and this time it was local wine wizard Johnny Goedhuis who joined Hugh and me on the podium. Just before the start, our young grandchildren, Oliver, Thomas and Milla, took to the stage, all three quite ready to join in the festivities.

My involvement with Brooks's wine lunches and dinners extends over such a long period that I hardly know where to start. I will, however, single out our reciprocal wine committee dinners with the Garrick and Boodle's as being wonderful examples of inter-Club camaraderie. Some of our more off-piste excursions, such as Thomas Heneage's exotic Truffle dinner in October 2006, which reached the parts no other cuisine could reach, will stay with me forever.

The same applies to lunches and dinners at the Vintners' Company, of which my son Jamie and daughter Lucy are now Liverymen. The sheer thrill of attending a black-tie dinner at Vintners' Hall never pales, from walking up the imposing stairs to being introduced to the current Master, from the ancient ceremony of the Loving Cup to the final, uplifting rendition of the Vintners' Song. And then there are the wines... tonight Rauzan-Ségla 2000, tomorrow Graham's 1977.

One of the oldest institutions devoted solely to the enjoyment of wine is the Saintsbury Club, founded in 1931 and named after Professor George Saintsbury, whose *Notes on a Cellar-Book* (1920) is part of wine lore. Among the club's founder members was the legendary André Simon, who also founded the International Wine & Food Society. It meets twice a year, usually in the Court Room of Vintners' Hall, and membership is strictly limited to 50 – just the right number to enjoy a jereboam of posh claret.

The members of the Saintsbury Club are mostly wine and literary person-alities, as deeply into their wines as they are into conversation, and the wines, which are always top-notch, are gifted to the club's cellar. Recently I took over from Merlin Holland, Oscar Wilde's grandson, as Editor. Each member also takes it in turn to act as chairman for a dinner, which I did in October 2019, and there is often a guest speaker. On that occasion Lord Menzies performed the speaking duties while we indulged in Pol Roger 2002, Château Léoville Barton 1996 and Château Lafite Rothschild 1995 among other delights.

Way back in 1970, six of us who had met whilst working for Watney's, which included my own firm of Brown & Pank, decided that it would be fun to meet up for lunch once a year. We heroically christened ourselves the Watney Mann Junior Board Lunch, since none of us were directors of anything at the time. We all went on to became very close friends. Although two of us, our self-appointed chairman, Angus Fraser, and Tim MacDowel, are sadly no longer with us, Jim Corbett, Jeremy Fraser, Al Sinclair and I continue to keep up the 'JBL' tradition. Covid prevented us from celebrating our 50th anniversary, planned to take place the island of Mull, but the spirit of adventure lives on. Although no one drinks beer on such occasions, the wine cup most definitely runneth over; 50 years of friendship is indeed something to be celebrated.

Another similar gathering with a special place in my heart is the 63ers Club – that core group of friends who first met all those years ago among the vineyards of Europe and who continue to dine together to this day, usually at Brooks's or Boodle's. We also still visit the odd vineyard together. Our last outing was to Jerez in October 2018 with Rodney and Cristal Briant Evans, David and Rosalie Butler Adams, Robin and Lavinia Byers, David and Sue Orr and Clarissa and me. There to greet us in Jerez were Peter and Menene Dauthieu. Sadly absent were Jeremy and Celia Burroughes, Nick and Moira Clarke, Willy and Sylvia Knight, and Sam and Belinda Sandbach – even so, not a bad show of friendship for over 50, going on 60, years. The wine vein still runs deep. At most of these gatherings, David Orr brings along a bottle of Cockburn 1963 and I bring along a Croft 1963, just to see how the other is getting on. We all know that the Croft 1963 was heralded as one of the best vintage ports of this outstanding year, but annoyingly it is Cockburn 1963 that now fetches higher prices at auction. Is there no justice?

It would be invidious (or would it?) to share all the invitations and menus that I have kept over the years. They currently sit in a drawer, or several drawers to be exact, in my study. I kept them partly as an *aide memoire* of where I had been and what I had enjoyed, usually at someone else's expense, and partly because many of them contain largely incoherent notes on particular wines. Most of all, though, they are a lasting record of the somewhat gilded life that Clarissa and I have led thanks to the humble vine.

During my Morgan Furze days, I was regularly asked to lunch at Justerini & Brooks' elegant dining room in St James's Street where, in return for a small wager, you had to guess the vintage of the port, the pot being shared between the winner and a trade charity, the Benevolent Fund. It is alleged that when HM the Queen Mother was so entertained, she suggested that the ante should be upped, or even doubled. Cannily, she had guessed that the vintage served that day would be the year of her birth, 1900. She was right, and scooped up the winnings with great pleasure.

Also, while I was at Morgan Furze, I found myself invited to a banquet at the Royal Pavilion, Brighton, in June 1984, to commemorate the 200th anniversary of the birth of Antonin Carême, the father of French cuisine. After this great bonanza, replete with Croft 20-year-old tawny port, Robin Byers and I somehow found each other on the beach early in the morning. Bizarrely, Robin discovered a German officer's hat. We then missed our train back to London.

As I said, at Morgan Furze we always listed the guests' names on each menu, which was another good reason to take them home. Berry Bros & Rudd, also in St James's Street, do the same. In November 2011, Simon Berry invited me and McKee Nunnally, who had flown over from the US specially, for first tastes of the pioneering Scion 1855 harvest port from Taylor's. My scribbled tasting note reads: 'Enveloping cascades of the Douro bake and unctuous fruit of love… always supremely balanced and a deep draft of a drink.' It obviously made sense to me at the time. I had known Simon for many years, during which I had worn many different hats. On one occasion at Vintners' Hall, he told me: 'I am never exactly sure what you do – but you always seem to be where it matters.'

The wine trade is full of generous folk. Looking through my collection, I recall Graham Chidgey of Laytons, who once kindly organized 'A wine trade lunch for Les Frères Roux' at their London offices where Château Lafite 1962 was followed by Comte Georges de Vogüé Musigny 1961 and topped off with Rabello Valente 1935. My copy of the menu is signed by both Michel and Albert, the latter's signature heavily underlined for some strange reason. Another menu, from the opening of the London Wine Trade Fair in May 1985, is signed by the chefs Roger Vergé and Anton Mossiman.

Among the countless other souvenirs is an invitation to The Wine Guild of the United Kingdom's Winter Banquet to honour Harry Waugh's 90th birthday at the Four Seasons Hotel in November 1994, when we dined on a brace of Latours – 1967 en magnum and 1981. Then there was the dinner to celebrate the 30th Anniversary of Christie's wine department 1966–96, where we sampled Pol Roger 1986 en magnum, González Byass oloroso Añada 1966, Château Lafite 1966 in jereboams and Graham's 1966. Or Steven Spurriers's *Decanter* Man of the Year Award lunch at Le Gavroche in March 2017, where his own splendid Bride Valley Rosé Bella 2014 was on the list.

Tim Stanley Clarke's retirement lunch at Mossiman's in March 2015 was an extremely jolly affair, as anyone who knew 'Filing' Clarke can imagine. Tim's day job was pulling legs but he also moonlighted as an ambassador for Symington's port – or was it the other way round? Another great character was London restaurateur Michael Proudlock, who with his business partner, Rex Leyland, created the appropriately named Foxtrot Oscar in Chelsea. The menu for Michael's Coterie lunch at Brinkleys in May 2019 states: 'Culinary skills have been significantly lowered in order to maintain Foxtrot Oscar standards'.

Looking back through my menu collection, I am reminded of how very much better wines taste on their home terroir, along with good food and in the company of like-minded souls. My eyes light on a menu from Hennessy's magnificent Château de Bagnolet in June 1982, where Michel Roux and I enjoyed glasses of Château Beychevelle 1970 before sampling the Hennessy itself. At Château Loudenne in March 1983, I notice that Château Latour 1955, Château d'Yquem 1962 and Croft 1945 were all served. One handwritten menu from Château Latour, dated May 1991, shows that we enjoyed Château Léoville Barton 1961 and Château Latour 1961 with the cheese; another one, from only a month later, records that we had Château Latour 1953 with the roast lamb, Château Latour 1949 with the cheese and Château d'Yquem 1962 with the raspberries. How lucky we were – and how dismal were the days of Covid, when convivial gatherings such as these suddenly became out of the question and the world was turned so abruptly on its head.

Since the pandemic, as part of my continuing efforts to connect people in the wine world, Zoom calls and webinars have become very much part of my stock in trade. While both undoubtedly have their place, I have to admit that they don't hold quite the same magic as sipping vintage port in a Manhattan restaurant, or watching the sun set over Beijing as I spoon the last few precious drops of Essencia to my lips.

Last year, as things finally returned to normal, Clarissa and I ventured to Georgia, where an underground quervi was opened in our honour and to neighbouring Armenia, where we stood in the recently excavated 6,000-year-old Areni-1 cave – formerly home to the oldest grape pip ever unearthed. And in February 2023, I skied for the Vintners' in an annual Inter-Livery Company Ski Championships in Morzine. In the ensuing giant slalom, which took place in almost a white-out, I collected a Gold Medal for being the oldest competitor to finish the course, plus a mounted 'bladder syringe' courtesy of the Company of Apothecaries.

Glancing at my diary, I note that it is now over 60 years since I rolled up at the Phipps Brewery in Northampton to start my first job in the wine trade. How time flies.

Ben's 1963 Vintners' Scholar Reports

Reproduced by kind permission of The Vintners' Company

1 BORDEAUX

Introduction

I was determined to follow Rabelais' advice — "Ne bois pas inutilement" — and largely thanks to my main hosts Louis Eschenauer I was able to seize upon every opportunity to further my knowledge in the divers Bordeaux wines. Within two days of my arrival, I was witnessing the vintage at Château d'Yquem and towards the end of my stay I actually had to refuse dégustations laid on so kindly by various firms, as I ran out of time.

The 1963 harvest was almost over when I arrived, but I did manage to see some grapes being picked in the Médoc and Graves districts, and I had mixed reports on how good it was. There seems no doubt that the Merlot grapes suffered enormously in the St. Emilion district at the hands of storms, but the outlook looks more optimistic than at first feared. There being produced so many individual wines, many with their unique characteristics, that a comprehensive and intimate knowledge of all would require one's life work, and yet, I would like to try, by different stages, to analyse the salient features which determine the continual successes of the Bordeaux wines. This necessitates firstly looking at the various wine regions to see why they produce such dissimilar wine, secondly finding out about what happens to the wine at the Château and then at the Chai.

The Wine Districts

There are over 320,000 acres of Bordeaux vineyards in the Gironde, and although the city of Bordeaux (the fifth in France) is definitely the centre of the industry, it is not the only hub. Each district: Médoc, Graves, Sauternes, St. Emilion, Pomerol, Entre deux Mers and Blaye to name the main ones, is individual and unrelated to the other.

The Médoc district to the north of Bordeaux is probably the best known, and is divided up into two sections — Médoc and Haut Médoc. The latter houses such famous red wine growths as Château Lafite, Château Margaux and Château Latour and acts as the mecca for the Bordeaux wine lover, whilst the more northern section of Médoc does not enjoy the pebbly terrain to such an extent and its wines are less elegant. I was fortunate enough to visit a few Châteaux in all the principal districts: Margaux, Moulis, St. Julien-Beychevelle, Pauillac and St. Estephe, and, if allowed, tasted the 1961, 1962 and the 1963 wines from the cask.

The classification of the Médoc growths took place in 1855, and still stands today, although there seem to be several wines which could have their growth rating and therefore their price altered. Château Mouton-Rothschild is now generally accepted to rank with the first growths.

It is the soil, or lack of it that gives a Bordeaux wine its inimitability, and the gravelly soil of the Médoc together with the weather conditions combine to ensure a constant quality, however the last word rests with the proprietor, and the Médoc can be grateful for having such wealthy patrons to look after its wine, through its different stages. Although some châteaux, such as Château Latour, show only remnants of their former majesty as their owners cannot afford to keep them up, the actual vineyards take on a military appearance in their neatness.

The cépages in the Médoc are generally from Cabernet Sauvignon or Merlot stocks grafted onto American roots. In spite of the unusually good weather in October, the leaves clung to the vines later this year, but I was able to witness that most important act — pruning. As the vines are no more than 2'6" high, and strung on wire trellisses, and as it takes five years to train a man properly to prune, this operation, carried out throughout the winter can make or mar the following year's wine. However, if the pruning and weather are perfect, then one might expect an ideal vintage, and benefit from the unparalleled elegance of the greatest wines in the world.

The Graves region extends along the left bank of the River Garonne from Bordeaux, to about twelve miles southwest of the city. Contrary to popular conception, "Graves" does not equal "White Bordeaux", but owes its name to the type of gravelly soil in which the vines are grown. Possibly the most famous château in the Graves region is Château Haut-Brion, whose vineyards are virtually within the city limits of Bordeaux, which produces red wine of classified first growth. In fact more red wine than white wine is produced in the north of Graves from such Châteaux as Château Haut-Brion, Château La Mission Haut-Brion, Château Smith Haut-Lafitte and Château Haut-Bailly, each of which have their own characteristic bouquet and finesse.

I spent several afternoons at Château Olivier during

and after the vintage, and followed the grapes through the
fermenting process to the taking of samples by the chemist
for analysing. The wine is bought by wine brokers (courtiers)
on the baume (sugary content, which ranges between 10° and
15° as this decreases while the wine is fermenting). It is
fascinating to put one's ear to the bunghole of a cask, thus
following its final stages of fermentation.

The exquisite dry Graves wines give way, geographically,
to the incomparable, though often imitated, rich luscious
wines of the Sauternes and Barsac districts. Here, even the
shunner of sweat wines must come and pay homage to the king
and the Premier Grand Cru Classé Château d'Yquem.

> *"Las Dieux le boivent debout, Las dames*
> *assises...et nous a genoux".*
>
> **(Gaston Roupnel)**

The vintaging in Sauternes is unique amongst Bordeaux
wines, in that the picking is done several times, and
only the grapes covered with the "pourriture noble" are
individually picked and taken, with a host of flies, to the
château. This "botytris cinerea" is in fact a mould, which
grows on very ripe grapes when the climatic conditions
are suitable: as in Sauternes. The actual grapes look
alternately hairy and roasted, but the foundation for a
true Sauternes has been laid. The sugar is concentrated,
and acidity is lowered and glycerine is formed. After
pressing the grapes, a thick sugary must is extracted
which starts to ferment, but the ferments cannot work with
so much sugar, and fermentation stops when the alcoholic
degree eaches 15° or 17°. The residual sugar thus giving
the wine its natural liquor.

The Sauternes district also comprises such well known

châteaux as: Château Rieussac, Château Guiraud and Château Coutet, which are renowned the world over for their soft, luscious, golden products. Again it is the happy combination of soil, sun, topography and care that has maintained the noble lineage of Sauternes.

To the east of Libourne, on the northern side of the river Dordogne, lie the districts of St. Émilion and its smaller western counterpart — Pomerol. On undulating slopes, the vines of the former district give a full bodied red wine that atones perhaps for its less subtle characteristics by being robust and fruity. The two great châteaux of St. Émilion are Château Cheval Blanc and Château Ausone, part of whose vineyards are built on a graveyard.

The Saint-Émilion red wines are considered to be the oldest in France, and the charter for the 'present day appellation of "St. Émilion" was given to Falsisse on July 8th, 1199 by the King of England. Saint Émilion itself is full of historical interest with its monolithic church, its cloisters, arches, bells etc., and even produces its own unique macaroons. The appellation laws are very strict in St. Émilion, and each year all wine desiring an "appellation contrôllée St. Emilion" has to undergo a triplicate degustation comprising growers, wine brokers and shippers, to ensure that the name of St. Émilion is not debased in quality. This year, as so much hail damage was done, the quantity of wine allowed to be called St. Émilion will doubtless be less than in previous years.

The vineyards of Pomerol are on a plateau and cover 650 hectares; here again, the soil is gravelly and sometimes sandy. Its wines have distinct Burgundian traits, in that they are well balanced and full with a powerful bouquet, and yet remind the Bordelais drinker somewhat of a Saint-Émilion, with the finesse of a Médoc. It is an intriguing wine, and the 'cru exceptionnel' of Château Petrus is indeed a delight, though an enigma to drink. Like its neighbour, St. Émilion, Pomerol has witnessed the feudal system, and now presents a well contented and prosperous air.

The huge expanse of vineyards between the River Garonne and the River Dordogne, is appropriately called, in true Gascon style, Entre deux Mers. Not affecting to be pretensious, the wine here produced is an honest dry white wine that has a reputation of being an excellent partner to Arcachon oysters. However, surrounding Entre deux Mers are several districts which enjoy European, if not international renown, the Premères Cotes de Bordeaux, bordering the Garonne; Loupiac, where Ansonius built his villa in the fourth century; Sainte Croix de Mont, whose wines have unfortunately completely failed this year, and to the north, Graves de Vayres, which produces fine velvety white wines.

On the right bank of the River Gironde lie the Blayais, Bourgeais and Bouzuguais vineyards. Facing the Médoc, with only the river between them they produce fine, sound red and white wines which are not to be ranked with their Médoc counterpart, but which are to be considered as a true Bordeaux wine. Château Bellevue's wines keep well in bottle and are often exported to other countries; the other wines produced are often drunk rather young, as good "vins ordinaires". The hilliness of the Bourgeais vineyards have earned them the name "Girondine Switzerland", and, true to their epithet, produce full bodied and colourful wines.

The Châteaux

Although there are an increasing number of wine
co-operatives being built, the château indisputably still
remains a real force amongst the quality Bordeaux wines.
The list of châteaux is impressive to the wine merchant,
and often overwhelming to the layman. It is on the name of
his Château that a merchant's fortunes can rise or fall.
In wine, they are unique to Bordeaux and surely partially
responsible for the continued affection for these great
wines. I met several shippers who boasted an excellent
wine, but an impossible name (e.g. Château Malescot-Saint-
Exupéry) for the wine list, and so were prevented from
exporting it.

At Vintage time, the grapes are brought from adjoining
vineyards to the château (which may in effect be a farm
house) and after they have been destalked, are led through
pipes into wooden cuves of different sizes. It takes about
four days for the must to ferment in a cuve (eighteen days
in a barrique) before it is run off into barrels, to await
the "cortier's ebulliometre" to determine the future of
the wine. The remainder of the pips, skins and residue
are pressed hydraulically — vertically or horizontally,
under the watchful eye of the "maltre de chai" and then go
to join the wine from the first pressing, if it is up to
standard.

A typical château (if there is one) is managed by an
often ebullient "maitre de chai" who is responsible for
carrying out the orders of the proprietor and running the
château efficiently. His knowledge is often indispensable as
to the timing of the vintage, the temperature of the must,
the vigilance of the new wine in cask right through to the
"mise en bouteille au Château" two years later.

There can be few better places to have lunch than in one of these châteaux, and with excellent food properly served, the wines of Bordeaux can be really shown off.

The Chais
In Bordeaux, I visited and was taught much by the following firms: Louis Eschenauer S.A., Calvet, de Luze, Sichel et Cie., Schroder et Schyler, Dourthe Frères, Ed Kressmann, Bouchard Père, Cruse et Fils Frères, Lemaire and Min. Marceau. Each have their own chai in Bordeaux (with the exception of Dourthe Frères in Moulis-Médoc) and many are situated on the quay. However, one can learn something on each tour of a chai, and it was most interesting seeing barrels upon barrels lying in state, ageing continually and improving to perfection.

The wine has to be constantly watched for an intrusion of bacteria and is racked three times each year. As the barrels are generally stacked four high, the traditional method is generally used. The wine is run off by means of a pipe and by gravity and a pump, fills a barrel that has just been rinsed out and sulphured. This method disturbs the wine the least, and does not interfere with its lees.

The majority of Bordeaux chais are above ground, as unfortunately there is water just beneath the surface as a result of the river. This makes it difficult for the Bordeaux shipper to materially expand in the city, as his Burgundian counterpart is only too well aware. However, the main aim of a chai is to give the wines a peaceful existence, keeping them free from outside noise such as traffic and maintaining a constant temperature of around 13°C. The Bordeaux chai achieves this admirably.

The wines are also bottled under these conditions, but

modern installations have vastly helped this operation. The wine is fined first, generally in large wooden or cement cuves, and then filtered either through pads or chemically, before it finally reaches the bottle. This is general practice, but for good growth wines the wine is bottled straight from the cask, whereas for a vin ordinaire (which is much younger) the process is quickened to produce about 2,000 bottles an hour. For white wines, however, many shippers freeze their wine at 0°C. for three or four days to let all the superfluous particles fall to the bottom and then bottle it; this is becoming more widespread as it prevents the danger of the wine becoming cloudy in a foreign climate.

To England, though, the majority of Bordeaux wines are shipped in cask after two years, when it is bottled over here and left to mature in bottle. Utmost care is taken by the shipper to ship the wine in peak condition, and in many firms, he himself will check every barrel that goes out. However the words "mise en bouteille au Château" are becoming increasingly known in this country, as a château bottled claret has an unmistakeable stamp of guarantee upon it.

The Tastings
Dégustations form a vital, integral part of the wine shipper's work, and Bordeaux is no exception. I benefited from several different tyres of dégustation, ranging from the 1961, 1962 and 1963 in cask, 1962 wines from different regions for making comparison, 1959, 1960, 1961, 1962 of one particular wine from bottle and trying to distinguish white Bordeaux from white Burgundy.

I found the 1961 Médocs, especially, quite superb, and Château Palmer insisted it to be one of the great vintages of the century. It had elegance and body, whereas the 1962s were fruity but will not last as long in bottle. I also compared the 1961s and 1962s at Château la Conseillante and Château Cheval Blanc amongst others and found the criticism the same, although the St. Émilions had relatively more body.

Louis Eschenauer run a degustation every week, very kindly, for all "stagiaires" in Bordeaux if they wish to come, and although it is on a Monday morning, competition is keen and the winner receives a bottle. I also had invaluable dégustations at Calvet, Bouchard Père, Dourthe Frères, Kressmann and Cruse, and began to appreciate the finer distinctions of similar wine — the difference between a Pauillac and a Margaux, spotting a Pomerol, deciding which was a Sauternes and which was just a sweet white wine, trying in vain to criticise Château Haut-Brion.

At Calvet we tasted the 1959, 1960, 1961, 1962 Château La Tour du Roc Millon (Pauillac) and unanimously voted 1959 and 1961 as the better years, though 1959 was a bit disappointing, but the 1961 excellent — fruity, full and elegant. No two wines ever seem to be alike, and it is this perhaps that incites such enthusiasm over a Bordeaux dégustation. There was a mixture of white Bordeaux and white Burgundies at Sichel et Cie, but even after spending a year or so in Bordeaux as one person had, only four out of the eight wines were spotted correctly. Every Frenchman thinks his wines to be the best, and rather than tending towards disillusionment, one is often overcome by the powers of persuasion and exults a wine that one might condemn — albeit unknowingly — the next day.

Conclusion
Bordeaux is an expansive field to cover, and without the

help and guidance notably of two Bordeaux devotees — M. Georges Lung of Louis Eschenauer and M. Jean Soula, the president du Syndicat d'Initiative, I might still have been hovering on the perimeter. M. Lung prepared numerable tastings for me and put me to work in the laboratory. I found this most revealing and somewhat refreshing, after so many Frenchmens' superfluous praise of wines that were good, but not excellent.

M. Jean Soula also gave me several comprehensive tastings and taught me much about the overall picture of Bordeaux wine. I also drank a unique bottle of 1892 Château Smith Haut-Lafitte with him, which had stood up remarkably well, refusing to wane.

The hospitality of the Bordelais is proverbial — long may it continue — and I very much enjoyed my stay in Bordeaux. The kindness of the many shippers out of office hours made me appreciate fully the delights of the city of Bordeaux. Whilst it is unfortunate that the 1963s in general will not be great wines, it seems unlikely that Rabelais will be proved wrong in the near future: "On rencontre plus de vieux ivrognes que de vieux médecins".

However, I would like to end this, my last report, on a totally grateful and sincere tone. I would like to thank the Master and Warders of the Vintners' Company for enabling me to benefit so fully from this magnificent opportunity. My own knowledge has decidedly increased, and I trust the link between various European countries and our own has been maintained for the good.

Ben Howkins, December, 1963

2 BURGUNDY

Introduction

Some forty kilometres south of Dijon in the Côte d'Or, lies
the heart of the Burgundy industry, Beaune. Flanked to the
north by the Côte de Nuits and to the south by the Côte
de Beaune, this small town has established itself as the
centre of one of the greatest wine areas in the world.

I arrived at Beaune on June 28th, and it was to be my
home for three weeks, I had been told that Beaune was
an enigma, and I found it to be. All the world-renowned
Burgundian maisons were clustered in this town. The
villages surrounding it were names made internationally
famous by the fine wines they produced, and yet the majority
of the inhabitants were not even aware that their wine,
that they had so carefully looked after, might be shipped
to a place they had never heard of 3,000 miles away. Yet it
is in this atmosphere that one studies the great Burgundian
wines, and one soon realises how complex the study can
become.

Interwoven into Burgundy are such creations as the Hotel
Dieu, where "la plus grande vente du charité du monde" —

L'Hospices de Beaune, takes place on the third Sunday every November. This enables the Sisters of Mercy to continue their work of looking after the sick as they have for 500 years. Also such magnificent sights as Château Clos da Vougeot, Aloxe-Corton and La Musée du Vin" and lighter aspects such as the casino at Santenay and the famed "Vin blanc cassis" aperitif, affectionately called "kir" after one of its great patrons the Mayor of Dijon, and the pillar of strength to all Burgundians.

Historically, Burgundy is important as an influential ambassador of France. Geographically Burgundy is fascinating, as its myriads of proprietors are kept under control by the appellation laws, and as to why some "cépages" in some years can produce totally different wines is often beyond man's control.

Historic Background
It is difficult to say exactly when wine was first produced in the Burgundy region, but we do know that by the sixth century there were many monasteries in the area "dont l'oevre vigneronne fut remarquable". The monks of Citeaux were foremost in this art, and by the twelfth century they had raised enough money to put the wines of Burgundy on the market. Happily for the Burgundians, Louis XIV's doctor, Monsieur Fagon, prescribed their wines for the king's health, and thus burgundy became recognised throughout France and demand necessitated supply.

Thus a majority of the leading firms in Beaune were founded at the beginning of the Eighteenth Century, Bouchard Aîné in 1750, Patriarchs in 1780 and Calvet in 1818. Soon firms were established in Dijon and Nuits St. Georges, and the market expanded overseas.

However in 1874, the one disease at which all proprietors shudder — phylloxera, made itself known in Beaujolais. Originally from America, this dreaded pest had been slowly creeping up from Orange in Vaucluse since 1863. There was no cure to stop "ce redoubtable insecte", which devastated the magnificent Côte d'Or vineyards to such an extent that Stendhal's phrase written in 1837 could well be applied:- "Cette cote n'etait qu'une petite montagne bian seche et bien laide".

But the Bourguignons were not going to give up the only way of life many of them knew without a struggle. By 1886 they had started replanting their treasured vineyards with French shoots grafted onto American plants. The latter had been found to be phylloxera-resistant, and by the end of the century, the damage caused thirty years previously became no more than a bad memory.

It must be noted moreover, and just tribute paid to the Burgundians, that such years as 1881, 1885 and 1894 could be favourably compared with the equally great years of 1904, 1909 and 1911, after the reconstruction of the vineyards. The last vineyard to have pre-phylloxera vines, the great Romanée-Conti vineyard in the Côte de Nuits, was unfortunately destroyed during the last war as there was a lack of carbonic disulphide, needed to protect the vines. It was replanted in 1945 with grafted shoots, which was not a mammoth task, as I measured it to be sixty-three yards long and it only covers 2.5 acres in all.

Geography

Burgundy is traditionally thought of as the strip of land between the north of France and the Midi. More precisely "La Bourgogne Viticole" was defined on April 29th 1930 as comprising the following four departments:-

Yonne - famous for the dry white wine of Chablis. Best orientation south-east.

Côte d'Or - Côte de Nuits and Côte de Beaune which stretch for 50kms from Dijon to Chagny.
Best orientation East-South-East.

Saône et Loire - the Mercurey (almost unknown in England) and Mâconnais districts.

Rhône - Beaujolais, which although it was never in the old province of Bourgogne, is now recognised in the Bourgogne Viticole. Best orientations East and South.

The vineyards, in fact, stretch from Dijon to Villefranche, a total of two hundred kilometres, and oddly enough all the better vines from Dijon to Chagny are grown on the west of the main road. They are to be found at a height between 200 and 500 metres on a gentle slope. The reason for the various preferred expositions is that, in this way, the vineyards are better able to resist frost, are sheltered from the strong westerly winds, can get the maximum amount of sun and are not choked by the humid air.

However, breaking down these departments into a comprehensible form is a monumental task, and I think can best be explained by a short history of the laws "des Appellations d'origine".

After the phylloxera disaster in 1878 the honesty of the vignerons rapidly decreased and the "law of diminishing returns" was passed on August 1st 1905 which forbade any deceit relating to the quality, type and origin of a particular wine. Unfortunately, the 1914-18 war prevented this law from being practised fully, and what little scruples the vignerons still possessed went by the board. Thus, in 1919 a law defining the "appellations d'origine" was passed, but a third crisis was on its way, that of the great depression. This state of affairs necessitated another law in 1935, which controlled the "appellations d'origine", and so each vigneron knew the limits of the wine to be "appellation controlée". This law still stands today, and — as is not commonly known — not only defines the region from which the wine has to come, but also defines the area of production, the type of grape, the maximum wine allowed to the hectare and the minimum degree of alcohol. There are four classifications:

1. Les Appellations géneriques — Bourgogne
2. Les Appellations de Villages — Fleurie, Mâcon, Chablis, Beaune, Volnay.
3. Les Premiers Crus - The best climats in each vineyard can either add the names of the village or put "premier cru" on the label, e.g. Pommard, les Rugiens-Bas.
4. Les Grands Grus - individual climats of the highest quality, e.g. Chambertin.

When one sees "appellation controllée" on a bottle label, one seldom realizes with what difficulties this has been achieved. There are loopholes, as négociants in Beaujolais are the first to admit, but no better solution has yet been found to ensure that the public are not deceived as to the quality of the wine that they buy. Burgundy is wrapped up in appellation laws, and even though the naked eye finds it difficult to differentiate between Pommard and Volnay, Romanée Conti and Romanée St. Vivant or between Corton and Pernand-Vergelesses, one's palate might.

From Chablis (North) to Villefranche (South): a quick glance at the wines in detail.

Chablis, the odd man out, lies some 150 kilometres to

the north-west of Dijon and is divided into Chablis Grand Cru, Chablis and Petit Chablis. The cépages are César and Trésor; it is a pity that the demand for Chablis has exceeded the supply.

However, the most northerly commune of the Côte de Nuits is Fixin, with Gevrey-Chambertin a few miles farther south. The Chambertin, to many, is Bacchus' nectar itself, which 'mêle la grace a la vigueur" (Gaston Roupnel). Then Morey St. Denis, whose vines were partially destroyed by hail this year and I photographed vines in water, an experience I could well do without. Next door is Chambolle Musigny, with its distinctive vinosity and whose vines come right up to the wall of Château Clos de Vougeot. The latter covers an area of about 100 acres and yet there are more than fifty proprietors. The Château was bought and is now used as their principal seat. Still further south is Vosne-Romanée, "il n'y a point à Vosne de vins communs" (Courtépée). One of my favourite wines, it has the robust quality of a great burgundy. Then the last great village of the Côte de Nuits hoves in sight — Nuits—St-Georges, a wine now known the world over.

The wines of the Côte de Beaune, beginning at Ladoix-Serrigny, are in general not as great as those of its northern cousin, and can be drunk sooner as they are generally softer. Aloxe-Corton, Ladoix and Pernand-Vergelesses are so close together on two sides of a hill and in the dale, that only the propriétaires can tell where one starts, and the other finishes. The famed Corton Charlemagne is judged to be the Chambertin of the White Burgundies and it is here that one comes across the presshouse and cellar amongst the vineyards, belonging to Louis Latour — certainly a worthwhile visit. Passing

through Chorey-Lès-Beaune and Savigny, one comes to the
gentle slopes of Beaune itself, comprising 528 hectares.

The next villages — Pommard, the beautifully fruity wine
of the Côte de Beaune and Volnay, distinctly lighter in
body and yet no more than a few hundred yards away — give
way, bypassing the almost hidden Monthélie, nestling behind
a hill, to the great white Burgundies, Meursault, Puligny-
Montrachet and Chassagne-Montrachet. Meursault covers 416
hectares, but Montrachet, according to Berthal, can be
favourably compared to the Château d'Yquem of the Bordelais
as the greatest of the two regions. Veering away from the
main road, one sees Santenay, whose rich, almost matted
characteristics are so admirably shown in the 1er cru Clos
des Gravières. The wine known in England as Côte de Beaune
Villages has in fact to be a blend of at least two wines
selected from sixteen appellations ranging the length of
the Côte de Beaune, and must not be confused with the Côte
de Beaune.

The cépages which truly makes the red wines of the
Côte d'Or great, is the Pinot, which "produit des grapes
compactes d'un beau noir violace dont les petits grains
serres contiennant un jus abondant, incolore et sucré". It
is, of course, the same cépage as used in the champagne
country. The Chardonnay cépage has, in the same way, made
the white wines of Montrachet and Meursault etc. so famous.
Leaving Chagny to the north, there are five important
communes in the Saône et Loire district. Rully, whose fine
white wines are gathered from the Chardonnay grape and
whose other Aligoté grapes go to make sparkling burgundy;
Mercurey, almost unknown in England and yet whose wines
can rival those of the Côte de Beaune; Givry and Montagny,
"vin blanc qui tient la bouche fraîche et la tête libre".

Further down the RN6, the abundant Mâcon district spreads itself over the rolling hills and whose white Pouilly Fuissé is now a household word. Here the red wines owe their reputation to the hardy Gamay grape.

Leaving Mâcon to the north, I spent three days in the Beaujolais district — whose wine has now almost become "the favourite wine of the Englishman". Here the vines sprawl (they are not strung along Palissages) around such villages as Julienas, Chenas, Moulin à Vent, Fleurie, Brouilly, and Morgon. The better Beaujolais wine, Beaujolais Villages, comes from the upper half of the district and goes down to Villefranche; to the south it is known as Beaujolais or Beaujolais Supérieur. The difference is mainly due to the soil, which noticeably becomes redder at St. Julien, and which therefore is not so beneficial to the Gamay grape.

Beaujolais covers 15,000 hectares of vines and is the largest "appellation controlée" vignoble in Burgundy. Still, unfortunately, demand exceeds supply. The countryside is beautiful, and vast slopes are often completely covered with vines.

Thus geographically, Burgundy consists of a complex structure of varying types of grape, types of soil, types of village and types of greatness. But right from the northernmost commune in the Côte de Nuits down to Villefranche in the south, there exists a passionate love and care of wine amongst all the inhabitants.

Le Vin (1)
Vintage time in Burgundy usually starts halfway through September, but this year as a result of the severe winter, the grapes may well not be gathered until October.

There are so many propriétaires in Burgundy that they cannot all have their own presses, and these sell direct to négociants, and they in turn will buy from several propriétaires. A few négociants are also propriétaires, but this combination strains the integrity of the weak, and is discouraged.

The "Caves co-operatives" almost unknown in the Côte d'Or, are prevalent the further south one goes, and these enable the very small propriétaires as well as the larger ones who do not want to bring up their wine, to sell directly to the regional co-operatives. The majority of propriétaires are shareholders, and this system is virtually universal in the Côte du Rhône, with such co-operatives as Rasteau holding 100,000 hectolitres of wine and whose largest cement vat holds 2,075 hectolitres.

In Burgundy, however, although cement cuves are decidedly being used today, they are mostly for younger wines (such as Beaujolais) to conserve their freshness and vitality. The diffident attitude to cement cuves lined with glass, held by true Burgundians, can be likened to a similar attitude held by true Champenois about crown corks. They do not like to admit they are here to stay.

But back to Burgundy wine. The unification of the red wine is achieved through various processes in the cuverie. The grapes are first of all thrown into a mechanical machine "the fouloir-égrappoir", which bursts their skins and then takes their stalks off (this is to prevent the burgundy wines from having excess tannin). The latter process is achieved by means of a sieve through which the pips and skins and juice fall, leaving the stalks discarded. The former are then pumped into a "cuve", whether it be ideally in oak or cement, and the fermentation takes place as the must boils with the rise in temperature. The ideal temperature is between 22° and 30°C and this is kept constant, if need be, by a heating or refrigeration system.

It is now common practice to sulphurate the wine to neutralise bacteria, and after five or six days, the "decuvage" takes place. This is the first racking and separates the now transformed must from the "marc". Most of the sugar has been transformed into alcohol by now, and this now waits to be blended with the "vin de goutte". This is accomplished (as the name implies) by pressing, whether in a vertical or horizontal press. The blend is then pumped into casks to finish its fermentation.

However, with the white burgundies, not having to be coloured, there is no need to let the wine take on the hue of the skins in a cuve, and so the fermentation takes place directly in casks. The grapes first of all are crushed, than pressed with their stalks, pressed again free from stalks, pips and skins and put into casks. Their fermentation takes nearly three weeks at a temperature of 15°-18°C. New horizontal pneumatic presses are being used now with great success, it seems.

Theoretically these processes should always produce pleasing wines, but often there is something lacking to make the wine truly great — be it lack of sugar, acidity, colour or tannin. Burgundy is one of the few districts where one can add sugar during fermentation to increase the alcoholic strength, but no more than 9 kilograms of sugar for each 3 hectolitres of "vendage". If there is a lack of colour, one has to heat a part of the "vendage" which darkens the colour.

Now the wine is in cask and three important operations have to be carried out. Racking, in order to draw the wine off its lees, refilling the casks with wine periodically to counteract the loss in evaporation and fining, in order to clear the wine by spreading a filmy substance (white of egg or gelatin) on the surface of the wine which sinks to the bottom, draining all impurities with it. The Burgundians are putting their wine into bottle sooner now, and four years is the maximum the wine should remain in cask, ideally two. The wine is thus filtered, bottled and left to age by itself.

This is one of the fascinating mysteries of wines, 'WHAT makes one wine ideal to drink in five years, another in ten years and yet another in twenty or thirty years? They remain in cellars at a constant temperature throughout the year, around 14°C, and when judged to be ready for drinking, are taken from their bins, cleaned, labelled and despatched to various parts of the world. Some great wines are decanted before they are despatched, to ensure a clarity particularly desired by the American market.

Le Vin (2)
Burgundy is undoubtedly one of the finest and noblest of the red wines "You will drink four or five bottles of truly first class burgundy in your whole life..., but you can drink claret of the highest class several times in the year: claret that should be drunk kneeling" (Mr. Maurice Healy). Unfortunately I have not been to Bordeaux, but I shall certainly take note of the last phrase.

I visited the following maisons in Beaune:-

Bouchard Aîné

Bouchard Père

Calvet

Patriarche

Bichot

Latour

Chanson

Poulet

Also, Reynier in Nuits St. Georges, Rodet in Mercurey, Chagny in Beaujolais, Piat in Mâcon, and Berthier in Chablis, amongst others. I was extremely fortunate in tasting a vast cross-section vintage wise and quality wise. I also visited a Cassis factory in Nuits St. Georges and a sparkling Burgundy maison in Rully. Although I was always most interested to taste the 1959s or before, and the 1961s from bottle, nothing so immersed me in the art of wine as tasting "en fût", i.e. from the wood. Darting back and forth across cellars, up stairs and behind bastions comparing say a Beaune, Clos du Roi 1961 with a Beaune, Clos du Roi 1962, which although still young, was fruity, velvety and pleasant on the palate.

I shall never forget the discussions that we had over a "Hospices de Beaune" wine that was almost vulgarly robust, or the description given to a Chambolle Musigny 1961 as "fruity grown inside" by an admiring Californian wine student, or the indecision on the part of us students about the pronouncement of a wooded white Meursault 1962, or the critical glances when I tasted my first Beaujolais in the Beaujolais district. I even tasted from two fûts containing identical wine, but one was from old vines (25 years) and the other fût had vines only 7 years old. I enjoyed the great Corton Charlemagne 1961 but preferred the more luscious Montrachet, which is luxuriant on the nose.

I could expound for ever on the fascinating disparities
between two seemingly identical wines, but suffice it to
say, in the words of Courteline, "Vin égale vie". Wine, as
man, is individual and psychologically different from his
fellows, and each adds something extra to his world, often
not understood.

Conclusion

Although the words of Aristophanes "Le vin est le lait
d'Aphrodite", may seem a little outmoded today, surely
in essence we still all agree with him? However much
one may talk, write or read about wine, its complete
enjoyment is achieved only by personal satisfaction. So
many words have been lost, so many phrases unfinished, so
many gesticulations made on the merits of an individual
wine, that the art of wine is ensured for many future
generations.

Burgundy will continue to be placed amongst the finest
wines of the world, its Chambertin, its Romaneé Conti,
its Montrachet will always hold affectionate places in the
hearts of mankind. The Mâconnais and the Beaujolais will be
drunk in abundance, and for many will act as the first rung
in the ever ascending ladder of fine Burgundy wines.

The very fullness and robust qualities of burgundy
will always be sought after, and the bourguignon cuisine
with its "coq au vin", escargots, écrevisses, escalopes
et perdreaux" will always be the fitting complement to the
great wine.

I enjoyed Burgundy, not only for its wine, but also for
its uniqueness. Love and care of the vines is universal
throughout the world. Yet the Bourguignons, perhaps because

they own such scattered smallholdings, take tremendous
individual interest in all their wines.

Ben Howkins August, 1963

3 CHAMPAGNE

Introduction

"La Champagne, when good, is the best sparkling wine in the world". (André Simon). The reputation of Champagne is global. It is drunk on festive occasions and is the gayest of all wines. It sparkles and it is expensive.

Many books have been written extolling the virtues of CHAMPAGNE, many people love to drink CHAMPAGNE and many adventures have been launched with CHAMPAGNE. However, I would like to give my impression of 'La Champagne', whose vineyards represent hardly a hundredth part of the land which is given over to the cultivation of the vine in France, and yet where is produced the unique sparkling wine 'La Champagne'.

History

Although there have been vineyards in La Champagne since the very early days, the wine produced from the grapes was a red wine, which did not keep nor travel well. Indeed in A.D. 92, the Emperor Domitian, fearing that his Roman soldiers would drink the wine in excess, and thus become incapable of guarding the frontiers of the Empire, ordered the destruction of all the vines in Gaul, especially those in Champagne. However this decree was abolished two centuries later and the vines flourished to such an extent that Charles VI drank so much Champagne, that, overcome by the fumes of wine, he signed everything that was put before him.

It was not until the end of the 17th Century that the sparkling white wine, as we know it today, was produced. At this time, Dom Pierre Pérignon, who is undoubtedly Champagne's most famous historical personality, realised the means of a second fermentation of the wine in the bottle during the warm weather and understood the use of cork as a stopper to the bottle, whereas a wad of cloth had been used formerly.

Dom Pierre Pérignon was the cellarer in the Abbey of Hautvillers, which is a few kilometres north of Épernay. Today the Abbey itself is a ruin, with only the cloister standing, and is used as the village church of Hautvillers. The history of the Abbey is interesting:

650 - Founded by St. Nivard
841 - Tentqize brought back remains of St. Helena from Rome
882 - Burnt by Normans.
952 - Reconstructed.
1449 - Burnt down in 100 Years War.
1507 - Reconstructed completely.
1544 - Burnt and pillaged by Charles V.
1562 - Pillaged by Huguenots.
1570 - Catherine de Medici gave money for its restoration.
1791 - Monks leave Abbey, as again pillaged.
1813 - Partially destroyed during Napoleonic Wars.
1870 - Burnt during Franco-Prussian war.
1914 and **1940** - Bombarded by shells.

Thus, Dom Pérignon invented the way of making Champagne which, apart from technical advances has not changed for two centuries. "Never was a man more skilful in the production of wine" (a contemporary admirer). In the museum in Épernay, one can follow the historical advances made, such as the evolution of the stopper in the bottle. First a wad of cloth, then a cork banged in by hand, then the cork put on by machine and still the 'agrafe' put on by hand, and then both put on by machinery.

The beginning and the end of the discovery of the making of modern Champagne, rests with Dom Pérignon in that he discovered how to control fermentation, and thus keep and ensure a 'Non Vintage' wine, in a manner which has not yet been surpassed.

The Maison Moët et Chandon in Épernay has many historical associations, partly because the Marne Valley was the gateway to Paris from the East. Jean-Rémy Moët was a great personal friend of Napoleon I, and it is said that he directed three of his greatest battles, Champaubert, Vauchamps and Montmirail from the study of Jean-Rémy Moët, and won them on account of the excellence of the Champagne. He also went to the Maison Moët in February 1814, before his abdication at Fontainebleau. Recently when Mr. Krushchev visited Moët's cellars, the wine served was an 1893 which was, as was sorrowfully expressed, not the year of Mr. Khrushchev's birth but the year he was conceived, "a sad year for all".

Geography
The three great regions of the "Appellation Champagne" lie around Reims and Épernay and can be divided into the Montagne de Reims, from Villedorauage to Ambonnay, the

Vallée de la Marne from Vincelles to Mareuil-sur-Ay, and
the famed Côte des Blancs from Chavot to Vertus.

   In these regions, the ideal orientation is South or
South East on a gradual slope — steep enough to catch
maximum sun, "but not too steep to prevent a horse from
ploughing or a Champenois' car from taking him to his place
of work." Just as important as the climate is the actual
vine and the soil (or lack of it) as often there are only
four inches of soil before giving away to chalk. The chalk
is vitally important not only for Le Champagne, but also
for La Champagne as in addition to helping reflect the sun
back onto the vine, it enables the roots of the vine to
breathe and give it that individual quality. There are
about 300 miles of underground cellars and the chalk has
saved time, money and labour in their construction and
upkeep.

   I even saw a new vineyard being planted on the Côte des
Blancs, which had formerly been a forest and there were
still old roots and stones on the surface. However, since
there was chalk underneath, the 'top' soil did not matter
and this vineyard will probably produce fine grapes. The
average vine lasts between 25-30 years which means that far
more work is entailed now than formerly, as all shoots now
have to be grafted with American vines, as a result of the
disastrous disease phylloxera in 1870. There are three main
types of grapes, the Pinot Noir, the Pinot Meunier and the
Chardonnay, and in a bottle of Champagne the average is 2/3
Pinot and 1/3 Chardonnay. The annual cycle of the vine is
interesting:

February — One cuts the American wood in the South of
France and selects French wood from the Champagne area.

March — The woods are prepared for grafting and the pruning takes place (of old vines).

April — Plant 1st year plants from nursery and actual grafting takes place in hot rooms (stratification period is twenty days). 1,500 grafts in each box.

May — Plant grafts in nursery and 1st year plants are re-earthed and trodden. Sulphur spraying on all vines.

June — The 'palissage' takes place and continual hoeing and spraying. Flowering begins and in 100 days one picks the grapes.

However since it rained a good deal of the two weeks that I was in Champagne, I was often confined to the car and only inspected the vines in discomfort.

Making of the Wine

Fortunately or unfortunately the making of the Champagne wine is intricately executed. Fortunate for the true Champagne lover, unfortunately for the consumer who has to pay.

One hundred days after the flowering (I was amazed how little the flowers were) the grapes are gathered and brought to the firms' winepresses. These may be actually in the vineyard or more likely, in a part of the Maison itself. The presses hold 4,000 kgs. of grapes, which will be extracted in successive presses, 572 gallons of juice corresponding to 13 casks of 44 gallons each. The best Champagne "Vin de Cuvée" is obtained from the first ten casks and the rest is called "tailles" — used by some firms and not by others.

Now the Champagne wine begins its unique history. It is kept in these casks in a room at a temperature of 20°

centigrade and thus its first frothy fermentation takes place. It is then racked and within six weeks the grape juice has become wine. Around November the doors are opened (yes, literally!) to let the cold air in, and thus cause the yeast to become numbed and inactive for the winter.

By April the "Chef de Caves" will have decided which vintages, the proportion of red to white grapes and the different vineyards he will use to make the Cuvée. The wine is then pumped into mixing vats, a balance of sugar from Martinique is added and the wine is then bottled.

Cork and agrafe or crown corks? I found the answer to my simple question to be intriguing. The larger Maisons dismissed the idea that the crown cork affected the wine adversely, but I noticed that even they who scorned still bottled their best vintage wine by using the cork and agrafe. One house even told me they still used the cork and agrafe for psychological reasons.

However, when the bottle is laid in a warm part of the cellar, the second fermentation takes place; but the cork (be it cork or crown) in the bottle prevents the gas from escaping (as it did through bungs in the first fermentation casks) and thus sparkling wine is born.

The stacks of bottles (Moët et Chandon have 28 million, Lanson 9 million, and Irroy 2 million) are then moved every six months to keep the yeast alive and fermenting. The pressure on these bottles can reach 90 lb. per square inch — equivalent to that of a bus tyre. However, after three, four or five years perhaps, Champagne starts on its most well known journey, through the 'remuage' the 'dégorgement' and then the 'Labillage'.

For the 'remuage' the bottles are placed on pupitres and every three days for three months, the remueurs shake and turn around 35,000 bottles each. In fact, if one merely turns the bottle, an experienced remueur can do 100,000 bottles each day (and probably more when dreaming at night). This operation is carried out to shake the sediment lying on the side of the bottle down into the cork, and yet at the same time to keep the yeast active in the wine. A true remueur is so dedicated to his seemingly unending work that he would burst into tears if he was given another job.

The bottles are now vertical, with the sediment (dead yeast and salts and minerals which have fallen out of the wine) adjacent to the cork — 1/2 inch thick. They are then "mise en point", which entails putting them neck downwards in rows on the floor in the traditional old cellars (one of the uses of the punt, or putting them neck downwards on trolleys in the more modern cellars). They remain thus for two or three months and then undergo their "dégorgements".

I was interested to discover that even the most conservative of Champagne Maisons, that of Krug, now uses the iced water method for this tricky operation (with the reservation — "of course you realise, sir, that for special customers we do not freeze the sediment".) After the dégorgement, during which five or six centilitres of wine has been lost, the Champagne is topped up with wine of the same cuvée and the dosage is added.

I soon realized that the dosage added i.e. the amount of sugar added to the Champagne to achieve different degrees of sweetness, or not, as in the case of a true Brut

Champagne, was vitally important. Each firm has to decide on the amount of dosage for each separate market in advance, and gauge the different trends in drinking. The French like a light wine with plenty of sparkle, the English like fine dry wines and the Mediterraneans prefer sweeter wines. One can talk in terms of Brut, dry, extra sec, demi sec or doux and one can make approximations of how much dosage is added for an extra sec or a demi sec, ranging from 3/4% to 8%, but the exact amount is a carefully guarded secret. Let it remain so!

After the bottle has been finally corked and capsuled, it is then left for a minimum of three months before shipment, to allow dosage and wine to marry in their own good time. Then it is 'dressed' in a foil cap (always put on by hand), a vintage slip or a non-vintage, a label, denoting the comparative sweetness or dryness of the wine and the overall label. It is then wrapped up in paper, to prevent the labels from being harmed, and put into cardboard cartons. Some firms are more automated than others, but the finished article sooner or later emerges, and is ready to be shipped to the four corners of the earth.

Conclusion

In these two weeks in Reims and Épernay I became fascinated by Champagne in all its different aspects. This was greatly enhanced by the hospitality and knowledge that I derived from the different Champagne firms that I visited.

Reims

— Lanson
— Irroy
— Heidsieck et Monopole
— Krug

190

Épernay

— Moët et Chandon
— Bollinger
— Pol Roger

At Lanson I tasted the 1955 which I found to be full bodied and pleasant on the nose, the 1959 which although obviously young is a great wine and the Black Label, which was light and refreshing and could be drunk at all times. M. François Lanson was still getting the taste of Californian wines out of his palate.

At Irroy I tasted their "Blanc de Blancs" recently changed to "Marie Antoinette", which was the first Champagne that I tasted in France and set a high standard, the 1955 which I found to be sweeter, and their 1959.

I tasted the 1955 Heidsieck and it was also this house that introduced me to "Le Marc", which I could have well done without. I also sampled the Brut 1959 Krug with M. Henri Krug, which with 3/4% dosage seemed strongly alcoholic and could be a very great wine.

In Épernay, I must confess, I derived much of my Champagne knowledge from Maison Moët et Chandon, whose generosity exceeded all bounds and whose Château de Saran is an inspiration to all. I tasted an extremely good 1911 there, which was still powerful and a true vintage wine. This proved that a great Champagne will last longer than the five or ten years it is expected to.

The Maisons Bollinger and Pol Roger entertained me extremely well. At the former I saw the only surviving pre-phylloxera wines, and at the latter drank Sir Winston Churchill's favourite Champagne.

I was also most fortunate to see M. Oller's cork factory in Reims and there I learnt the intricate composition of the Champagne cork. Each cork is carefully scrutinised, after it has been baked and rounded, by women who ensure the cork does not give any bad odour that may upset the wine. The cork comes from Spain and is generally over sixty years old. The best corks have three separate pieces next to the wine and are then agglomerated to a single piece, with paraffin smeared on the outside to make it slip into the bottle more easily. The cork is perfectly cylindrical, two inches long, and just over one inch in diameter. A bad cork could ruin a bottle of Champagne and waste much labour, therefore, a lot of care is taken to put corks into the bottle faultlessly and this is not always done by machine.

Several extra curriculum facts interested me, not least that Krug does not own any vineyards itself, but they buy from the same "propriétaires" year after year. If it is not a good year, they do not buy. Moët et Chandon own 1,100 acres of vineyards, but this is only one quarter of the vines they need each year.

The still wines of Champagne, which can only be procured locally, are extremely pleasant — to wit, the red Bouzy and the white Cramant.

The price of Champagne grapes was last fixed in 1944 by giving to each commune a 'pro rata' coefficient on which each year's harvest is paid for. There are seven coefficient categories:
Outstanding — 100% Ambonnay, Bouzy, Avize, etc.
First Category — 90%-98% Mareuil sur Ay, Oger, etc.
Second Category — 80%-88% Avenay, Vertus, etc.

Third Category — 70%-78% Moussy, Verzy, etc.

Fourth Category — 60%-68% Châtillon, Dormans, etc.

Fifth Category — 50%-58% Basse, Montaget, etc.

Sixth Category — The departments of the Aube and Aisne, except for the canton of Conde en Brie.

Even for a great vintage like 1959, only half the grapes of that year are used as the vintage wine, the remaining 50% are put into reserve vats and will go to make up a future non-vintage wine that has to remain constant. The qualities that lack in a certain year can be made up by the wine of another year.

Generally the storage vats are lined with glass, and the fermenting vats with polyester.

These facts, coupled with a visit to the "Musée du Vin'' in Épernay, and the fact that the chef at Château de Saran uses the Bouzy '28 for the "Coq au Vin" and the guests have to be content with the Bouzy '59 to drink at the table, made my two weeks in La Champagne unforgettable. They were most educational.

Ben Howkins July, 1963

4 PORT

Introduction

I drove into Porto from Jerez on September 21st, having successfully thwarted all Portuguese car drivers, who, it seemed, were determined that I should not live to enjoy my stay in that town. My first thanks must go to Sr. Alfredo Calem of A .A. Calem y Filho, my main hosts, for educating and entertaining me so well in Porto, Vila Nova de Gaia and the Douro Valley. I was also hospitably received by many other firms, and altogether spent twelve days in the Douro Valley at four different "Quintas". "When not in the Douro I stayed at the British Club, which admirably suited my needs.

After giving the background of port wine, the report falls naturally into two parts, the vintage and "quintas" in the Douro Valley, and the port shippers' lodges in the Vila Nova de Gaia. It seems that the port trade is not quite sure of its future clientele at the moment, and I hope to give my impressions of the present situation at the end of the report.

Port Wine

Port is a wine made entirely from grapes grown in the

demarcated port area of the Douro district, which is over forty-five miles east of Porto. It is fortified with wine brandy distilled from Portuguese grapes, and no wine in the world is so rigorously protected against fraud. However this has not always been the case.

Vines were being cultivated in the mountainous region of the Douro, as can be ascertained by seeing the wine-making utensils in the Fonte de Milho district, in early Roman times. However the Methuen Treaty of 1703, which gave preferential duties to port, gave rise to port wine shipments to Great Britain. But the relationship between farmer and shipper was never a happy one. Even though the Marquis de Pombal founded the Royal Oporto Wine Company in 1756, to prevent farmers selling wine not grown in the Duoro Valley, and Joas Franco demarcated the Douro wine region in 1907 after the phylloxera ravage in 1868, it was not until 1932 that the government took over the burden of organising under strict control the production of port and its trade.

Three separate bodies were founded which today are in complete control of the Port Wine Trade. The "Casa do Douro", which has its headquarters in Regua and to which all growers have to belong, looks after the national interest and enforces the laws; the "Gremio dos Exportadores de vinho do porto", which ensures the quality of Port wine and looks after the shippers' interests; and the "Institute do Vinho do Porto" which checks all Port leaving the "Entreposto" of Vila Nova de Gaia, issues a "certificate of origin" seal, and deals with the technical matters. I visited all three institutions end was most impressed by the efficiency and care with which each seemed to exercise their duties.

Geographically, the port wine region consists of approximately 860 square miles, but not all of whose wine is made into port. The River Douro runs through the centre of this schistous rocky region, which reaches heights of over 3,500 ft. and port is produced on both sides of the river but not above 500 metres. The climate is one of extremes, with only 20 inches of rain per annum, and the sun can be extremely hot. The sun shone the entire time I was there, which, coming after a few rainfalls in early September, greatly increased the chances of 1963 being declared a vintage year by many shippers.

Due to the hard schistous rock, often blasted by dynamite, the grower has to plant his vines in terraces. I have seen anything up to two hundred terraces on the slopes rising from the river Douro, with as little as one line of vines on each.

Nowadays, the increasing shortage of labour has necessitated many farmers to construct longer terraces — still built by hand and with no cement — but on a gentle slope, so that he hopes that the rain will not wash the soil down and yet he is saving labour.

Unlike any other wine region, the vines used here are all mixed, and the characteristics of one may complement the defects of another. The main red vines (naturally grafted on American shoots) are: Taurige, Alvaralhão, Bastardo, Sonzão and Tinto Francisca, and the white: Codega, Malvazia, Fina. To prove my point, the Tinto Francisca vine simply produced no grapes this year for some reason.

The Douro Region is split into two halves at the river

Corgo, into the "Cima Corgo" and the "Baixo Corgo". The former stretches further to the east, and is imposing in its ruggedness. Here, one thousand vines produce about a pipe of port of high quality. The shipper will generally choose his vintage and tawny wines-to-be from this region. The "Baixo Corgo" extends towards the west and produces a greater quantity of wine and therefore not such good quality, as can be seen from the prices asked. Here, one may buy one's future ruby and cheaper tawny ports.

In the Spring, the new wine is taken down to Vila Nova de Gaia and put straight into the shippers' lodges. There the port wine will mature in pipes or vats until it is ready to be sold.

The Douro Valley

My first journey to the Douro Valley, some sixty miles from Porto, was at the kind invitation of Croft y Cia, who have the delightful "Quinta da Roêda" at Pinhão. The train journey, on the single line track, took upwards of four hours, as we stopped at every other station to load and unload the men and women who still manage to scrape a living from the Douro Valley. The sheer majesty of the vine and olive covered mountains rising abruptly from the valley, snatched my breath away, and far exceeded my previous conception of this unique, giant, vineyard.

On arrival at Pinhão, I went to see the actual pressing of the grapes in the lagars. The ever-present problem of labour is rearing its ugly head in the Douro at an alarming rate, and many firms are having to buy mechanical aids which are not as good as the traditional methods, as their results seem to indicate.

Traditionally, the bands of peasants used to willingly come many miles by foot to take part in the vintage that their forebears always participated in, to sing and play the accordion for the joy of it, to carry baskets on their shoulders containing upwards of sixty kilos of grapes and transport them on foot to the central press house. There to be tipped into huge granite lagars holding roughly twelve to fifteen pipes and trodden by men in shorts (and I even saw one lagar full of women of three generations) to start the fermentation, to keep treading or to use monkey sticks to get the Baume from 12° or 13° down to 71/2°, then to run off the juice into wooden tonels, adding brandy at the same time at a ratio of 100 litres of brandy to every 450 litres of must, and finally to leave the must there until it is ready to be transported down to Vila Nova de Gaia by boat, a 'barco rebelo'.

Assuredly, all the above methods are still used in some parts of the Douro Valley today, but mechanisation is creeping in. The peasants often come by lorry for the vintage season. They have trucks to help them carry the grapes from the terraced vineyards to the presshouse and now there are various methods used for the actual pressing. Two of the largest firms in Porto use extensively the fermentation tank system, which entails — all by machines — taking off all the stalks, pumping the pulp into concrete tanks, which hold 10 to 40 pipes, and then by means of a water valve enact an artificial fermentation similar to that of a soda syphon bottle. The advantages lie in the speed of the operation, the saving in labour, and the good results. I was most impressed by the two fermentation centres I saw in travail. Some firms use just the centrifugal machine to take the stalks off, and then, by means of a pipe, fill the lagar and use monkey sticks to make the ferments work,

whereas others solely use a kind of mangle to gently
squeeze the grapes to make the "cutting" or first treading
easier. One firm has a mechanical foot, but I gather the
compact grapes forces the leg to be lifted, and I never saw
it work.

White port from white grapes, is made in exactly the
same fashion as red port, except that for a sweet port, the
must is run off from the lagars at a higher sugar content
and then brandy is immediately added to arrest further
fermentation and thus keep the national sweetness. Red
port is run off at 7 1/2° Baume, as 1° is lost when brandy
is blended with the wine. The brandy used is strictly
controlled, and 77% comes from Douro wine; this year,
the Casa do Douro have fixed the price even higher than
previously, to help subsidise the Douro farmer. However, a
few firms do not add their quota of brandy all at once, as
they maintain it "burns" the immature wine. This being the
case, they add the remaining brandy after a few months,
as two gallons of brandy per pipe raises the wine by 1%
of alcohol. The wines then undergo their first racking in
December or January, and slightly more alcohol is added to
counteract evaporation.

I stayed at Cockburn's "Quinta da Tua", Silva and
Cosen's "Quinta da Bonfim" and Calem's "Quinta dal Figeira"
in the Douro valley, and was kindly taken to visit many
other Quintas from Regua to the Spanish frontier. I smelt
some magnificent tonels and I smelt some quite revolting
tonels. I tasted a deliciously dry 1870 port straight from
the wood and was fond of many ports that had the "Douro
bake". As the rainfall in the Douro is half that in Porto,
the wines left in the Douro all their life mature twice as
fast and acquire a burnt flavour that is most pleasant in
moderation. This is also the reason why most epicurean port

directors keep their cigars at their quinta.

Vila Nova de Gaia
In 1926 the entrepôt of Vila Nova de Gaia, the town
opposite Porto on the south side of the river Douro, was
created. This meant that all wine lodges had to be within
the town's limit, and thus became more easily controlled.
But even before the new wine arrives from the Douro Valley
by train or boat, every single pipe is checked at Regus by
the Casa do Douro to defy fraud.

There is no set time to bring the wines down to the Vila
Nova de Gaia, and indeed some shippers leave wine in the
Douro valley to let it mature quicker and gain a slight
bake, but generally the wine arrives in the lodges in the
spring. Port wine must be aerated to keep it alive, and
it enjoys three rackings the first year, two rackings the
second year, and one the third year. No port can be sold
under two years old and an "old" wine is classed as being
over ten years old. The wines are also refreshed from time
to time with younger wine having the same characteristics.

Most lodges consist of unconventional tiers of pipes
- the shippers "lots", blending vats whether in concrete
or wood (Warre's have one in wood holding 244 Pipes), a
cooperage for making the pipes from Memel or Yugoslavian
oak, a laboratory and a few shippers have invested in a
refrigeration system to stabilise the wine. It is the
responsibility of the tasting experts in each firm to
decide, not only which wine to blend with which, but
whether the wine would best be sold as a young ruby, a
young tawny, a tawny, a light tawny or as a crusted port.

Often six or seven wines go to make up a blend, which

will be the best possible combination of colour, alcoholic strength, sugar strength and taste. To keep a young ruby fresh and alive, the wine is often subjected to a below-zero temperature for ten days in a brine-insulated tank so that all impurities may fall to the bottom. The wine is then put into shipping pipes and shipped.

The public have often mistakenly confused "tawny" with "age", and thus the demand for tawny port has visibly increased. However, the public was only willing to pay "ruby" prices, and so nowadays a cheaper tawny port is often a blend between red and white wines. This is perfectly legal, and demonstrates that the customer is always right. But a wine left to age for more than fifteen years takes on a natural tawny colour, and can be a delicious wine if left even longer to become a light tawny. I honestly found it most difficult sometimes to differentiate between a genuine old light tawny and an old white port that has matured in wood and gained considerably in colour. A crusted port is one that has had six or seven years of its life in wood as a blended wine; it is then bottled and drunk by those who perhaps cannot afford a true vintage wine, but nevertheless appreciate the characteristics of one.

If the year has yielded a particularly good wine, the shipper may declare it to be a "vintage year". This being so, he will select the best wine from that year and after two years in wood, he will put it into bottle. The bottle will then remain on its side, so that the crust can form on the bottom leaving the wine clear. The vintage wine will be at its most exquisite in about twenty-five to thirty years time, when it will be extremely carefully decanted, poured into the glass and, one hopes, be praised as the perfect climax to an excellent dinner. A vintage Port bottled later than two years in wood has to show on the label words to the effect, 1935 bottled in 1938. The port will mature quicker, and perhaps is the answer to prevent people from drinking vintage port too young.

I visited the following lodges in Vila Nova de Gaia: Calem, Cockburn Smithes, Sandeman, Silva & Cosens, Warre, Taylor, Fladgate & Yeatman, Grahams, Croft and Mackenzie. I was most hospitably received by all the shippers, and will certainly miss my M.P. at the end of the traditional lodge lunch.

The Port Trade
The pipe line of the port trade lies not, as one may think, in the Douro Valley, but in the streams of samples that foreign merchants send to Vila Nova de Gaia to be matched. The blending to match an established mark, or the following on of lots, is one of the principal tasks of the port shipper, and it is on his ability to do this that his reputation is made or marred.

For instance, an old full wine needs to have been robust in the beginning, but if not naturally, then it must be a blend of a tawny and a young wine. A sweet white port is usually achieved by the addition of Geropiga wine (7°-8° sugar), and an old tawny is often revived by adding a soupçon of a young tawny of the same characteristics. Although the laboratory is now helping the shipper, he must still be aware that tastes are tending towards lighter drinks, that France drinks more port as an aperitif than Great Britain drinks altogether, that politically Portugal is not absolutely stable and that he must maintain his reputation of quality.

The Port Trade is also controlled by the law, which
states that each shipper must have in stock double that
which he sells; if he sells 100 pipes on a Wednesday,
he has to prove that he has a further 200 pipes in his
lodge on the same date. This means that vast capital sums
are tied up in some of the bigger lodges that may well
be wanted by the owners to expand into England or into
Jerez de la Frontera. Even the growing shortage of labour
throughout the trade necessitates higher and higher wages
and new machines to replace manual labour.

No doubt, the three Government bodies aforementioned are
dealing with these problems, and far from painting the
future of the port trade black, I, for one, will look
forward to shooting partridges in the Douro Valley again
and to the day when one will again be able to say to
Jeeves:
> *"How goes the time?*
> *'Tis five o'clock; go fetch a pint o' port".*

Ben Howkins November, 1963

5 SHERRY

Introduction

I arrived in Jerez de la Frontera in the Province of Cadiz on August 12th, and for four and a half weeks, I was not only taught a tremendous amount about sherry, but also survived the Vendimia Fiesta.

My main hosts were Messrs. A.R. Valdespino S.A., who looked after my car and myself extremely well. I am indebted to them for showing me my first glimpse of a wine harvest in their well known Machanudo vineyard. My enjoyable stay was only marred by the out of season weather that we had at the beginning of September and my subsequent temperamental catarrh.

Whilst still on a personal note I would also mention that my predecessor, Michael Maguire, who is now working in Jerez was most helpful to me both inside and outside the bodega, and prevented me from falling into many a tourist trap.

Since sherry wine is certainly unique as a subject matter, I would like to give a rapid sketch of the background of sherry and then break the report down into

four sections: the vineyards, the vinification, the wine and
the vendimia.

General

"To every Spaniard sherry brings the real necessities of
life: it imparts wisdom to the foolish, cheerfulness to the
sad, assurance to the shy and a knowing self-confidence to
the ignorant". Thus, if we were to take Don Antonio Frates
Sureda literally, sherry is indispensable to our general
well-being. But in a more serious vein, sherry is always
more fascinating to drink, if one appreciates how sherry is
in fact made and how one can achieve so many varied blends,
for so many varied palates throughout the world.

It is essential to realise that sherry is a fortified
wine, and comes only from the delimited region in Andalusia
bordered by three towns, Jerez de la Frontera in the north,
Puerto Santa Maria in the south, and Sanlúcar de Barrameda
to the West. These towns form a triangle which comprises
over 20,000 acres of vineyards. It is between these three
towns that the necessary chalky albariza soil is found,
which gives the wine its inimitable characteristics. The
three basic types of Sherry - fino, amontillado and oloroso
together with brandy are blended and matured in Jerez and
Puerto Santa Maria, whereas the only wine that can be
matured in San Lucar is the bone dry manzanilla. A true
manzanilla can only be found in San Lucar, as this type of
sherry is entirely dependent on the salty breezes that waft
through the majestic bodegas overlooking the Atlantic.

Historically, it might almost be true to say that there
have been as many arguments over the origin of the name
'sherry' as over the wine itself. Suffice it to say that
Theopompus called the town Xera, the Phoenicians, Ceret,

the Visigoths, Serit and the Moors Sherrison or Saris. This
is not to dismiss the subject abruptly, but unfortunately
the full etymological theories lie outside the scope of
this report.

Sherry was shipped to the British Isles as early as the
twelfth century and by the fourteenth century, England
had become the world's largest consumer of sherry. Indeed
the English trade was so important that in 1491 there was
a proclamation that Spanish and foreign merchants could
export wine by sea without paying customs duty, which was
followed in 1517 by the Duke of Medina Sidonia conceding
special privileges to the English merchants at Sanlúcar.
By Elizabeth I's reign "Sherry Sack" was acclaimed as a
firm favourite, and there is a bust of Shakespeare just
outside Jerez by the 'El Bosque' restaurant to commemorate
Falstaff's appreciation of the wine.

However, the large bodegas as we know them today were
not founded until the late eighteenth century. Prior
to this the wine trade was in the hands of individual
merchants but such firms as Domecq, Garvey, Osborne, De la
Riva and Misa were all founded at the turn of the century
and so a new era in the wine trade was born.

The Sherry export trade has fluctuated considerably and
whereas now the export figures are very favourable, i.e.
over 50,000 butts per annum (over 80% to Europe), it must
be remembered that sherry has hit its nadir more than once.

The Vineyards
The vineyards of Jerez are basically divided into three
main classes, depending wholly on the type of soil. The
chalky, white, firm albariza soil provides the best wine,

whereas the darker barro soil and the sandy arena type, progressively produce an inferior quality of wine.

Essentially, it is the albariza, or "tierra de anafas", "tierra blanca", or "tosca" as it is sometimes referred to, that gives sherry its distinctive and original flavour. Consequently the best must is to be obtained from correspondingly good albariza vineyards. The four important "pagos" are Macharnudo (best amontillados), Varrascal (best olorosos), Balbaina and Anina (best finos). The Pedro Ximenez sweet wine is also produced in the above zones, whilst the equally sweet Muscatel comes from Chipiona, nearer the sea.

The glare caused by the chalk reflecting the sun is most beneficial to the grapes, but blinding to the eyes. The average yield is about three butts per acre, which is almost half the yield from the other types of soil.

The barro soil stretches from Sanlúcar right along the coast to Gibraltar, and gives a coarser wine, but greater quantity; the arena soil is mostly sand, which is easier to cultivate, but which produces more inferior wine.

Now, having established what and where the vineyards are that produce sherry, let us turn to the types of vine and the care taken in the vineyards during the year. Too many people take the harvesting for granted, without appreciating the toil and sweat given during the other eleven months.

The principal vine is the Palomino Blanco, from which the majority of sherry must be obtained. The grapes are light green, fairly sweet, medium sized and are harvested during the first half of September. This year however the vintage was late due to the poor weather at the beginning of September, and many firms did not start until the fifteenth of the month. The other vine which is essential for the blending of sherry is the legendary Pedro Ximenez, commonly referred to as P.X. This is to be found lower down on the albariza vineyards, and produces a superb rich wine, mostly used for the blending of sweeter sherries. The other important types of wine are Moscatel Gordo Blanco, which has its own distinctive honey flavour, Albillo Castellano, Meatus Castellano and Perruno.

The average life of a vine giving a useful yearly production is between twenty-five and thirty-five years. As in other wine regions, this is the result of grafted shoots from American vines, made necessary after the scourge of the "vine louse" phylloxera in 1894. Like the Burgundians, the Jerezanos refused to abandon the business which their ancestors had handed down through so many centuries, and fought the plague with stalwart determination. So much in fact, that now not only is there more ground covered by vines than previously, but the quality is just as excellent.

There are two different systems - both widely used - for the planting of new vines: the Marco Real or square system and the Tresbolillo or diagonal system. Both have advantages and disadvantages, but the latter is more generally used as it produces fifteen per cent more vines and gives a uniform distance between adjacent vines. The vines themselves are not, as is common in France and Portugal, supported by wire trellises, but rather have wooden supports to uphold the magnificently full bunches of grapes, which would otherwise weigh the branches down to the soil, and allow them to rot.

There is a guard in each vineyard to stop would-be
pilferers. Although nicknamed "bienteveo" (l see you well),
I never saw one that was not having an extended siesta.

I had the good fortune to visit several vineyards,
and talking to the farmers in their isolated, spotlessly
white farms, situated in the middle of their vineyard,
I realised the devotion that each one held for his own
vines. In theory, and very nearly in practice, the Jerezano
farmer has no other ambition than to produce the best of
everything. I will never forget being offered and accepting
a truly luscious melon in the middle of the serene
Macharnudo vineyard, at eleven o'clock one morning. For an
instant time stood still, all cares were forgotten and the
sun benignly smiled down, encouraging us to drink in the
glory of the ages past.

But the farmer's life is far from being idyllic, and as
is shown in the following chronological synopsis, he is
busy the year round. The year's work starts immediately
after harvesting:
October — "Repaso": to see if any vines have failed to
produce grapes, usually about 10, "Deserpia": digging pits
around each vine to catch the all-important rainfall.

November — "Desbraga": cutting off unwanted shoots.
December - "Injerta": grafting of American and national
vines (2nd year).
January — "Injerta de yeura": second grafting if first is
unsatisfactory; not as good. Ground is levelled.
February — "Carabien": earth hoed to ten inches.
March — "Abonado": ground is manured.

April — "Golpe lleno": earth hoed to seven inches to keep weeds down.

May — "Castra": vines pruned and tidied.

June — end of blossoming and grapes appear.

July — spraying vines against mildew with Bordeaux mixture. "Bina": earth broken, hoed again in order to trap any rain or natural moisture.

August — "Rebina": cracks caused by sun are filled up.

Spraying (six or seven times a year depending on the state of the vine).

Thus, one can see that the principal aims of the farmer are to absorb all the rain he can, and prevent it from evaporating, to kill all weeds and suckers, and to keep the vines free from parasites and mildew. These tasks are mostly carried out manually with a roman hoe, as it is difficult to make proper use of machinery on the slopes and amongst the narrow spaces between the vines.

I have not explained the pruning system in detail, as it is so important as to warrant a paragraph to itself. The traditional method is called "de vara y pulgar", which entails leaving the sticks (vara) with seven or eight knots which will produce the year's grapes, whilst the thumb (pulgar) is a young shoot waiting to become the vara of the following year. This may sound easy, but in practice this combination takes many years to achieve and varies with each farmer. A longer vara produces lighter wines, whereas a vara well pruned back will give the wine more body and fullness. Bad pruning can ruin a crop.

By September, provided that the vines have escaped such diseases as chlorosis, oidium, mildew and they are free from insects, that there has been enough rain to swell the grapes and enough sun to raise the auger content to around 12° Baume and that the pickers have not gone on strike, the vintage will begin.

The Vinification
Briefly, the grape is picked, pressed, run off into new casks, transported to Jerez where it undergoes first a tumultuous, then a slow fermentation, classified in January, blended with grape spirit, classified again, left in an anada system until next September, racked, then put into the last criadera and run through the scale until the final solera. For the moment I would like to go as far as the addition of grape spirit and thus deal with the unadulterated must — "mosto".

The day eventually arrives for the start of the vintage. Bands of gaily singing men and women, armed with clasp knives, cut the grapes from the branches all day and fill wooden or cane baskets weighing about thirty pounds. These are then transported to the press house by mule, horseback or in the modern way by truck. The Palomino grapes are then left out in the sun (if there is any) for twenty-four hours or so, on round esparto grass mats, in order to raise their sugar content. However the Pedro Ximinez grapes are left in the sun much longer, anything up to three weeks, so that they will carry an extremely high proportion of sugar and end up like raisins.

Jerez, rather like the Douro, is undergoing a miniature industrial revolution, and the methods of obtaining juice of the highest quality are varied. However, traditional treading in the lagar by four "pisadores" wearing cowhide boots, whose soles are nailed with tacks, still accounts for much of the must produced. Each lagar holds 1,500 lbs.

of grapes, enough to fill one butt. The grapes are lightly sprinkled with gypsum, which improves the quality of the must, and then trodden until all the juice has been run off. The residue is then heaped around the centre screw, esporto grass wrapped around the conical pile and then given a second pressing by two men gently squeezing the residue by means of a clamp.

But more and more machines are being used now: horizontal presses, centrifugal machines, together with the much-used vertical press. The Co-operative at Sanlúcar is typical of the modern methods. There the grapes are pushed into a centrifugal machine by means of an automatic screw, whirled around to such an extent that all the stalks are thrown out of the machine and pumped into huge concrete vats, where the very weight of the grapes against each other produces the first must. The remaining juice, skin and pips are then shovelled by two men into hydraulic vertical presses for the second pressing. The third pressing produces aguapie, whilst the remains are either fed to pigs or used as a fertilizer.

The grape juice is run off into new oak casks (the ideal way to season a future shipping cask) after being filtered through generally a rather primitive sieve, and then taken to the respective bodega in Jerez or Puerto Santa Maria.

After a few hours (this year being cooler, after a few days) with the must between 12° and 15° Baume, the tumultuous fermentation sets in. This lasts for three or four days, during which time the temperature rises, the froth bubbles over the loosely fitting bung and Jerezanos try not to breathe. The excitement dies down after a few days and the must undergoes the slow "lenta" fermentation for about three weeks.

For the next three months the wine does exactly what
it wants. If 'flor' appears on the surface of the must, it
will most likely be a future fino, as it does not grow on an
oloroso. The 'flor', a white, nauseating film of yeast cells
can easily be killed, but can never be induced to grow
artificially. It is, in fact, Jerez' trump card to ensure
that true sherry comes from Spain.

In January or February, the "capataz" (foreman, master
story teller and expert taster) of each bodega will take
samples from each butt with a venencia, and categorise
the must into varying classes. He, in fact, wants to know
if the must is good, bad or indifferent, and marks the
butt accordingly. If he can trace vinegar, the butt is
immediately removed.

The wine is then racked off its lees, checked for
alcoholic content, usually about 12° Baume, and blended
with the same quality of its type, i.e. a superb fino is
blended not just with all other finos, but with another
fino of the same high quality, before being fortified with
alcohol. A fino is brought up to 15°/15½°, an oloroso to
16½°/17°.

The Wine
For a small blend the alcohol or industrial spirit, is
still mixed in butts, but nowadays more and more concrete
vats are being used for blending larger quantities. A fifty-
fifty mixture of alcohol and matured sherry shocks the wine
less than pure alcohol, and after the wine has been allowed
to settle for a few days, the second classification ensues.
The actual divisions of this classification often vary from

bodega to bodega, but the object is to mark each butt with a symbol that will give an indication as to how the wine will develop, whether to a fino, palo cortado, amontillado or oloroso.

Whether there are two or four basic types of sherry, experts will never agree, but below is a classification of the main types of sherry wine, which I hope at this stage may help clarify misunderstandings.

Manzanilla — Very dry salty sherry at 15°-16° that can only be matured in Sanlucar. Loses characteristics when travels.

Fino — Straw coloured and delicate 15°-17°. Aroma imparted by flor. To be drunk young and fresh.

Amontillado - Nutty and pungent, 17°-18°. Salleron. Could be derived from old fino type name derived from Montilla, a village near Cordoba.

Palo Cortado — Rare, but often bastardised for sale, bouquet of amontillado, body of oloroso perhaps three butts per annum of genuine palo cortado.

Oloroso — Darker vinosity on palate, full body. 16°-20° Salleron. Trace of sweetness, yet clean to the nose.

All these wines are completely dry as they are fully fermented and it is only with blending the above with a naturally sweet wine, that one can talk about degrees of sweetness or dryness. It is unfortunate that the general English public should equate oloroso with sweet sherry. I am sure a majority simply would not believe me if I told them my favourite sherry in Jerez was a dry oloroso. It was. I list the sweet wines below.

Pedro Ximenez — Very sweet and dark, 22°-25° Baume. Grapes left in the sun, so high in sugar content. "Ferments are inhibited by the alcohol they produce before all the sugar has been used up". Blended with oloroso to make cream sherries.

Moscatel — As above, but with its own distinctive flavour. Essentially a blending wine.

Vino de Color - Dark wine, syrup obtained by concentrating unfermented must over a slow wood fire in a pot. When mixed with 1/3 must, tumultuous fermentation follows and "color de macetilla" emerges — the best type.

With the above types of wine, it is possible to produce almost every blend of sherry on the market. This is made possible by the solera system, which is essential to maintain the standard of sherry.

After the wine has been fortified and classified for the second time, it is put into an "anada" (from ano — year). This means the wine will stay as it is until the capataz has decided once and for all the character of each individual butt. Thus, after one or two years, the rows, usually four tiers high, of new wine will be run off into the last "criadera".

A solera system may have as many as nine criaderas, which simply means that the wine has to pass from the ninth to the eighth to the seventh, etc., until it reaches the first criadera and ultimately into the solera itself. It is only from the solera that wine can be drawn off for blending, about three times a year, and as no more than 2/3 of wine is drawn from any one cask, the new wine coming in always takes on the exact characteristics of the old wine, and thus the quality is maintained.

A criadera may comprise two or two hundred butts, it may be four hundred yards away in another bodega from its next criadera and thus have to be run off through long nylon pipes, though generally the wine is transported in "arrobas" - a measure of about 31/2 gallons and thirty to a butt. However, there are certain standard rules, with which most shippers comply.

Finos are placed in the bottom tiers nearest the ground, in order that they may draw more humidity for the flor and the coolness keeps the wine fresh. It is uneconomical, from a labour and temperature angle, to place butts into more than four tiers, even though the bodegas are so awe-inspiring in their vastness. I spent many instructive hours roaming at will through through many bodegas, drawing off wine in all stages with my venencia. Some of it reached the glass, some did not, but it was always fascinating trying to place the different criaderas and solera in their correct chronological order and seeing how each matured consistently.

It is thus impossible to tell, accurately, how old any sherry is. When, for instance, a fino is drawn off from the solera, it may be blended with other wines and put in a shipping solera, or blended and shipped straight away, or put into an amontillado criadera and take on amontillado characteristics.

Williams and Humbert have kept up an experiment since 1920 by keeping one butt of sherry from the same vineyard each year without fortifying or refreshing it at all. I was privileged to see the range and astonished at their variance — for instance 1934 has turned out to be fino viejo, 1935 palo cortado, and 1936 oloroso. Just this alone proves the necessity for a solera system.

Perhaps the antithesis to the above is revealed in each bodega's prized "sacristia". Jealously guarded, often behind locked doors, really old wines repose in all their glory. One is told in almost conspiratorial undertones that this wine saw the repeal of the Corn Laws and that one, the Battle of Waterloo. But these wines are essential for each bodega to own, as without them, the quality of sherry would soon slip. It is true that some casks are kept as curiosities for the tourists, but from many of them come those necessary few drops to give genuine age to a good sherry. A mere drop of some old olorosos could transform a fino into an oloroso, but this would not be practical as a policy.

I have endeavoured to pursue the ultimate sherry wine through all its stages, which I believe to be vital in understanding sherry itself.

The Vendimia
During my stay in Jerez I visited the following firms: Valdespino, González Byass, Sandeman, Garvey, Domecq, Williams & Humbert, Manuel Fernandez, Mackenzie, Zoilo Ruiz-Mateos, Misa and de la Riva. I was made to feel at home with all of them, and gratefully accepted their offers of freelancing with a venencia and copa.

I nosed the youngest mosto (and to taste they are not delicious) to the oldest sacristia wine, and many times a full solera scale. Once, in the San Patricio bodega, I had three scales laid out for me: fino, amontillado and oloroso, and the one point that still fascinates me is if and when a "fino" can be termed an "amontillado". There I was informed, and at the end of three hours practically ordered, that a fino, a true fino, will never become an amontillado! However, I am certain of one thing; that sherry drunk in Jerez is perfection attained. Whether a dry fino or dry oloroso, whether a "tapa" of shrimps, or an omelette, whether in Hotel Los Cisnes or in Bar Victoria, the result is always the same — a feeling of contentment and approval of Spanish time.

Happily the sale of sherry is still on the increase — 370,209 hectolitres in 1961, and I sincerely hope that the zenith has not yet been reached. Whilst I was at González Byass, an American importer was trying to persuade the directors that sherry could replace the dry martini. I wish him the best of luck.

This year Norway were the guests of the sherry shippers for the Vendimia Festival, and it would seem unbalanced to write a report on sherry without mentioning the Fiesta. This year, the sixteenth Fiesta, again including bullfights, (which I watched, sipping Spanish sparkling wine, that somehow or other in the excitement found its way down someone's neck); the treading of the first grapes (that had been brought from Chiclana as the vintage was so late) and the releasing of pigeons, that symbolically is one of the most enthralling acts I have ever witnessed, and the customary speeches, dances, patio competition, flamenco and horse riding expertise. It would also be interesting to work out how much the home sales of sherry rise for just those four days during September.

I could not have wished for a more instructive four and a half weeks than I enjoyed in Jerez, but unlike my predecessor I have the willpower to refrain from including my ditties on sherry wine!

Ben Howkins October 1963

Index

Acknowledgements

To those friends mentioned in the book, a huge thank you for helping to make this long journey so memorable and such fun; to those friends and colleagues not in the book, you know who you are and again an equal thank you for adding to life's rich pageant and being part of this story. Friendships made in wine are made for life.

Sincere thank yous to Hugh Johnson who sowed the seed for the outline of the book and to Simon McMurtrie, founding publisher of AdVL, who kindly proposed that 'this is a story that should be told'. I have much enjoyed working with Académie du Vin Library's energetic managing director, Hermione Ireland and editor in chief, Susan Keevil, who is probably the most distinguished editor of wine books today.

My special thanks must go to Martin Preston at Académie du Vin Library, who helped me to launch *Sherry* in 2019 and who has so tirelessly guided me through my manuscript to make it a much better read. We often found that a copita or two of *fino* cleared our thinking.

Above all, almost none of this would have happened were it not for the deep love and encouragement of my wonderful family, which includes my late mother and father. And so many thanks and love to my wife Clarissa; Jamie and Annabelle and their three, Oliver, Thomas and Milla; Lucy and Gav and their two, Rosa and Bobbie and also to my fine literary brother and sister in law, John and Ariane, for such happy support throughout.

'And thank you for reading it, if you do' with apologies to Dennis Nordern.

* *

Royal Tokaji, one of the most admired wine brands in the world, has partnered with Wilson Daniels, one of the most respected wine importers in the USA, for over 30 years. Hugh Johnson was the creator and founder of Royal Tokaji and Ben Howkins brought this legendary wine to market. This enviable continuity of mutual trust has determined an unshakeable bond between these two ultra-luxury wine specialists. In turn, the author wishes to acknowledge and thank these two iconic companies for their support in bringing *Adventures in the Wine Trade* to market.

Waddesdon Manor is the iconic 19th century Rothschild chateau sitting within the rolling Buckinghamshire countryside. Waddesdon, especially the Wine Cellars, has played a significant part in my life and I would like to sincerely thank all those at Waddesdon Manor for their wonderful support in bringing this book to market. The publication date of this book happily coincides with the opening of the renovated Wine Cellars.

I would also like to thank Marc Nadeau of Toronto, Canada for his unstinting support.

    WILSON DANIELS